5 STEPS TO A

500

AP Physics C Questions

to know by test day

Also in the 5 Steps series:
5 Steps to a 5: AP Physics C

Also in the McGraw Hill 500 Questions Series
500 ACT English and Reading Questions to know by test day
500 ACT Math Questions to know by test day
500 ACT Science Questions to know by test day
500 SAT Math Questions to know by test day
500 SAT Reading, Writing, and Language Questions to know by test day
5 Steps to a 5: 500 AP Biology Questions to know by test day
5 Steps to a 5: 500 AP Calculus AB/BC Questions to know by test day
5 Steps to a 5: 500 AP English Language Questions to know by test day
5 Steps to a 5: 500 AP English Literature Questions to know by test day
5 Steps to a 5: 500 AP European History Questions to know by test day
5 Steps to a 5: 500 AP Human Geography Questions to know by test day
5 Steps to a 5: 500 AP Macroeconomics Questions to know by test day
5 Steps to a 5: 500 AP Microeconomics Questions to know by test day
5 Steps to a 5: 500 AP Physics 1 Questions to know by test day
5 Steps to a 5: 500 AP Physics 2 Questions to know by test day
5 Steps to a 5: 500 AP Psychology Questions to know by test day
5 Steps to a 5: 500 AP Statistics Questions to know by test day
5 Steps to a 5: 500 AP U.S. Government & Politics Questions to know by test day
5 Steps to a 5: 500 AP U.S. History Questions to know by test day
5 Steps to a 5: 500 AP World History Questions to know by test day

5 STEPS TO A >5™

500
AP Physics C Questions
to know by test day,
Second Edition

Hugh Henderson

Jeff Steele

New York Chicago San Francisco Athens London Madrid
Mexico City Milan New Delhi Singapore Sydney Toronto

ISBN   978-1-265-02644-8
MHID   1-265-02644-0

e-ISBN   978-1-265-02657-8
e-MHID   1-265-02657-2

McGraw Hill products are available at special quantity discounts to use as premiums and sales promotions or for use in corporate training programs. To contact a representative, please visit the Contact Us pages at www.mhprofessional.com.

McGraw Hill is committed to making our products accessible to all learners. To learn more about the available support and accommodations we offer, please contact us at accessibility@mheducation.com. We also participate in the Access Text Network (www.accesstext.org), and ATN members may submit requests through ATN.

CONTENTS

INTRODUCTION

Congratulations! You've taken a big step toward AP success by purchasing *5 Steps to a 5: 500 AP Physics C Questions to Know by Test Day, Second Edition*. We are here to help you take the next step and score high on your AP exam so you can earn college credits and get into the college or university of your choice.

This book gives you 500 AP-style multiple-choice questions that cover all the most essential course material, in addition to short essay questions at the end of each chapter similar to those on the AP exam. Each question has a detailed answer explanation that can be found at the back of the book. These questions will give you valuable independent practice to supplement your regular textbook and the groundwork you are already doing in your AP classroom. This and the other books in this series were written by expert AP teachers who know your exam inside and out and can identify the crucial exam information as well as questions that are most likely to appear on the test.

You might be the kind of student who takes several AP courses and needs to study extra questions a few weeks before the exam for a final review. Or you might be the kind of student who puts off preparing until the last weeks before the exam. No matter what your preparation style is, you will surely benefit from reviewing these 500 questions, which closely parallel the content, format, and degree of difficulty of the questions on the actual AP exam. These questions and their answer explanations are the ideal last-minute study tool for those final few weeks before the test.

Remember the old saying "Practice makes perfect." If you practice with all the questions and answers in this book, we are certain you will build the skills and confidence needed to do great on the exam. Good luck!

—Editors of McGraw Hill

5 STEPS TO A 5™

500

AP Physics C Questions
to know by test day

Diagnostic Quiz

GETTING STARTED: THE DIAGNOSTIC QUIZ

The following questions refer to different units in this book. These questions will help you test your understanding of the concepts tested on the AP exam by giving you an idea of where you need to focus your attention as you prepare. For each question, simply circle the letter of your choice. Once you are done with the exam, check your work against the given answers, which also indicate where you can find the corresponding material in the book.

Good luck!

DIAGNOSTIC QUIZ QUESTIONS

1. The position of a particle is described by the function $x = \frac{1}{6}t^4 - \frac{2}{3}t^3 - 8t^2 + 12t - 7$, where x is in meters and t is in seconds. When is the acceleration of the particle zero?

   (A) 2 s
   (B) 3 s
   (C) 4 s
   (D) 5 s
   (E) 6 s

2. A ball is thrown along a level range with an initial velocity v_0 at an angle θ to the horizontal. Beginning with the expression $y = y_0 + v_{0,y}t + \frac{1}{2}a_y t^2$, derive an expression for the maximum height the particle reaches in terms of v_0, θ, and fundamental constants.

3. A 2-kg mass is on a rough surface that is inclined at an angle of 30° to the horizontal. The coefficients of static and kinetic friction between the mass and the surface are 0.4 and 0.2. The 2-kg mass is attached to a string that passes over a frictional pulley and is suspended vertically, as shown below.

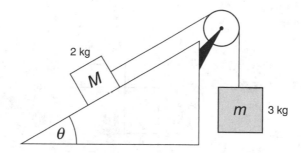

   (A) Show that the mass on the incline will slide, and determine which direction (up or down the incline).
   (B) Find the acceleration of the mass.

4. A variable force of air resistance $F = -kv$ acts on a 60-kg skydiver. What is the speed of the skydiver after 3 s if she begins from rest and $k = 6$ kg/s?

   (A) 22 m/s
   (B) 24 m/s
   (C) 26 m/s
   (D) 28 m/s
   (E) 30 m/s

5. A nonconservative force $\mathbf{F} = 2\hat{i} - 3\hat{j}$ does work on a 2.1-kg mass that moves through a displacement given by $r = t\hat{i} - 2t\hat{j}$. The amount of work done on the mass in the first 2 seconds this force is applied is

   (A) 12 N m
   (B) 14 N m
   (C) 16 N m
   (D) 18 N m
   (E) 20 N m

6. A 5-kg block is acted on by a conservative force described by $\mathbf{F} = -3x^2 - 2x$, where $\mathbf{F}$ is in newtons and x is in meters. The potential energy at $x = 0$ m is 0 J. What is the speed of the object at $x = 2$ m if the speed of the object at $x = 1$ m is -2 m/s?

   (A) 0
   (B) 1 m/s
   (C) 2 m/s
   (D) 3 m/s
   (E) 4 m/s

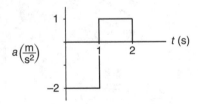

7. An acceleration-time graph is shown for a 2-kg mass above. If the initial velocity of the mass is -1 m/s, what is the velocity of the mass at 2 s?

   (A) -2 m/s
   (B) -1 m/s
   (C) 0 m/s
   (D) 1 m/s
   (E) 2 m/s

8. A small 1.5-kg explosive is sliding on a frictionless surface when it detonates into two pieces, a 1-kg piece traveling at 3 m/s in the positive y-direction and a 0.5-kg piece traveling in the positive x-direction. What is the original speed of the explosive?

(A) 1.11 m/s
(B) 1.83 m/s
(C) 2.05 m/s
(D) 2.37 m/s
(E) 2.98 m/s

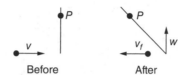

Before   After

9. A 3-kg, rigid, 1-meter-long uniform bar is at rest on a frictionless surface attached to a pivot one-quarter of its length from the top, as shown above. A 1-kg block is sliding toward it at a speed $v = 5$ m/s and collides elastically with the bar three-quarters of the distance from the top. The block rebounds at a speed v_f. What is the kinetic energy of the bar after the collision?

(A) 21.5 J
(B) 29.8 J
(C) 35.3 J
(D) 42.1 J
(E) 45.8 J

10. A physics student stands halfway from the center to the edge on a rotating platform on frictionless bearings that is rotating freely. She begins walking toward the outer edge. What happens when she reaches the outer edge?

(A) Her rotational kinetic energy and angular momentum have increased.
(B) Her rotational kinetic energy has increased and her angular momentum has remained constant.
(C) Her rotational kinetic energy and her angular momentum have remained constant.
(D) Her rotational kinetic energy has decreased and her angular momentum has remained constant.
(E) Her rotational kinetic energy and her angular momentum have decreased.

11. A planet of mass M, radius R, and uniform density has a tunnel drilled through a diameter of the planet. The force of gravity on a mass m at a distance r from the center of the planet is

    (A) $\dfrac{GmMr}{R^3}$

    (B) $\dfrac{GmM}{r^2}$

    (C) $\dfrac{GmM}{R^2}$

    (D) $\dfrac{GmMr}{(2R)^3}$

    (E) $\dfrac{GmM(2r)}{R^3}$

12. Two asteroids (mass m and $2m$) are separated by a distance r and are initially at rest. A gravitational attraction between the masses pulls them together. When they are a distance $\dfrac{r}{2}$ apart, what is the speed of the more massive asteroid if the smaller asteroid is 1×10^{12} kg and the asteroids are initially 1 km apart?

    (A) 0.15 m/s
    (B) 1.5 m/s
    (C) 15 m/s
    (D) 150 m/s
    (E) 1,500 m/s

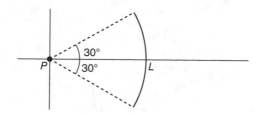

13. A uniformly charged arc with total charge $+Q$ spanning $60°$ ($30°$ on each side of the x-axis) is a distance L away from a point P, as shown above. The electric field at P is

(A) $\dfrac{2kQ}{\pi L^2}$

(B) $\dfrac{3kQ}{L^2}$

(C) $\dfrac{3kQ}{\pi L^2}$

(D) $\dfrac{kQ}{L^2}$

(E) $\dfrac{kQ}{\pi L^2}$

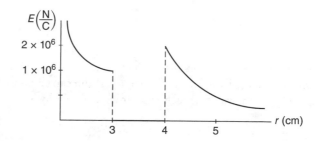

14. A charged particle is placed in the center of a spherical shell. A graph of the electric field as a function of distance is shown above. What is the magnitude of the charge in the center of the shell?

(A) 120 nC
(B) 240 nC
(C) 360 nC
(D) 480 nC
(E) 600 nC

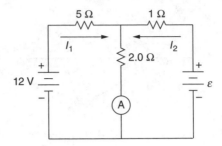

15. A circuit consists of a 12-V battery, a second battery with an unknown emf, a 5-ohm resistor, a 2-ohm resistor, and a 1-ohm resistor, as shown above. The current through the ammeter is 1 A and travels from the 2-ohm resistor to the ammeter (down). What is the emf of the unknown battery?

   (A) 1 V
   (B) 2 V
   (C) 3 V
   (D) 4 V
   (E) 5 V

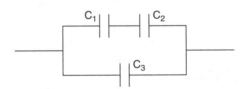

16. A system of three capacitors is shown above. When 12 V is put on the system, the energy stored is 8.64×10^{-4} J. If the capacitances have equal values, what is the value of each capacitor?

   (A) 2 μF
   (B) 4 μF
   (C) 6 μF
   (D) 8 μF
   (E) 10 μF

Questions 17–18. A positive charge is placed between two charged plates and accelerated from rest toward the negative plate through a uniform electric field *E*. The negative plate has a small hole in it through which the charge passes, where it then enters a magnetic field of magnitude *B* directed out of the page.

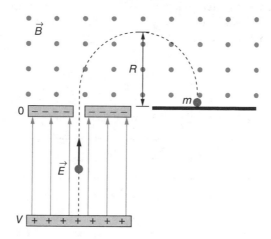

17. If the charge is a proton and it enters the electric field with a speed of 2.5×10^5 m/s, what is potential difference between the two plates?

(A) 75 V
(B) 129 V
(C) 197 V
(D) 282 V
(E) 326 V

18. What is the radius of the curved path of the proton in the magnetic field if *B* = 4 mT?

(A) 0.5 m
(B) 0.65 m
(C) 0.80 m
(D) 0.95 m
(E) 1.05 m

19. A circular loop of wire has a resistance of 2.0 Ω and a radius of 0.2 m. The loop is placed into a magnetic field that is described by $B = 4t^2 - 2t + 10$, where a positive magnetic field indicates that the field is out of the page. The magnitude and direction of the current in the loop at $t = 2$ s are

    (A) 0.88 A, clockwise
    (B) 0.88 A, counterclockwise
    (C) 0.95 A, clockwise
    (D) 0.95 A, counterclockwise
    (E) 0 A

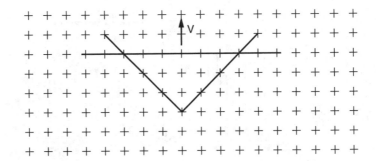

20. A conducting bar is placed horizontally across two conducting bars that form a right angle. At $t = 0$, the horizontal bar is at the point where the right angle is formed. The arrangement is in a magnetic field $B = 20$ mT, and the horizontal bar is slid upward at 2 m/s. The emf at $t = 2$ s is

    (A) 0.08 V
    (B) 0.16 V
    (C) 0.24 V
    (D) 0.32 V
    (E) 0.40 V

DIAGNOSTIC QUIZ ANSWERS

1. (Chapter 1: Kinematics)

(C) The velocity function is the first derivative of position; the acceleration function that needs to be found is the second. The acceleration needs to be set equal to zero and solved for time:

$$v = \frac{dx}{dt} = \frac{2}{3}t^3 - 2t^2 - 16t + 12$$

$$a = \frac{dv}{dt} = 2t^2 - 4t - 16 = 0$$

$$2(t^2 - 2t - 8) = 0$$

$$(t-4)(t+2) = 0$$

$$t = 4 \text{ s} \quad \text{or} \quad t = -2 \text{ s}$$

The negative solution is discarded because negative times are not in the domain of the position function.

2. (Chapter 1: Kinematics)

The initial vertical velocity is the component of the initial velocity vector, or $v_{0,y} = v_0 \sin\theta$. An expression for the time it takes to reach the highest point can be found by recognizing that the vertical velocity is zero at the top of a projectiles path, and

$$v = v_{0,y} + a_y t$$

$$0 = v_{0,y} + a_y t$$

$$t = -\frac{v_0}{a_y} = -\frac{v_0 \sin\theta}{-g} = \frac{v_0 \sin\theta}{g}$$

The maximum height is found by using the kinematic equation for position as a function of time:

$$y = y_0 + v_{0,y}t + \frac{1}{2}a_y t^2 = 0 + v_0 \sin\theta \left(\frac{v_0 \sin\theta}{g}\right) + \frac{1}{2}(-g)\left(\frac{v_0 \sin\theta}{g}\right)^2$$

$$y = \frac{v_0^2 \sin^2\theta}{g} - \frac{v_0^2 \sin^2\theta}{2g} = \frac{2v_0^2 \sin^2\theta}{2g} - \frac{v_0^2 \sin^2\theta}{2g} = \frac{v_0^2 \sin^2\theta}{2g}$$

3. (Chapter 2: Dynamics: Newton's Laws of Motion)

(A) Begin by examining the 2-kg mass. The component of the weight of the 2-kg block perpendicular to the surface is $mg \cos 30° = (2\ \text{kg})\left(10\ \dfrac{\text{m}}{\text{s}^2}\right) \cos 30° = 17.3\ \text{N}$ and is equal to the normal force. The maximum static frictional force is $f_s = \mu_s F_N = 0.4(17.3\ \text{N}) = 6.9\ \text{N}$ and is directly opposite the attempted slide. The component of the weight of the 2-kg block that is parallel to the surface is $F_x = mg \sin 30° = (2\ \text{kg})\left(\dfrac{9.8\ \text{m}}{\text{s}^2}\right) \sin 30° = 10\ \text{N}$ and directed down the incline. If the system is at rest, the tension in the string is equal to the weight of the hanging mass: $T = mg = (3\ \text{kg})\left(10\ \dfrac{\text{m}}{\text{s}^2}\right)$ and is directed up the incline. It is not specified whether the block slides up or down the incline. If the block slides down the incline, with down as positive, the net force before the block begins to slide is $F_x - f_s - T = 10\ \text{N} - 6.9\ \text{N} - 30\ \text{N} < 0$. Because this is a negative sum, the block cannot slide down the incline. If the block slides up the incline, the net force before the block begins to slide (with up the incline as the positive direction) is $T - f_s - F_x = 30\ \text{N} - 6.9\ \text{N} - 10\ \text{N} = 13.1\ \text{N}$. Since this is greater than zero, static friction is not enough to prevent the block from sliding up the incline.

(B) Apply Newton's second law to the system of the two blocks, where the only force in the positive direction (up the incline) is the weight of the 3-kg block, and kinetic friction and the parallel component of the 2-kg weight act down the incline:

$$a = \frac{F_{\text{net}}}{m} = \frac{30\ \text{N} - (0.2)(17.3\ \text{N}) - 10\ \text{N}}{5\ \text{kg}} = 3.3\ \frac{\text{m}}{\text{s}^2}$$

4. (Chapter 2: Dynamics: Newton's Laws of Motion)

(C) Make the downward direction positive, and Newton's second law gives $a = \dfrac{dv}{dt} = \dfrac{mg - kv}{m} = g - \dfrac{kv}{m}$. To solve for the velocity, separate variables, substitute, and integrate:

$$\frac{dv}{g - \dfrac{kv}{m}} = dt, \quad \text{substitute } u = g - \frac{kv}{m}, \quad \text{so } \frac{du}{dv} = -\frac{k}{m}$$

$$\frac{du}{u} = -\frac{k}{m} dt$$

$$\int \frac{du}{u} = \ln u = \int -\frac{k}{m} dt = -\frac{k}{m} t + C$$

$$u = g - \frac{kv}{m} = e^{-\frac{k}{m}t + C} = Ae^{-\frac{k}{m}t}$$

$$v = \frac{mg}{k} - Ae^{-\frac{m}{k}t}$$

Using the initial condition that $v = 0$ at $t = 0$, $A = \dfrac{mg}{k}$, and thus $v = \dfrac{mg}{k}\left(1 - e^{-\frac{k}{m}t}\right)$,

so at $t = 3$ s, $v = \dfrac{(60\ \text{kg})\left(10\ \dfrac{\text{m}}{\text{s}^2}\right)}{6\ \dfrac{\text{kg}}{\text{s}}}\left(1 - e^{-\frac{6\ \text{kg/s}}{60\ \text{kg}}(3\ \text{s})}\right) = 26\ \dfrac{\text{m}}{\text{s}}.$

5. (Chapter 3: Work, Energy, Power, and Conservation of Energy)

(C) Work is the integral of the dot product of force and displacement:

$$W = \int_0^2 \left(2\hat{i} - 3\hat{j}\right)\left(t\hat{i} - 2t\,\hat{j}\right) dt = \int_0^2 (2 \times t + (-3)(-2t))\, dt = \int_0^2 (8t)\, dt = 4t^2 \Big|_0^2$$
$$= (16 - 0)\ \text{N m} = 16\ \text{N m}$$

6. (Chapter 3: Work, Energy, Power, and Conservation of Energy)

(A) The change in potential energy from $x = 1$ m to $x = 2$ m is

$$\Delta U = -\int_1^2 F(x)\, dx = \int_1^2 (3x^2 + 2x)\, dx = (x^3 + x^2)\Big|_1^2$$
$$= [(2)^3 + (2)^2] - [(1)^3 + (1)^2] = 10\ \text{J}$$

The kinetic energy of the block at $x = 1$ m is $K = \dfrac{1}{2}mv^2 = \dfrac{1}{2}(5\ \text{kg})\left(-2\ \dfrac{\text{m}}{\text{s}}\right)^2 = 10\ \text{J}.$

The increase in potential energy of 10 J, because the work is done by a conservative force, results in a decrease of kinetic energy of 10 J, so the kinetic energy at $x = 2$ m is 0 J.

7. (Chapter 4: Impulse, Linear Momentum, and Conservation of Linear Momentum)

(A) The impulse is the area under a force-time curve. The given graph, if the vertical axis is multiplied by the mass ($\mathbf{F} = ma$), becomes a force-time graph, so the force of this particle would be $(2\ \text{kg})(-2\ \text{m/s}^2) = -4\ \text{N}$ from 0 to 1 seconds, and the force from 1 to 2 seconds is 2 N. From 0 to 1 second, the impulse is

$(-4\ \text{N})(1\ \text{s}) = -4\ \text{N s}$ and from 1 to 2 seconds is $(2\ \text{N})(1\ \text{s}) = 2\ \text{N s}$. The total impulse is then $J = -4\ \text{N s} + 2\ \text{N s} = -2\ \text{N s}$. Impulse equals change in momentum, so $\Delta v = \dfrac{J}{m} = \dfrac{-2\ \text{N s}}{2\ \text{kg}} = -1$ m/s. Given the initial velocity of -1 m/s, the final velocity is -2 m/s.

8. (Chapter 4: Impulse, Linear Momentum, and Conservation of Linear Momentum)

(D) The momentum of the first piece is $mv = (1.5\ \text{kg})(3\ \text{m/s}) = 4.5\ \text{kg}\cdot\text{m/s}$ in the positive y-direction, and the momentum of the second piece is $(0.5\ \text{kg})(3\ \text{m/s}) = 1.5\ \text{kg}\cdot\text{m/s}$ in the positive x-direction. Momentum is a vector, and these two momenta are at right angles, so the total momentum of the system is

$$\sqrt{\left(4.5\ \text{kg}\ \frac{\text{m}}{\text{s}}\right)^2 + \left(1.5\ \text{kg}\ \frac{\text{m}}{\text{s}}\right)^2} = 4.7\ \text{kg}\ \frac{\text{m}}{\text{s}}.$$ Momentum is conserved in an explosion, so this is also the momentum before the explosion; thus, the original speed is $v = \dfrac{p}{m} = \dfrac{4.7\ \text{kg}\ \frac{\text{m}}{\text{s}}}{1.5\ \text{kg} + 0.5\ \text{kg}} = 2.35$ m/s.

9. (Chapter 5: Circular and Rotational Motion)

(C) Angular momentum is conserved in the collision, so with

$$I = \int_{\frac{L}{4}}^{\frac{3L}{4}} \frac{m}{L} r^2 dr = \frac{mr^3}{3L}\Bigg|_{\frac{L}{4}}^{\frac{3L}{4}} = \frac{m}{3L}\left[\left(\frac{3L}{4}\right)^3 - \frac{L}{4}3\right] = \frac{m}{3L}\left(\frac{27L^3}{64} + \frac{L^3}{64}\right) = \frac{7mL^2}{48} =$$

$$\frac{(7)(3\ \text{kg})(1\ \text{m})^2}{48} = 0.4375\ \text{kg m}^2$$

$$L_i = L_f$$
$$rmv = -rmv_f + I\omega$$
$$(1\ \text{m})(3\ \text{kg})\left(5\ \frac{\text{m}}{\text{s}}\right) = -(1\ \text{m})(3\ \text{kg})(v_f) + (0.4375\ \text{kg m}^2)\omega$$
$$v_f = \frac{(0.4375\ \text{kg m}^2)\ \omega - 15\ \text{kg}\ \frac{\text{m}^2}{\text{s}}}{3\ \text{kg m}} = (0.1458\ \text{m})\ \omega - 3\ \frac{\text{m}}{\text{s}}$$

The collision is elastic, so energy is also conserved:

$$K_i = K_f + K_r$$

$$\frac{1}{2}mv^2 = \frac{1}{2}mv_f^2 + \frac{1}{2}I\omega^2$$

$$mv^2 = m\left[(0.1458 \text{ m})\omega - 3\ \frac{\text{m}}{\text{s}}\right]^2 + I\omega^2$$

Expanding and using the quadratic equation, we get

$$\omega = 12.7\ \frac{\text{rad}}{\text{s}}$$

$$K_r = \frac{1}{2}I\omega^2 = \frac{1}{2}(0.4375 \text{ kg m}^2)\left(12.7\ \frac{\text{rad}}{\text{s}}\right)^2 = 35.3 \text{ J}$$

10. (Chapter 5: Circular and Rotational Motion)

(D) Because the platform is rotating freely on frictionless bearings, there is no external torque, and angular momentum will remain constant. The rotational inertia of the girl is found by $I = mr^2$, because she can be treated as an extended rotating body. Thus, when she walks to the edge of the platform, she doubles her distance from the axis of rotation r, and her new rotational inertia is $I = m(2r)^2 = 4mr^2$, or four times the rotational inertia. Because angular momentum ($I\omega$) is conserved, with four times greater rotational inertia, her angular velocity will be one-quarter of the original value after the motion.

11. (Chapter 6: Oscillations and Gravitation)

(A) At a position r inside the plane, the portion of the planet that is outside r will produce a zero net gravitational force, so using the universal law of gravitation, $F = \dfrac{GmM_{\text{ins}}}{r^2}$, where M_{ins} is the mass of the planet inside the distance r. This mass inside can be found by using the constant density of the planet:

$$M_{\text{ins}} = \rho V_{\text{ins}} = \left(\frac{M}{\frac{4}{3}\pi R^3}\right)\left(\frac{4}{3}\pi r^3\right) = \frac{Mr^3}{R^3}$$

Thus,

$$F = \frac{GmM_{\text{ins}}}{r^2} = \frac{Gm\left(\dfrac{Mr^3}{R^3}\right)}{r^2} = \frac{GmMr}{R^3}$$

12. (Chapter 6: Oscillations and Gravitation)

(A) Momentum and energy are conserved in this interaction. The momentum of the system is zero because both asteroids are initially at rest:

$$p_i = p_f$$
$$0 = mv_1 + 2mv_2$$
$$v_1 = -2v_2$$

Applying conservation of energy, we get

$$U_i = U_f + K_1 + K_2$$

$$-G\frac{(m)(m)}{r} = -G\frac{(m)(m)}{\dfrac{r}{2}} + \frac{1}{2}mv_1^2 + \frac{1}{2}(2m)(v_2)^2$$

$$G\frac{m^2}{r} = \frac{1}{2}m(-2v_2)^2 + mv_2^2 = 3mv_2^2$$

$$v_2 = \sqrt{\frac{Gm}{3r}} = \sqrt{\dfrac{\left[6.67 \times 10^{-11}\left(\text{N} \cdot \dfrac{\text{m}^2}{\text{kg}^2}\right)\right](1 \times 10^8 \text{ kg})}{3(1{,}000 \text{ m})}} = 0.15 \text{ m/s}$$

13. (Chapter 7: Electric Force, Field, Potential, Gauss's Law)

(C) By symmetry, the electric field will point along the negative x-axis. Using a differential slice of the rod, we get $dE_x = \dfrac{kdq}{r^2}\cos\theta$. Because the arc is uniformly charged, the charge density $\lambda = \dfrac{dq}{ds}$ or $dq = \lambda ds$. For any arc, $s = r\theta$, so $dq = \lambda ds = \lambda L d\theta$, given that $r = L$. The electric field is thus

$$E = \int_{-30}^{30} dE_x = \int_{-30}^{30} \frac{k}{L^2}\cos\theta(\lambda L d\theta) = \frac{\lambda k}{L}\sin\theta\Big|_{-30}^{30} = \frac{\lambda k}{L}(\sin 30 - \sin(-30)) = \frac{\lambda k}{L}$$

Given $\lambda = \dfrac{Q}{s} = \dfrac{Q}{L\theta} = \dfrac{Q}{L\dfrac{\pi}{3}} = \dfrac{3Q}{\pi L}$, $E = \dfrac{\lambda k}{L} = \dfrac{3kQ}{\pi L^2}$.

14. (Chapter 7: Electric Force, Field, Potential, Gauss's Law)

(C) The electric field inside a conducting material is zero, so it can be seen that the shell has an inner radius of 3 cm and an outer radius of 4 cm. At 4 cm from the graph, the electric field is 2×10^6 N/C. Using Gauss's law and a spherical Gaussian surface at $r = 4$ cm, we get

$$q_{enc} = \varepsilon_0 EA = \left(8.85 \times 10^{-12} \ \frac{F}{m}\right)\left(2 \times 10^6 \ \frac{N}{C}\right)(4)(\pi)(0.04 \ m)^2 = 360 \ nC$$

15. (Chapter 8: Electric Circuits, Capacitors, Dielectrics)

(A) Kirchoff's loop equations for the loops on the left and the right are

$$12 \ V - (5 \ \Omega)I_1 - (2 \ \Omega)(1A) = 0$$
$$(2 \ \Omega)(1A) + (1 \ \Omega)I_2 - \varepsilon = 0$$

A node equation for the currents is $I_1 + I_2 = 1$ A. Solving the system of equations gives

$$\varepsilon = 1 \ V$$

16. (Chapter 8: Electric Circuits, Capacitors, Dielectrics)

(D) The equivalent capacitance needs to be found. First, C_1 and C_2 are in series, and thus

$$C_{12} = \left(\frac{1}{C_1} + \frac{1}{C_2}\right)^{-1} = \frac{C_1 C_2}{C_1 + C_2} = \frac{C^2}{2C} + \frac{C}{2}$$

using C for the value of each capacitor. These are in parallel with C_3, so $C_{eq} = C_{12} + C_3 = \frac{C}{2} + C = \frac{3C}{2}$. Energy in a capacitor is $U = \frac{1}{2}C_{eq}V^2$, so $C = \frac{2U}{V^2} = \frac{(2)(8.64 \times 10^{-4} \ J)}{(12 \ V)^2} = 1.2 \times 10^{-5}$ F and $C = \frac{2}{3}C_{eq} = \frac{2}{3}(1.2 \times 10^{-5} \ F) = 8 \times 10^{-6}$ F.

17. (Chapter 9: Magnetic Fields and Forces)

(E) Energy is conserved as the charge accelerates:

$$U = K$$

$$qV = \frac{1}{2}mv^2$$

$$V = \frac{mv^2}{2q} = \frac{(1.67 \times 10^{-27} \ kg)\left(2.5 \times 10^5 \ \frac{m}{s}\right)^2}{(2)(1.602 \times 10^{-19} \ C)} = 326 \ V$$

18. (Chapter 9: Magnetic Fields and Forces)

(B) The particle is accelerated by a magnetic force, and Newton's second law can be applied in the centripetal direction:

$$F_c = ma_c$$

$$qvB = \frac{mv^2}{r}$$

$$r = \frac{mv}{qB} = \frac{(1.67\times10^{-27}\ \text{kg})\left(2.5\times10^5\ \dfrac{\text{m}}{\text{s}}\right)}{(1.602\times10^{-19}\text{C})(4\times10^{-3}\ \text{T})} = 0.65\ \text{m}$$

19. (Chapter 10: Electromagnetic Induction, Inductance, and Maxwell's Equations)

(D) The emf is found by

$$\varepsilon_{\text{ind}} = A\frac{dB}{dt} = \pi r^2 (8t-2) = \pi(0.2\ \text{m})^2\,[8(2\ \text{s})-2] = 1.76\ \text{V}$$

The magnetic field is negative at $t = 2$, while the rate of change is positive, meaning that the field is into the page and decreasing. The induced emf will produce a current that will oppose this change, so into the page and increasing. In a circular loop, this would be a clockwise current, and Ohm's law can be used to find the magnitude:

$$I = \frac{V}{R} = \frac{1.76\ \text{V}}{2.0\ \Omega} = 0.88\ \text{A}$$

20. (Chapter 10: Electromagnetic Induction, Inductance, and Maxwell's Equations)

(D) The emf will be found by $\varepsilon_{\text{ind}} = B\dfrac{dA}{dt}$. At $t = 2$ s, the bar has moved (2 m/s) (2 s) = 4 m. Given that the triangle is an isosceles right triangle, it can be determined that the length of the horizontal bar is twice the altitude of the triangle (the distance from the horizontal bar to the vertex), so the area of the triangle is $A = \dfrac{1}{2}bh = \dfrac{1}{2}(2h)(h) = h^2$. Thus $\dfrac{dA}{dt} = 2h\dfrac{dh}{dt} = 2hv$. With the given information at $t = 2$ s, $\varepsilon_{\text{ind}} = B\dfrac{dA}{dt} = (20\times10^{-3}\ \text{T})(2)(4\ \text{m})\left(2\ \dfrac{\text{m}}{\text{s}}\right) = 0.32\ \text{V}$.

CHAPTER 1

Kinematics

On all of the questions in this book, you may neglect air resistance and use $g = 10$ m/s^2 unless otherwise noted.

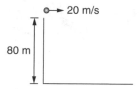

Questions 1–3

A ball of mass m is launched horizontally from the top of a cliff of height h with an initial speed of v_0 at time $t = 0$.

1. Which of the following is an expression for the horizontal distance x the ball travels before striking the ground?

   (A) $x = v_0 \sqrt{\dfrac{2h}{g}}$

   (B) $x = v_0 \sqrt{\dfrac{h}{g}}$

   (C) $x = v_0 \sqrt{\dfrac{h}{2g}}$

   (D) $x = \dfrac{v_0^2}{g}$

   (E) $x = \dfrac{2v_0^2}{g}$

2. Which of the following graphs best represents the vertical speed v_y of the ball from $t = 0$ until just before the ball strikes the ground?

(A) v_y

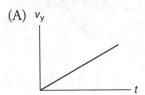

(B) v_y

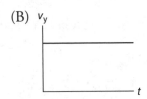

(C) v_y

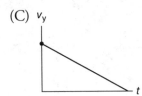

(D) v_y

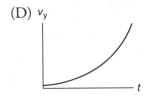

(E) v_y

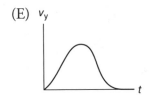

3. The speed of the ball just before striking the ground is

(A) v_0

(B) $v_0\sqrt{\dfrac{2h}{g}}v_0$

(C) $\sqrt{2gh}$

(D) $\sqrt{v_0^2 + 2gh}$

(E) $2v_0$

Questions 4–5

A sprinter starting from rest runs a 100-m race on a straight track. The sprinter accelerates for the first 2 seconds at a constant rate and then maintains a constant top speed for the remainder of the race. The entire race takes 11 seconds.

4. What is the acceleration of the runner during the first 2 seconds?

(A) 1 m/s²
(B) 2 m/s²
(C) 4 m/s²
(D) 5 m/s²
(E) 6 m/s²

5. A second runner has a nonconstant acceleration described by the function $a(t) = 10t^{1.5}$. Given that this runner also accelerates for 2 seconds, what is the distance this runner covers while accelerating?

(A) 5 m
(B) 6.5 m
(C) 8 m
(D) 9.5 m
(E) 10 m

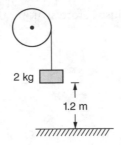

6. A block of mass 2 kg is attached to a string that is wrapped around a pulley of negligible mass and allowed to descend from rest a vertical distance of 1.2 m in a time of 1.5 s. The acceleration of the block is most nearly
    (A) 0.2 m/s²
    (B) 0.6 m/s²
    (C) 1.1 m/s²
    (D) 1.4 m/s²
    (E) 1.5 m/s²

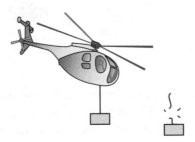

7. A helicopter raises a package with an upward constant speed of 3 m/s. The rope suddenly breaks when the package is 8 meters above the ground. Neglecting air resistance, calculate the speed at which the package strikes the ground.
    (A) 13 m/s
    (B) 26 m/s
    (C) 84 m/s
    (D) 169 m/s
    (E) 202 m/s

8. A ball is attached to a string of length 0.8 m and is swung in a vertical circle. The bottom of the circle is 0.2 m above the floor. If the string breaks at the top of the circle when the speed of the ball is 5 m/s, the horizontal distance the ball travels before striking the floor is

(A) 0.8 m
(B) 2.3 m
(C) 3.0 m
(D) 5.0 m
(E) 13.2 m

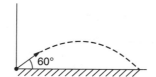

9. A golf ball is hit from level ground and has a horizontal range of 100 m. The ball leaves the golf club at an angle of 60° to the level ground. What is the speed with which the golf ball is hit?

(A) 15 m/s
(B) 20 m/s
(C) 25 m/s
(D) 30 m/s
(E) 35 m/s

10. A small cart is moving with an initial positive velocity of 4.0 m/s on a track of negligible friction when it rolls up the ramp, just makes it over the top, and rolls back down the ramp. The cart then rolls along the level track. Which of the following graphs best represents the velocity vs. time graph for the entire trip?

(A)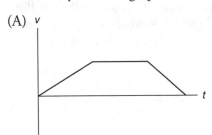

(B)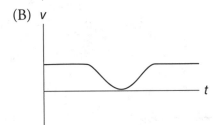

(C)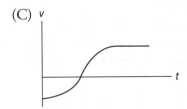

(D)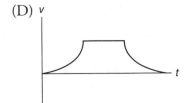

(E)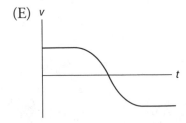

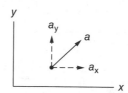

Questions 11–12. A particle moves on a horizontal surface with a constant acceleration of 6 m/s² in the *x*-direction and 4 m/s² in the *y*-direction. The initial velocity of the particle is 3 m/s in the *x*-direction.

11. The speed of the particle after 4 s is
   (A) 16 m/s
   (B) 27 m/s
   (C) 31 m/s
   (D) 44 m/s
   (E) 985 m/s

12. The displacement of the particle from its initial position is
   (A) 16 m
   (B) 32 m
   (C) 60 m
   (D) 68 m
   (E) 92 m

13. A space explorer throws a tool downward on a planet with an initial velocity of 2.0 m/s from a height of 6 m above the surface. The tool strikes the surface in a time of 2 s. The magnitude of the acceleration due to gravity on the planet is
   (A) 1 m/s²
   (B) 2 m/s²
   (C) 3 m/s²
   (D) 4 m/s²
   (E) 10 m/s²

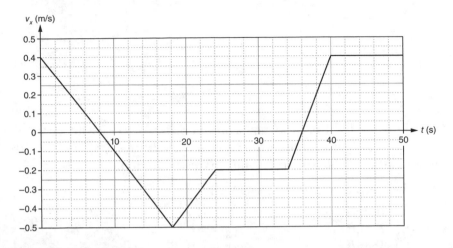

Questions 14–15

The graph shown represents the motion of a cart rolling along a horizontal track.

14. The time(s) at which the object is at rest is

(A) zero

(B) 8 s and 36 s

(C) 18 s and 40 s

(D) 24 s and 34 s

(E) 40 s and 50 s

15. The time(s) at which the cart changes direction is

(A) zero

(B) 8 s and 36 s

(C) 18 s and 40 s

(D) 24 s and 34 s

(E) 40 s and 50 s

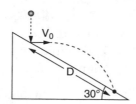

16. A rubber ball is dropped from rest onto a plane angled at 30° to the horizontal floor and bounces off the plane with a horizontal speed v_0. The ball lands on the plane a distance D along the plane, as shown. In terms of v_0, D, and g, the speed of the ball just before striking the plane is

    (A) v_0

    (B) $\left(v_o^2 + 2D\sin\theta g\right)^{\frac{1}{2}}$

    (C) $\left(v_o + \dfrac{D\sin\theta}{g}\right)^{\frac{1}{2}}$

    (D) $\left(v_o^2 + \dfrac{2D\sin\theta}{g}\right)^{\frac{1}{2}}$

    (E) $(2D\sin\theta g)^{\frac{1}{2}}$

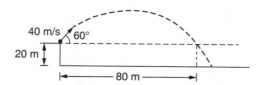

17. A projectile is launched from a platform 20 m high above level ground. The projectile is launched with a velocity of 40 m/s at an angle of 60° above the horizontal. The projectile follows a parabolic path and reaches its original height at a horizontal distance of 80 m, but moves past the height of the cliff to strike the ground below. The total time from the launch until it strikes the ground is

    (A) 2 s
    (B) 4 s
    (C) 6 s
    (D) 9 s
    (E) 10 s

Questions 18–20

An object is moving on a horizontal surface at a constant speed v_0 when it encounters a fluid at time $t = 0$. The fluid causes an acceleration to act on the object according to the equation $a = -kv$, where k is a positive constant.

18. The velocity of the object through the fluid as a function of time is
    (A) $-kv^2$
    (B) $-\frac{1}{2}kv^2$
    (C) $-k$
    (D) $\ln(kt)$
    (E) v_0e^{-kt}

19. Which of the following best represents the graph of velocity vs. time from $t = 0$ until the filters reach terminal velocity?

    (A)

    (B)

    (C)

    (D)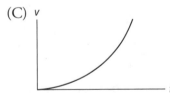

    (E)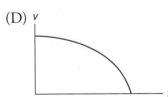

20. The object is initially moving at 12 m/s, and the positive constant k has a value of 1 s^{-1}. When the object has reached half its initial velocity, how far has the object traveled?
    (A) 4 m
    (B) 6 m
    (C) 8 m
    (D) 10 m
    (E) 12 m

Questions 21–22. A car of mass m travels along a straight horizontal road. The car begins with a speed v_o but accelerates according to the velocity function $v = \left(v_o^2 + \dfrac{Ct^2}{m} \right)$, where t is time.

21. The speed of the car is zero at a time t of
    (A) zero
    (B) $2t$
    (C) $4t$
    (D) $\sqrt{8t}$
    (E) The speed of the car is never zero.

22. The acceleration of the car as a function of time is

    (A) $\left(v_o^2 + \dfrac{Ct^2}{m} \right)$

    (B) $\left(v_o^2 + \dfrac{2Ct}{m} \right)$

    (C) $\left(v_o + \dfrac{2Ct}{m} \right)$

    (D) $\left(\dfrac{2Ct}{m} \right)$

    (E) $\left(\dfrac{2Ct^2}{m} \right)$

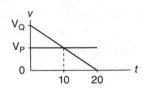

Questions 23–24. The graph shown represents the velocity vs. time graphs for two cars, P and Q. Car P begins with a speed v_P, and Car Q begins with a speed v_Q, which is twice the velocity of Car P; that is, $v_Q = 2v_P$.

23. Which of the following is true at a time of 10 s?
    (A) The cars occupy the same position.
    (B) Car P is at rest.
    (C) $v_Q > v_P$
    (D) $v_P > v_Q$
    (E) Car Q is ahead of Car P.

24. At what time do the cars have the same displacement?
    (A) Between $t = 0$ and $t = 10$ seconds
    (B) $t = 10$ s
    (C) Between $t = 10$ and $t = 20$ seconds
    (D) $t = 20$ seconds
    (E) At no time between $t = 0$ and $t = 20$ seconds

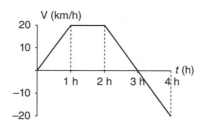

25. The velocity vs. time graph for a bike rider is shown above. At which two times is the rider in the same position?
    (A) $t = 0$ and $t = 3$ h
    (B) $t = 1$ and $t = 2$ h
    (C) $t = 2$ and $t = 4$ h
    (D) $t = 0$ and $t = 4$ h
    (E) At no time between $t = 0$ and $t = 4$ hours

26. A car is initially moving with a positive velocity of 16 m/s when it passes the origin at time $t = 0$ seconds. The car begins to accelerate according to the function $a = -8t$. The car comes to a stop at which time?
    (A) $t = 1$ second
    (B) $t = 2$ seconds
    (C) $t = 3$ seconds
    (D) $t = 4$ seconds
    (E) $t = 5$ seconds

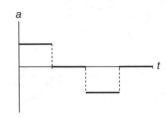

27. Which of the following pairs of graphs could show the position vs. time and velocity vs. time graphs for the acceleration vs. time graph shown above? Assume $v = 0$ and $x = 0$ at $t = 0$.

(A)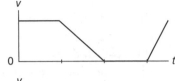

(B)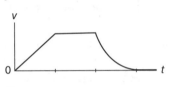

(C)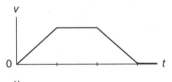

(D)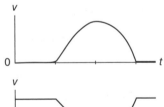

(E)

28. A small airplane can fly at 200 km/h with no wind. The pilot of the plane would like to fly to a destination 100 km due north of his present position, but there is a crosswind of 50 km/h east. How much time is required for the plane to fly north to its destination?

    (A) less than ½ h
    (B) ½ h
    (C) more than ½ h
    (D) 1 h
    (E) more than 1 h

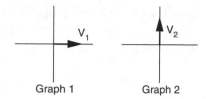

Graph 1   Graph 2

29. Two velocity vectors v_1 and v_2 each have a magnitude of 10 m/s. Graph 1 shows the velocity v_1 at $t = 0$ s, and then the same object has a velocity v_2 at $t = 2$ s, shown in Graph 2. Which of the following vectors best represents the average acceleration vector that causes the object's velocity to change from v_1 to v_2?

(A)

(B)

(C)

(D)

(E)

30. An object starts from rest at $t = 0$ and position $x = 0$ and then moves in a straight line with an acceleration described by the equation $a = 4t^2$ in m/s². What is the position of the object at $t = 3$ s?

(A) 6 m
(B) 18 m
(C) 27 m
(D) 54 m
(E) 108 m

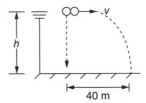

31. A ball is dropped from rest from the top of a cliff 80 m high. At the same time, a rock is thrown horizontally from the top of the same cliff. The rock and ball hit the level ground below a distance of 40 m apart. The horizontal velocity of the rock that was thrown was most nearly

(A) 5 m/s
(B) 10 m/s
(C) 20 m/s
(D) 40 m/s
(E) 80 m/s

32. A stone is dropped near the surface of Mars and falls with an acceleration of −3.8 m/s². This means that the

(A) distance the stone falls changes −3.8 meters for each second of fall
(B) derivative of the distance fallen with respect to time is −3.8 m/s
(C) derivative of the velocity with respect to time is −3.8 m/s²
(D) velocity is constant at −3.8 m/s
(E) derivative of the acceleration is −3.8 m/s²

33. An automobile moves with a position function described by $x(t) = 2t^3 - 3t^2 + 4t$, where x is in meters and t is in seconds. The average velocity of the automobile over the first 4 seconds is

   (A) 0 m/s
   (B) 12 m/s
   (C) 24 m/s
   (D) 72 m/s
   (E) 96 m/s

34. A passenger on a train moving horizontally at a constant speed relative to the ground drops a ball from his window. A stationary observer on the ground sees the ball falling with a speed v_1 at an angle to the vertical at the instant it is dropped from the train window, but the ball appears to be falling vertically with a speed v_2 at the same instant as viewed by the train passenger. What is the speed (magnitude of velocity) of the train relative to the ground after the ball is dropped? Neglect air resistance.

   (A) $v_1 + v_2$
   (B) $v_1 - v_2$
   (C) $v_1^2 + v_2^2$
   (D) $v_1^2 - v_2^2$
   (E) $\sqrt{v_1^2 - v_2^2}$

35. A ball is hit straight up into the air with an upward positive velocity. Which of the following describes the velocity and acceleration of the ball at the instant it reaches the top of its flight?

	Velocity	Acceleration
(A)	0	0
(B)	0	g
(C)	$2v_o$	g
(D)	½ v_o	0
(E)	0	½ g

36. A toy dart gun fires a dart at an angle of $45°$ to the horizontal and the dart reaches a maximum height of 1 meter. If the dart were fired straight up into the air along the vertical, the dart would reach a height of

    (A) 1 m
    (B) 2 m
    (C) 3 m
    (D) 4 m
    (E) 5 m

Questions 37–38
A projectile is launched at the angle and follows the trajectory shown below.

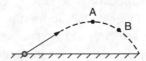

37. Which of the following indicates the direction of the velocity at point A?

    (A) ↑
    (B) ←
    (C) →
    (D) ↖
    (E) ↓

38. Which of the following indicates the direction of the acceleration at point B?

    (A) ↑
    (B) ←
    (C) →
    (D) ↖
    (E) ↓

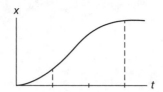

39. The graph above shows the displacement as a function of time for a car moving in a straight line. Which of the following graphs shows the velocity vs. time graph for the same time intervals?

(A)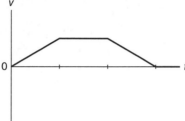

(B)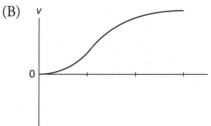

(C)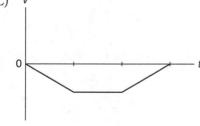

(D)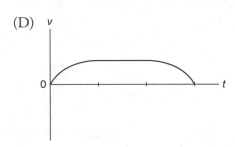

(E)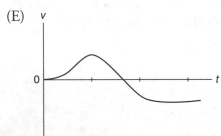

Questions 40–41

40. An object is released from rest and falls through a resistive medium. The resistance causes the velocity of the object to change according to the equation $v = 16t - \frac{1}{2}t^4$, where v is in m/s and time is in s. Which of the following is a possible equation for the acceleration of the object as a function of time?

(A) $16 - 2t^2$
(B) $16 - 2t^3$
(C) $16 - 2t$
(D) $8t^3 - 2t^2$
(E) $32t^3 - 2t^5$

41. What is the terminal velocity of the object as it falls?

(A) 5 m/s
(B) 10 m/s
(C) 24 m/s
(D) 32 m/s
(E) The object never reaches a terminal velocity.

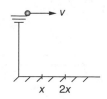

42. A student jumps off a cliff with an initial horizontal velocity v and lands in a lake below at a distance of x from the base of the cliff. In terms of his initial velocity v, how fast would he have had to jump to land a distance $2x$ from the base of the cliff?

    (A) $\sqrt{2}v$
    (B) $2v$
    (C) $4v$
    (D) $8v$
    (E) $16v$

43. An astronaut drops a hammer on a moon with no atmosphere. The hammer falls a distance of 2 meters in the first second. What is the acceleration due to gravity on this moon?

    (A) -1 m/s^2
    (B) -2 m/s^2
    (C) -3 m/s^2
    (D) -4 m/s^2
    (E) -8 m/s^2

44. A car travels 300 m in 60 s, then travels 200 m in 30 s. The average speed of the car is

    (A) 5.6 m/s
    (B) 5.0 m/s
    (C) 3.0 m/s
    (D) 2.3 m/s
    (E) 12.0 m/s

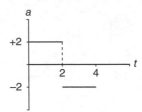

45. The motion of an object is represented by the acceleration vs. time graph above. Which of the following statements is true about the motion of the object?

    (A) The object returns to its original position.
    (B) The velocity of the object is zero at a time of 2 s.
    (C) The velocity of the object is zero at a time of 4 s.
    (D) The displacement of the object is zero at a time of 4 s.
    (E) The acceleration of the object is zero at a time of 2 s.

Free Response

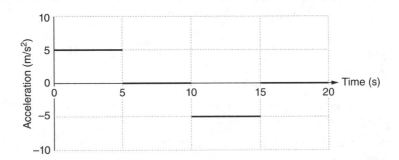

The acceleration vs. time graph shows the motion of an elevator during a 20-second interval. The elevator is at rest at time $t = 15$ seconds.

46. Find the instantaneous velocity of the elevator at $t = 0$ seconds.

47. During which time interval, if any, is the elevator moving down while slowing down?

48. On the axes below, sketch the graph that represents the velocity vs. time graph for the elevator for the 20-second time interval.

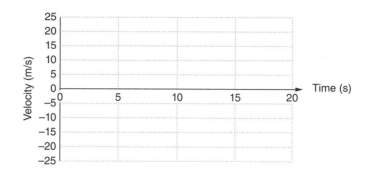

Questions 49–50. A particle follows a parabolic path with the equation $y = 2x^2$ as shown. The x-component of the particle's velocity v_x as a function of time t is 6; that is, the horizontal displacement is $x = 6t$.

49. Determine the y-component of the particle's velocity v_y as a function of time.

50. On the diagram below, sketch arrows to represent the horizontal and vertical components of the particle's acceleration at point P.

CHAPTER 2

Dynamics: Newton's Laws of Motion

On all of the questions in this book, you may neglect air resistance and use $g = 10$ m/s^2 unless otherwise noted.

51. Which of the following involves a net force?
   I. A ball on the end of a string travels in circular motion.
   II. A space probe travels with a constant velocity in a straight line between planets.
   III. An object has a constant horizontal velocity but a decreasing vertical velocity.

   (A) I only
   (B) I and II only
   (C) II and III only
   (D) I and III only
   (E) I, II, and III

52. A small moving block collides with a large block at rest. Which of the following is true of the forces the blocks apply to each other?
   (A) The small block exerts twice the force on the large block compared to the force the large block exerts on the small block.
   (B) The small block exerts half the force on the large block compared to the force the large block exerts on the small block.
   (C) The small block exerts exactly the same amount of force on the large block that the large block exerts on the small block.
   (D) The large block exerts a force on the small block, but the small block does not exert a force on the large block.
   (E) The small block exerts a force on the large block, but the large block does not exert a force on the small block.

53. Which of the following position vs. time graphs shows an example of the law of inertia?

(A)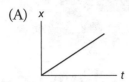

(B)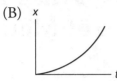

(C)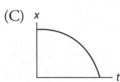

(D)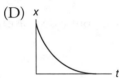

(E)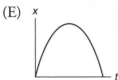

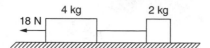

Questions 54–55. Two blocks, 4.0 kg and 2.0 kg, are connected by an elastic band, which can be treated as an ideal spring with a spring constant of 4 N/m. An applied force **F** of magnitude 18 N pulls the blocks to the left. The coefficients of static and kinetic friction between the blocks and floor are 0.2 and 0.1, respectively.

54. The acceleration of the 4.0-kg block is
    (A) 0.0 m/s^2
    (B) 2.0 m/s^2
    (C) 3.0 m/s^2
    (D) 4.0 m/s^2
    (E) 6.0 m/s^2

55. At a later time, the 18-N force is reduced to a value that has the two blocks moving at constant velocity. How much is the elastic band stretched from its equilibrium length at this moment?
    (A) 0.1 m
    (B) 0.2 m
    (C) 0.3 m
    (D) 0.4 m
    (E) 0.5 m

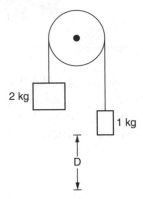

Questions 56–57. A system consists of two blocks having masses of 2 kg and 1 kg. The blocks are connected by a string of negligible mass and hung over a frictionless pulley, and then released from rest.

56. The acceleration of the 2-kg block is most nearly

(A) $\dfrac{2}{9}g$

(B) $\dfrac{1}{3}g$

(C) $\dfrac{1}{2}g$

(D) $\dfrac{2}{3}g$

(E) g

57. The speed of the 2 kg block after it has descended a distance D is most nearly

(A) $\sqrt{\dfrac{4D}{3}}$

(B) $\sqrt{\dfrac{2D}{3}}$

(C) $\sqrt{\dfrac{D}{3}}$

(D) $\sqrt{\dfrac{D}{2}}$

(E) $\sqrt{\dfrac{4D}{6}}$

Questions 58–59. A weight of magnitude W is suspended in equilibrium by two cords, one horizontal and one slanted at an angle of 60° from the horizontal, as shown.

58. Which of the following statements is true?
- (A) The tension in the horizontal cord must be greater than the tension in the slanted cord.
- (B) The tension in the slanted cord must be greater than the tension in the horizontal cord.
- (C) The tension is the same in both cords.
- (D) The tension in the horizontal cord equals the weight W.
- (E) The tension in the slanted cord equals the weight W.

59. The tension in the horizontal cord is
- (A) equal to the tension in the slanted cord
- (B) one-third as much as the tension in the slanted cord
- (C) one-half as much as the tension in the slanted cord
- (D) twice as much as the tension in the slanted cord
- (E) three times as much as the tension in the slanted cord

Questions 60–61. An object of mass m moves along a straight line with a speed described by the equation $v = c + bt^3$.

60. The initial velocity of the mass is
- (A) c
- (B) $ct + bt^3$
- (C) $ct + bt^4$
- (D) bt^2
- (E) bt

61. The net force acting on the mass at time T is
- (A) $3mbT$
- (B) $3mbT^2$
- (C) $3mbT^3$
- (D) $mc + 2mbT^2$
- (E) $mc^2 + 4mbT^4$

62. A wooden block slides down a frictionless inclined plane a distance of 1 meter along the plane during the first second. The distance traveled along the plane by the block during the time between 1 s and 2 s is
    (A) 2 m
    (B) 3 m
    (C) 4 m
    (D) 6 m
    (E) 8 m

63. A mass located at point P follows a parabolic path. Which of the following diagrams indicates a possible combination of the net force **F** acting on the mass, the velocity **v**, and acceleration **a** of the mass at point P?

    (A)

    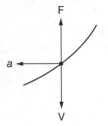

    (B)

    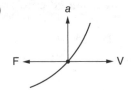

    (C)

    (D)

    (E)

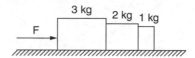

Questions 64–65. Three blocks, of mass 3 kg, 2 kg, and 1 kg, are pushed along a horizontal plane by a force **F**, described by $\mathbf{F} = 6t$, where **F** is in newtons and t is in seconds. The force is first applied at time $t = 0$ seconds. The coefficient of static friction between the blocks and the plane is 0.4, and the coefficient of kinetic friction is 0.2.

64. At what time t will the blocks begin to move?

(A) 1 s
(B) 2 s
(C) 3 s
(D) 4 s
(E) 5 s

65. At $t = 6$ s, the force that the 2-kg block exerts on the 3-kg block is

(A) 6 N
(B) 12 N
(C) 18 N
(D) 24 N
(E) 30 N

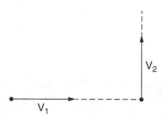

66. A hockey puck slides along horizontal ice with a velocity $\mathbf{v}_1$ when it is struck by a hockey stick, changing its direction, as shown. After the puck is struck, it has a velocity $\mathbf{v}_2$, which is greater than $\mathbf{v}_1$. Which of the following vectors best represents the direction the force of the hockey stick acted on the puck?

(A) ↑
(B) ←
(C) →
(D) ↖
(E) ↗

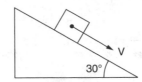

67. A block of mass 4 kg slides down a rough incline with a constant speed. The angle the incline makes with the horizontal is 30°. The coefficient of friction acting between the block and incline is most nearly

    (A) 0.1
    (B) 0.2
    (C) 0.3
    (D) 0.4
    (E) 0.6

68. An object of mass 3 kg moves along a straight line on the y-axis according to the equation $y = 8t - 4t^2 + t^3$, where y is in meters and t is in seconds. The net force acting on the mass is zero at a time of

    (A) $\dfrac{3}{4}$ s

    (B) $\dfrac{4}{3}$ s

    (C) $\dfrac{8}{3}$ s

    (D) 2 s
    (E) 4 s

69. A downhill speed skater experiences an air resistance force and kinetic friction on her skis as she slides downhill. The hill is a constant incline. At a time where her speed is increasing, which of the following is true about these forces that act on her?

    (A) There is a decreasing kinetic friction force and an increasing force of air resistance.
    (B) There is an increasing kinetic friction force and an increasing force of air resistance.
    (C) There is a decreasing kinetic friction force and a decreasing force of air resistance.
    (D) There is a constant kinetic friction force and an increasing force of air resistance.
    (E) There is a constant kinetic friction force and a decreasing force of air resistance.

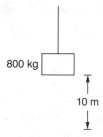

Questions 70–71

An 800-kg elevator is supported by a vertical cable.

70. The elevator accelerates upward for the first 10 m of travel, at which time it is moving at 7.1 m/s. The tension in the cable is most nearly

(A) 2,000 N
(B) 4,000 N
(C) 5,000 N
(D) 8,000 N
(E) 10,000 N

71. The elevator passes the 10-m height on the way up, stops, then begins its descent downward, having an initial velocity as it passes the 10 m height on the way down. If the tension in the cable is now 6,000 N and it comes to rest just before reaching the ground, the initial velocity at the 10-m height must have been most nearly

(A) 5.0 m/s
(B) 7.0 m/s
(C) 29.5 m/s
(D) 12.5 m/s
(E) 16.0 m/s

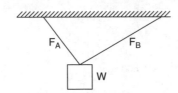

72. A weight W is hung from two threads, A and B, as shown above. The magnitudes of the tensions in each string are F_A and F_B, respectively. Which of the following describes the relationship between F_A, F_B, and W?

    (A) $F_A = F_B = W$
    (B) $F_A = F_B$
    (C) $F_A < F_B$
    (D) $F_A > F_B$
    (E) $F_A + F_B = W$

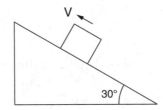

Questions 73–74
A 1-kg block slides down a rough 30° incline at a constant speed.

73. The coefficient of kinetic friction is closest to

    (A) 0.25
    (B) 0.39
    (C) 0.5
    (D) 0.57
    (E) 0.87

74. What force, applied parallel to the surface and directed up the incline, would be required to move the block *up* the incline at a constant velocity?

    (A) 5 N
    (B) 7 N
    (C) 10 N
    (D) 13 N
    (E) 15 N

75. A 2-kg object is moving with a velocity function given by $v(t) = 2t^2 - 3t$, where t is in seconds and $v(t)$ is in m/s. The net force acting on the object at $t = 4$ s is closest to

(A) 8 N
(B) 13 N
(C) 20 N
(D) 26 N
(E) 40 N

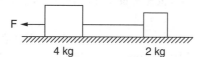

4 kg   2 kg

76. Two blocks are pulled by a force of magnitude F along a level surface with negligible friction as shown. The tension in the string between the blocks is

(A) $\dfrac{1}{4} F$

(B) $\dfrac{1}{2} F$

(C) $\dfrac{1}{3} F$

(D) F

(E) $2F$

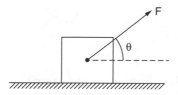

77. A force of magnitude F pulls up at an angle θ to the horizontal on a block of mass m. The mass remains in contact with the level floor and the coefficient of friction between the block and the floor is μ. The frictional force between the floor and the block is

(A) μmg
(B) $\mu(mg - F\sin\theta)$
(C) $\mu(mg + F\sin\theta)$
(D) $\mu(mg - F\cos\theta)$
(E) $\mu(mg + F\cos\theta)$

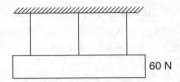

78. A uniform block weighing 60 N hangs from three ropes of negligible mass as shown. Which of the following statements is true?

    (A) Each rope has a tension of 60 N.
    (B) The tension in each rope is higher in the lower part than in the upper part of the rope.
    (C) The tension in each rope is higher in the upper part than in the lower part of the rope.
    (D) The rope in the center has a higher tension than the other two ropes.
    (E) Each rope has a tension of 20 N.

79. A stone is thrown straight upward through the air. While the stone is rising, the magnitude of the resistive force the air applies to the stone is given by the equation $F = cv$, where c is a positive constant and v is the speed of the stone. The acceleration of the ball is given by the equation

    (A) $c - g$
    (B) $c + g$
    (C) $-cv/m - g$
    (D) $cv/m - g$
    (E) cv/m

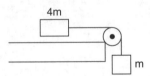

80. A block of mass $4m$ can move without friction on a horizontal surface. Another block of mass m is attached to the larger block by a string that is passed over a light pulley. The acceleration of the system is

    (A) $\dfrac{1}{5} g$

    (B) $\dfrac{1}{2} g$

    (C) $\dfrac{2}{3} g$

    (D) g

    (E) $5g$

81. The block of mass $4m$ in the previous question now moves on a rough surface. The frictional force between the surface and the larger block is equal to ½ mg. The acceleration of the system is now

(A) $\dfrac{1}{16} g$

(B) $\dfrac{1}{10} g$

(C) $\dfrac{1}{4} g$

(D) $\dfrac{1}{2} g$

(E) g

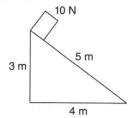

Questions 82–83. A 10-N block sits atop an inclined plane in the shape of a right triangle of sides 3 m, 4 m, and 5 m, as shown. The block is allowed to slide down the plane with negligible friction.

82. The acceleration of the block is most nearly
    (A) 2 m/s²
    (B) 4 m/s²
    (C) 6 m/s²
    (D) 10 m/s²
    (E) 12 m/s²

83. The normal force exerted on the block by the plane is most nearly
    (A) 2 N
    (B) 4 N
    (C) 6 N
    (D) 8 N
    (E) 10 N

Questions 84–85

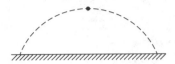

84. A projectile is launched at an angle and follows a parabolic path near the Earth's surface from left to right, as shown above. Which of the following best indicates the net force acting on the projectile at the top of its path?

(A) ↑

(B) ←

(C) →

(D) ↖

(E) ↓

85. The projectile in Question 84 now experiences air resistance. Which of the following best indicates the net force acting on the projectile on the top of its path?

(A) ↑

(B) ←

(C) →

(D) ↖

(E) ↓

Questions 86–87. The position of a 2-kg object is described by the equation $x = 2t^2 - 3t^3$, where x is in meters and t is in seconds.

86. The net force acting on the object at a time of 1 s is

(A) −4 N

(B) −8 N

(C) −14 N

(D) −20 N

(E) −24 N

87. The net force acting on the object is positive from $t = 0$ until a time of

   (A) 0.11 s
   (B) 0.22 s
   (C) 0.44 s
   (D) 0.67 s
   (E) 1.0 s

Questions 88–89. A particle of mass 0.5 kg moves in two dimensions according to the velocity equation $\mathbf{v} = 4t^3\mathbf{i} + 6t^2\mathbf{j}$ and has an initial position $\mathbf{r} = 2\mathbf{i} - 3\mathbf{j}$, where position is in meters, velocity is in m/s, and time is in s.

88. The position and acceleration of the particle at $t = 1$ s in m/s^2 is

   (A) $\mathbf{r} = 3\mathbf{i} - \mathbf{j},\ \mathbf{a} = 12\mathbf{i} + 12\mathbf{j}$
   (B) $\mathbf{r} = 2\mathbf{i} - 3\mathbf{j},\ \mathbf{a} = 12\mathbf{i} + 12\mathbf{j}$
   (C) $\mathbf{r} = 3\mathbf{i} - \mathbf{j},\ \mathbf{a} = 12\mathbf{i} - 12\mathbf{j}$
   (D) $\mathbf{r} = 3\mathbf{i} + \mathbf{j},\ \mathbf{a} = -12\mathbf{i} + 12\mathbf{j}$
   (E) $\mathbf{r} = -3\mathbf{i} - \mathbf{j},\ \mathbf{a} = -12\mathbf{i} - 12\mathbf{j}$

89. The magnitude of the net force acting on the particle at $t = 1$ s is most nearly

   (A) 6 N
   (B) 7 N
   (C) 9 N
   (D) 17 N
   (E) 36 N

90. A constant force acts on a particle in such a way that the direction of the force is always perpendicular to its velocity. Which of the following is true of the particle's motion?

   (A) The acceleration of the particle is increasing.
   (B) The acceleration of the particle is decreasing.
   (C) The speed of the particle is increasing.
   (D) The speed of the particle is constant.
   (E) The speed of the particle is decreasing.

91. A coffee filter is released from rest at a height of 3 meters above the floor. Which of the following graphs best describes the speed of the falling coffee filter as a function of time?

(A)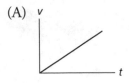

(B)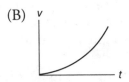

(C)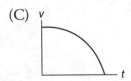

(D)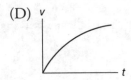

(E)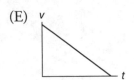

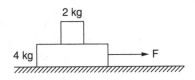

Questions 92–93. A block of mass 2 kg rests on top of a larger block of mass 4 kg. The larger block slides without friction on a table, but the surface between the two blocks is not frictionless. The coefficient of friction between the two blocks is 0.2. A horizontal force **F** is applied to the 4-kg mass.

92. What is the maximum force that can be applied such that there is no relative motion between the two blocks?

(A) Zero
(B) 1 N
(C) 2 N
(D) 4 N
(E) 12 N

93. What is the acceleration of the 2 kg block **_relative to the 4-kg block_** if a force is applied to the 4-kg block that causes the 4-kg block to accelerate at 3 m/s² to the right?

(A) 1 m/s² to the right
(B) 1 m/s² to the left
(C) 2 m/s² to the right
(D) 2 m/s² to the left
(E) Zero

Free Response

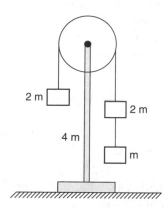

Questions 94–97. Three masses are connected by two strings as shown. One of the strings is passed over a pulley of negligible mass and friction. The pulley is attached to a stand that rests on a table. The smallest mass is m, the other two masses each have a mass of $2m$, and the mass of the stand is $4m$.

94. If the small mass m is removed, the other two masses hang in equilibrium. Determine the normal force the table exerts on the stand when the system is in equilibrium.

95. The small mass *m* is once again hung below one of the masses of mass 2*m*. Determine the acceleration of the system.

96. Determine the tension in the string between the block of mass 2*m* and the attached block of mass *m* while the system is accelerating.

97. While the system is accelerating, is the normal force exerted by the table on the stand greater than, equal to, or less than 8*mg*? Justify your answer.

_____ greater than 8*mg* _____ equal to 8*mg* _____ less than 8*mg*

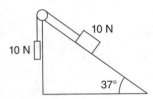

Questions 98–100. Two blocks weighing 10 N each are connected by a light string that is passed over a light pulley. One of the blocks rests on an inclined plane at an angle of 37° to the horizontal. The friction between the inclined plane and the block is such that the system remains at rest. The length of the ramp is 5 m.

98. Determine the tension in the string while the system is at rest.

99. Determine the frictional force between the block and the inclined plane while the system is at rest.

100. If the string is suddenly cut, what is the speed of the block when it reaches the bottom of the plane?

CHAPTER 3

Work, Energy, Power, and Conservation of Energy

On all of the questions in this book, you may neglect air resistance and use $g = 10$ m/s^2 unless otherwise noted.

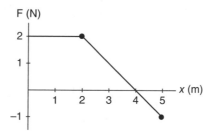

Questions 101–102. The graph shown represents a force F acting on an object vs. its displacement x.

101. The work done on the object between 0 and 4 meters is

(A) 2 J
(B) 4 J
(C) 6 J
(D) −2 J
(E) −6 J

102. The change in kinetic energy of the object from 0 m to 5 m is

(A) 4 J
(B) 5 J
(C) 5.5 J
(D) −5.5 J
(E) −6 J

103. An object of weight W is pulled from rest by a cable with tension T such that the velocity is described by the equation $v = 2t^{3/2}$. The magnitude of the average power the tension force supplies is represented by the equation

(A) $2Wt^{3/2}$

(B) $3Tt^{1/2}$

(C) $3t^{3/2}$

(D) $\dfrac{4}{5}Tt^{5/2}$

(E) $\dfrac{4}{5}Tt^{3/2}$

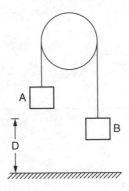

Questions 104–105. Two blocks of mass m_A and m_B are connected by a string that passes over a light pulley. The mass of A is larger than the mass of B.

104. The change in potential energy of the system just before block A reaches the floor is

(A) $(m_A + m_B)gD$

(B) $m_A gD$

(C) $m_B gD$

(D) $(m_A - m_B)gD$

(E) zero

105. The speed of mass A just before reaching the floor is

(A) $\sqrt{\dfrac{(m_A - m_B)}{(m_A + m_B)} gD}$

(B) $\sqrt{\dfrac{(m_A + m_B)}{(m_A - m_B)} gD}$

(C) $\sqrt{\dfrac{(m_A)}{(m_A + m_B)} gD}$

(D) $\sqrt{\dfrac{(m_B)}{(m_A + m_B)} gD}$

(E) $\sqrt{\dfrac{(m_A)}{(m_B)} gD}$

106. Which of the following force F vs. displacement x graphs below will cause the **least** change in kinetic energy of the object on which the force acts? All graphs are drawn to the same scale.

(A) F
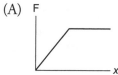

(B) F

(C) F
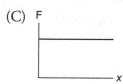

(D) F
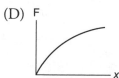

(E) F
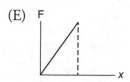

107. A particle of mass m moves according to the displacement equation $x = 2t^{5/2}$. The kinetic energy of the particle as a function of time is

(A) $10mt^{5/2}$
(B) $10mt^{3/2}$
(C) $5/2mt^3$
(D) $5mt^2$
(E) $2mt^{3/2}$

108. A 1-kg ball experiences a constant resistive force of 2.5 N as it descends through a thick fluid. The ball descends from rest with a velocity described by $v(t) = 2(1 - e^{-2t})$, where t is in seconds and v is in m/s. The magnitude of the energy lost due to resistance from the fluid for the first 3 s of descent is most nearly

(A) 10 J
(B) 12.5 J
(C) 15 J
(D) 17.5 J
(E) 20 J

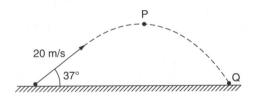

Questions 109–110. A 2-kg projectile is launched with a speed of 20 m/s from horizontal ground at an angle of 37° to the horizontal as shown. Point P is at the top of the path, and point Q is at the end of the path, just before the projectile again reaches the ground.

109. The work done by gravity from point P to Q is most nearly

(A) –144 J
(B) –72 J
(C) 0 J
(D) 72 J
(E) 144 J

110. If the projectile loses 120 J of energy due to air resistance over the entire path, what is the kinetic energy when the particle reaches point Q?

(A) 120 J
(B) 240 J
(C) 280 J
(D) 340 J
(E) 400 J

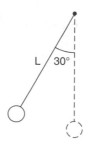

111. A pendulum of mass m swings from a vertical angle of 30° as shown. The length of the pendulum is L. If the pendulum is released from rest, the speed of the pendulum at the bottom of the swing is

(A) $2gL$
(B) gL
(C) $\sqrt{gL}$
(D) $\sqrt{2gL(L - \cos 30°)}$
(E) $\frac{1}{2}\, gL \cos 30°$

112. A 10-N weight is lifted by applying a 15-N upward force. The change in kinetic energy of the weight during this time is equal to the

(A) change in potential energy during this time
(B) the work done by the 10-N weight only
(C) the work done by the 15-N force only
(D) the work done by the 5-N net force
(E) the work done by the algebraic sum of the forces (25 N)

Questions 113–115. A 5-kg object moves along the x-axis with a potential energy function $U = 4x^2 - 2x + 3$, where x is in meters and U is in joules.

113. If at $x = 0$ the particle is at rest and energy is conserved, at what other location will the particle be at rest?

   (A) 0.25 m
   (B) 0.5 m
   (C) 0.75 m
   (D) 1.0 m
   (E) 1.25 m

114. The magnitude of the force acting on the object at $x = \frac{1}{4}$ m is

   (A) zero
   (B) 2 N
   (C) 4 N
   (D) 8 N
   (E) 16 N

115. If the total energy of the particle is 10 J and the particle has a mass of 2 kg, what is the speed of the particle at $x = 0$ m?

   (A) 1.7 m/s
   (B) 2.6 m/s
   (C) 3.2 m/s
   (D) 3.5 m/s
   (E) 4.1 m/s

116. A ball is thrown upward with an initial velocity. At a height of 5 m above the ground, the ball has a potential energy of 30 J relative to the ground. At this height, the ball has a kinetic energy of 20 J. Neglecting air resistance, the maximum height the ball will reach is most nearly

   (A) 6 m
   (B) 8 m
   (C) 10 m
   (D) 12 m
   (E) 20 m

Questions 117–118. A 2-kg crate is slid up an inclined plane with a force given by $\mathbf{F} = 4\hat{i} + 4y^3\hat{j}$, with x and y in meters and $\mathbf{F}$ in newtons.

117. The work done by the force as the particle moves from (0, 0) to (1, 3) is

(A) 4 J
(B) 81 J
(C) 85 J
(D) 117 J
(E) 200 J

118. The work done by gravity is

(A) −80 J
(B) −60 J
(C) 0 J
(D) 60 J
(E) 80 J

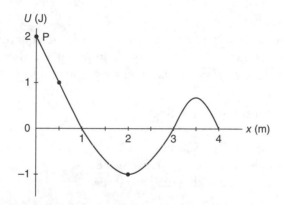

Questions 119–120 refer to the potential energy U vs. displacement x graph shown for a particle moving in one dimension. The force acting on the particle is conservative. The graph begins at point P. The kinetic energy of the particle at position $x = 2$ is 3.0 J. The graph is represented by a straight, diagonal line between $x = 3$ and $x = 4$.

119. The magnitude of the force acting on the particle between $x = 3$ and $x = 4$ is

(A) zero
(B) constant
(C) increasing
(D) decreasing
(E) equal to the weight of the particle

120. Which of the following is false about the particle?
- (A) The net force on the particle at $x = 2$ is zero.
- (B) The total energy of the particle at $x = 2$ is +2 J.
- (C) The particle, when moving to the left, stops at point P and begins to move to the right.
- (D) The kinetic energy of the particle at $x = 1$ m is 0 J.
- (E) The kinetic energy of the particle at $x = 1$ m is equal to the kinetic energy of the particle at $x = 4$ m.

121. The force acting on an object varies with the equation $F(x) = -3x^2 - 2x - 4$, where force is in newtons and displacement is in meters. The potential energy at $x = 2$ m is
- (A) zero
- (B) 20 J
- (C) 40 J
- (D) −20 J
- (E) −40 J

122. The potential energy of an object varies with the equation $U(x) = 2x^2 + x - 6$, where potential energy is in joules and displacement is in meters. A force F vs. displacement x graph would yield which of the following?
- (A) A straight, horizontal line
- (B) A parabola
- (C) An exponential decay curve
- (D) A straight line with a positive slope
- (E) A straight line with a negative slope

123. An object is moved from rest at point P to rest at point Q in a gravitational field. The net work against the gravitational field depends on the
- (A) mass of the object and the positions of P and Q
- (B) mass of the object only
- (C) positions of P and Q only
- (D) length moved between points P and Q
- (E) coefficient of friction

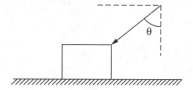

Questions 124–125. A force is applied to a block of mass m at a downward angle of θ to the vertical as shown. The block moves with a constant speed across a rough floor for a distance x.

124. The work done by the applied force on the block is

(A) $Fx\sin\theta$
(B) $Fx\cos\theta$
(C) $Fmx\sin\theta$
(D) $Fmx\cos\theta$
(E) zero

125. The coefficient of friction between the block and the floor is

(A) $\dfrac{F}{mg}$

(B) $\dfrac{F\cos\theta}{mg}$

(C) $\dfrac{F\cos\theta}{F\sin\theta + mg}$

(D) $\dfrac{F\sin\theta}{F\cos\theta + mg}$

(E) $\dfrac{F\cos\theta}{F\sin\theta}$

126. An electron travels in a circle (radius $= 3 \times 10^{-10}$ m) around a hydrogen nucleus at a speed of 2×10^6 m/s due to an electrostatic force. The work done by the electrostatic force acting on the electron after one complete revolution is

(A) 0 J
(B) 2.7×10^{-39} J
(C) 5.5×10^{-33} J
(D) 1.82×10^{-23} J
(E) 6.0×10^{-4} J

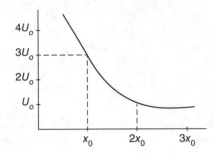

Questions 127–128. The potential energy curve shown refers to a particle having a mass m. The particle is released from rest at the position x_o.

127. The kinetic energy of the particle at position $3x_o$ is

(A) zero
(B) $2U_o$
(C) $3U_o$
(D) $4U_o$
(E) $-2U_o$

128. The particle is instead given a kinetic energy at x_0 of 2 J. The kinetic energy at $3x_0$ is closest to

(A) zero

(B) $\sqrt{\dfrac{U_0 + 2}{m}}$

(C) $\sqrt{\dfrac{U_0 + 1}{2m}}$

(D) $2\sqrt{\dfrac{U_0 + 1}{m}}$

(E) $2\sqrt{\dfrac{U_0 + 2}{m}}$

129. A block, $m = 4.0$ kg, is dropped from a height of 0.5 m onto a spring with a spring constant $k = 2,000$ N/m. What is the speed of the package when the spring is compressed to half its maximum distance?

(A) 2.5 J
(B) 2.8 J
(C) 3.4 J
(D) 3.6 J
(E) 3.9 J

130. A block slides down a smooth incline from a vertical height h so that the work done by gravity is 100 J. The block is then placed at the bottom of the incline and given an initial velocity so that it rises to the same height h before coming to rest. The work done by gravity as the block slides up the plane to a height h is

(A) 100 J
(B) zero
(C) −100 J
(D) −200 J
(E) The work done by gravity cannot be determined without knowing the mass of the block and the distance it slides along the plane.

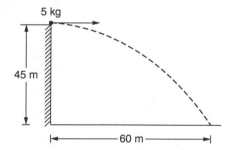

Questions 131–132. A 5-kg cannonball is fired with a horizontal velocity from a height of 45 m above level ground below. The cannonball strikes a target on the ground a horizontal distance of 60 m away.

131. The total energy of the cannonball is

(A) 1,000 J
(B) 2,250 J
(C) 3,250 J
(D) 4,000 J
(E) 4,750 J

132. The speed of the cannonball just before striking the ground is most nearly

(A) 12 m/s
(B) 21 m/s
(C) 36 m/s
(D) 45 m/s
(E) 90 m/s

Questions 133–134. A ball is thrown from level ground with a velocity at an angle θ above the horizontal so that it follows a parabolic path.

133. Which of the graphs below best represents the kinetic energy of the ball as a function of time until it again reaches the ground?

(A)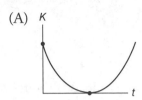

(B)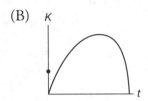

(C)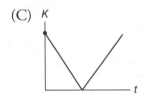

(D)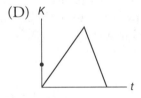

(E)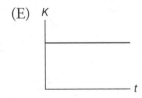

134. Which of the graphs below best represents the potential energy of the ball as a function of time until it again reaches the ground?

(A)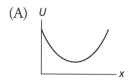

(B)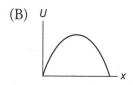

(C)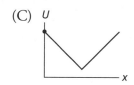

(D)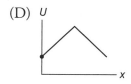

(E)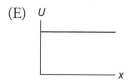

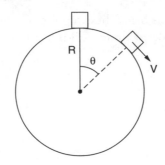

Questions 135–136. A small block rests on the top of a smooth sphere of radius R when it is given a light tap so that it just begins sliding on the sphere. When the block reaches the angle θ, it loses contact with the surface of the sphere.

135. The kinetic energy of the block as it leaves the surface of the sphere is
    (A) mgR
    (B) $mgR\cos\theta$
    (C) $mgR\sin\theta$
    (D) $mg(R - R\cos\theta)$
    (E) $mg(R - R\sin\theta)$

136. The speed of the block as it leaves the surface of the sphere is

    (A) $\sqrt{\dfrac{2g}{m}}$

    (B) $\sqrt{\dfrac{2gR}{m}}$

    (C) $\sqrt{2gR\cos\theta}$

    (D) $\sqrt{2g(R - R\cos\theta)}$

    (E) $\sqrt{2g(R - R\sin\theta)}$

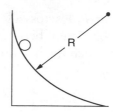

137. A small ball starts from rest and rolls down a quarter-circle ramp of radius R. The speed of the ball at the point halfway down the ramp is most nearly

(A) gR

(B) $2gR$

(C) $\sqrt{gR \sin 45°}$

(D) $\sqrt{2gR \sin 45°}$

(E) The speed cannot be determined without knowing the mass of the ball.

138. A machine can lift large weights according to the power equation $P(t) = 4t^3 + 3t^2 - 2$, where power is in watts and time is in seconds. The energy expended by the machine from $t = 0$ to $t = 10$ s is

(A) 1,260 J

(B) 3,630 J

(C) 9,240 J

(D) 10,080 J

(E) 18,150 J

139. A certain spring does not follow Hooke's law. The force required to stretch the spring a distance x meters is given by $\mathbf{F} = 3x^2 + 2x$, where $\mathbf{F}$ is in newtons. The work required to stretch the spring from $x = 0.25$ m to $x = 0.5$ m is

(A) 0.078 J

(B) 0.297 J

(C) 0.375 J

(D) 0.453 J

(E) 0.750 J

140. A boy pushes a crate of mass m across a level floor with a constant speed v. The coefficient of friction between the crate and the floor is μ. What is the rate at which the boy does work on the crate?

(A) μmg

(B) mgv

(C) μmgv

(D) $\mu mg/v$

(E) $\mu v/mg$

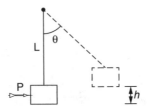

141. A ballistic pendulum consists of a dart that is launched into a block of wood hanging as a pendulum of length L as shown. When the dart enters the block of wood at point P, the dart and block (total mass m) have a speed v_o and the system is raised to a height h. At this height, the angle of swing is θ. Which of the following is the correct expression for the speed v_o in terms of the other given quantities?

(A) $\sqrt{\dfrac{2g}{m}}$

(B) $\sqrt{\dfrac{2gL}{m}}$

(C) $\sqrt{2gL\cos\theta}$

(D) $\sqrt{2g(L-L\cos\theta)}$

(E) $\sqrt{2g(L-L\sin\theta)}$

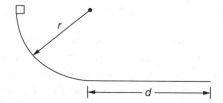

142. A block slides down a smooth quarter-circle ramp of radius r, then onto a rough flat surface at the bottom of the ramp. The friction on the horizontal surface causes the block to come to rest in a distance d. The work done by the frictional force on the horizontal surface is

(A) mgr

(B) $\sqrt{mgr}$

(C) $2mgr\cos\theta$

(D) $2mg(r - r\cos\theta)$

(E) $2mg(r - r\sin\theta)$

Questions 143–144. A 1-kg rubber ball is thrown vertically downward and strikes the floor with a speed of 12 m/s, bounces off the floor, and then rises to a height of 4 m.

143. The speed of the ball immediately after it strikes the floor is most nearly

(A) 4 m/s

(B) 9 m/s

(C) 12 m/s

(D) 16 m/s

(E) 80 m/s

144. The fraction of the ball's kinetic energy that is apparently lost during the bounce is

(A) 0.25

(B) 0.44

(C) 0.55

(D) 0.70

(E) 0.89

Free Response

Questions 145–147. A spring that does not follow Hooke's law is compressed horizontally by a 5-kg mass by 0.5 m. The force necessary to compress the spring is given by $F = 4x^3$, where x is in meters and F is in newtons. The surface beneath the spring is frictionless, and the surface in front of the spring has noticeable friction with $m_s = 0.4$ and $m_k = 0.2$.

145. Determine the work done to compress the spring 1.5 m.

146. How far has the mass moved when it is traveling at half its maximum speed?

147. If the surface beneath the spring is also the same rough surface as in front of the spring, determine the speed of the mass when it leaves the spring.

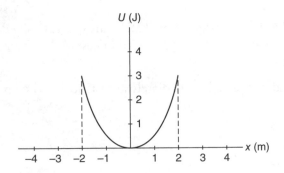

Questions 148–150. A 2.0-kg object's potential energy $U(x)$ is described by the graph shown. The object has a total energy of 3.0 J.

148. What is the farthest the object can move along the x-axis?

149. What is the object's kinetic energy when its displacement is −1 m?

150. What is the object's speed at $x = 0$?

CHAPTER 4

Impulse, Linear Momentum, and Conservation of Linear Momentum

On all of the questions in this book, you may neglect air resistance and use $g = 10$ m/s^2 unless otherwise noted.

151. A toy train car of mass 3.0 kg rolls to the left at 2 m/s and collides elastically with a 3.0-kg train car at rest. The velocity of the 3-kg car after the collision is

(A) 3 m/s to the left
(B) 1.5 m/s to the left
(C) 0 m/s
(D) 1.5 m/s to the right
(E) 3 m/s to the right

152. Two steel balls, one of mass m and the other of mass $2m$, collide and rebound in a perfectly elastic collision. Which of the following is conserved in this elastic collision?

(A) Velocity only
(B) Momentum only
(C) Momentum and kinetic energy only
(D) Momentum, velocity, and kinetic energy
(E) Kinetic energy only

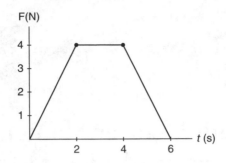

Questions 153–154. A 2.0-kg mass collides with a 4.0-kg mass for a 6-s time interval. The force that acts on the 2.0-kg mass is shown in the graph.

153. The change of momentum in the 4.0-kg mass from $t = 0$ s to $t = 6$ s is

   (A) −16 kg · m/s
   (B) −12 kg · m/s
   (C) 8 kg · m/s
   (D) 12 kg · m/s
   (E) 16 kg · m/s

154. If the initial velocity of the 4.0-kg mass is 4 m/s, what is its speed at the end of 6 s?

   (A) −4 m/s
   (B) −2 m/s
   (C) 0 m/s
   (D) 2 m/s
   (E) 4 m/s

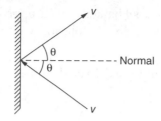

155. A rubber ball of mass m strikes a wall with a speed v at an angle θ below the normal line and rebounds from the wall at the same speed and angle above the normal line as shown. The change in momentum of the ball is

(A) mv
(B) $2mv$
(C) $mv\cos\theta$
(D) $2mv\cos\theta$
(E) zero

156. Two blocks are connected by a compressed spring and rest on a frictionless surface. The blocks are released from rest and pushed apart by the compressed spring. If one mass is twice the mass of the other, which of the following is the same for both blocks?

(A) Magnitude of momentum
(B) Acceleration
(C) Speed
(D) Kinetic energy
(E) Potential energy

Questions 157–158. A 1.0-kg basketball is dropped from a height of 1.8 m and rebounds from the floor. In the collision with the floor, the basketball loses 5 J of energy.

157. The magnitude of impulse delivered to the basketball by the floor is

(A) 0.9 kg · m/s
(B) 1.8 kg · m/s
(C) 5.2 kg · m/s
(D) 9.4 kg · m/s
(E) 11.1 kg · m/s

158. The average force the floor delivers to the basketball is 24 N. The basketball is in contact with the floor for what period of time?

(A) 0.46 s
(B) 0.59 s
(C) 0.66 s
(D) 0.81 s
(E) 0.89 s

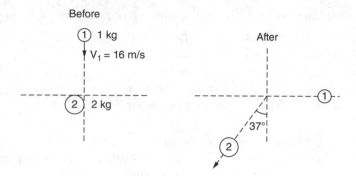

Questions 159–160. Two balls are on a horizontal billiard table. A 1.0-kg billiard ball moves downward along the y-axis with a speed of 16 m/s toward a 2.0-kg ball that is at rest. The balls collide at an angle and move along the lines shown. After the collision, the 1.0-kg ball moves at 9 m/s along the positive x-axis. The table below shows the x- and y-components of the two balls before the collision and of the 1-kg ball following the collision.

	p_{1x}	p_{1y}	p_{2x}	p_{2y}
Before collision	0	−16	0	0
After collision	+9	0		

159. Which of the following statements is true regarding the center of mass of the system?

(A) The velocity of the center of mass decreases following the collision.

(B) The velocity of the center of mass increases following the collision.

(C) The velocity of the center of mass remains constant following the collision with a value of 16 m/s in the negative y-direction.

(D) The velocity of the center of mass remains constant following the collision with a value of 8 m/s in the negative y-direction.

(E) The velocity of the center of mass remains constant following the collision with a value of 5.3 m/s in the negative y-direction.

160. The velocity of the 2.0-kg ball following the collision is

(A) 9.2 m/s, 39° below the negative y-axis
(B) 9.2 m/s, 61° below the negative y-axis
(C) 25 m/s, 39° below the negative y-axis
(D) 25 m/s, 39° below the negative y-axis
(E) 8 m/s, 61° below the negative y-axis

161. A 0.3-kg baseball at rest on a tee is struck by a bat. The bat does 70 J of work to the baseball. The magnitude of the impulse imparted to the baseball by the bat is most nearly

(A) 6.5 N s
(B) 7.0 N s
(C) 7.5 N s
(D) 8.0 N s
(E) 8.5 N s

162. Two blocks, with masses of 1 kg and 2 kg, are sliding together at 4 m/s. The blocks explode apart, with the 1-kg block sliding backward at 2 m/s. What is the ratio of initial to final kinetic energy of the system of two blocks?

(A) 24/51
(B) 4/7
(C) 1
(D) 7/4
(E) 51/24

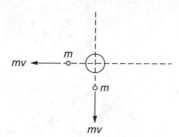

Questions 163–164. An object has a mass $4m$. The object explodes into three pieces of mass m, m, and $2m$. The two pieces of mass m move off at right angles to each other with the same momentum mv, as shown.

163. The speed of mass $2m$ after the explosion is

(A) $2v$

(B) $\sqrt{2}v$

(C) $\dfrac{\sqrt{2}}{2}v$

(D) $\dfrac{\sqrt{2}}{3}v$

(E) $\dfrac{\sqrt{3}}{2}v$

164. The direction of velocity of mass $2m$ is

(A) $\longrightarrow$

(B) $\swarrow$

(C) $\downarrow$

(D) $\nearrow$

(E) $\uparrow$

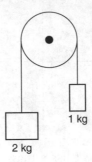

165. A system consists of two blocks having masses of 2 kg and 1 kg. The blocks are connected by a string of negligible mass and hung over a light pulley, and then released from rest. When the speed of each block is v, the momentum of the center of mass of the system is

(A) $(2 \text{ kg} + 1 \text{ kg})v$

(B) $(2 \text{ kg} - 1 \text{ kg})v$

(C) $1/3 \ (2 \text{ kg} + 1 \text{ kg})v$

(D) $½ \ (2 \text{ kg} - 1 \text{ kg})v$

(E) $(2 \text{ kg})v$

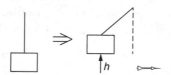

Questions 166–167. A ballistic pendulum consists of a dart imbedded in a block of wood in a spring-loaded dart shooter suspended from a string that shoots the dart out at speed v_0. The mass of the block/shooter system is M, and the mass of the dart is m. The spring dart shooter has a spring constant k, and when loaded, the spring is compressed to a distance d before the dart is fired. After the dart is fired, the pendulum swings backward, and the block is raised to a maximum height h.

166. Which of the following is a correct expression for the speed of the block immediately after the dart is fired in terms of the given quantities and fundamental constants?

(A) $-\dfrac{mv_0}{M}$

(B) $\dfrac{mv_0}{M}$

(C) $-\dfrac{Mv_0}{m}$

(D) $\sqrt{\dfrac{kd^2}{m}}$

(E) $\sqrt{\dfrac{kd^2}{M}}$

167. Which of the following is a correct expression for the height h in terms of the given quantities and fundamental constants?

(A) $\dfrac{m^2 v_0^2}{2M^2 g}$

(B) $\dfrac{m v_0^2}{2Mg}$

(C) $\dfrac{M^2 v_0^2}{2m^2 g}$

(D) $\dfrac{v_0^2}{2g}$

(E) $\dfrac{kd^2}{2Mg}$

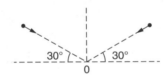

Questions 168–169. Two pieces of clay of equal mass m moving with equal speeds v_0, each traveling at an angle of 30°, collide and stick together at the origin O as shown.

168. The speed of the combined mass after the collision is

(A) v_o

(B) $\tfrac{1}{2} v_o$

(C) $\tfrac{1}{4} v_o$

(D) $\dfrac{\sqrt{2}}{2} v_o$

(E) $\dfrac{\sqrt{2}}{3} v_o$

169. The collision is instead elastic. Which of the following statements is false?

(A) The pieces will have the same speed before and after the collision.
(B) The pieces will rebound along the same path.
(C) The pieces have zero momentum in the horizontal direction following the collision.
(D) The pieces' velocity will have angles of 30° below the horizontal axis following the collision.
(E) The pieces will have a negative momentum in the vertical direction following the collision.

170. A small mass m is moving with a speed v toward a stationary mass $2m$. The speed of the center of mass of the system is

(A) $\left(\dfrac{m}{m+2m}\right)v$

(B) $\left(\dfrac{m+2m}{m}\right)v$

(C) $\left(\dfrac{m}{2m}\right)v$

(D) $\left(1+\dfrac{m}{2m}\right)v$

(E) $\left(1+\dfrac{2m}{m}\right)v$

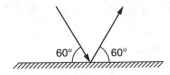

Questions 171–172. A ball has a mass of 0.5 kg and collides with a wall at an angle of 60°. The ball rebounds as shown in the figure above. The speed before the collision is 10 m/s, and the speed following the collision is 8 m/s. The ball is in contact with the wall for 0.1 s.

171. The momentum of the ball before the collision, in unit-vector notation, is

(A) $(-2.5\hat{i} - 4.3\hat{j})\dfrac{\text{kg} \cdot \text{m}}{\text{s}}$

(B) $(-2.5\hat{i} + 4.3\hat{j})\dfrac{\text{kg} \cdot \text{m}}{\text{s}}$

(C) $(2.5\hat{i} - 4.3\hat{j})\dfrac{\text{kg} \cdot \text{m}}{\text{s}}$

(D) $(2.5\hat{i} + 4.3\hat{j})\dfrac{\text{kg} \cdot \text{m}}{\text{s}}$

(E) $(4.3\hat{i} - 2.5\hat{j})\dfrac{\text{kg} \cdot \text{m}}{\text{s}}$

172. The impulse given to the ball by the wall, in unit-vector notation, is

(A) $(-0.5\vec{i} - 7.8\vec{j})\dfrac{\text{kg} \cdot \text{m}}{\text{s}}$

(B) $(-0.5\vec{i} + 7.8\vec{j})\dfrac{\text{kg} \cdot \text{m}}{\text{s}}$

(C) $(0.5\vec{i} - 7.8\vec{j})\dfrac{\text{kg} \cdot \text{m}}{\text{s}}$

(D) $(4.5\vec{i} - 0.8\vec{j})\dfrac{\text{kg} \cdot \text{m}}{\text{s}}$

(E) $(2\vec{i} + 3.5\vec{j})\dfrac{\text{kg} \cdot \text{m}}{\text{s}}$

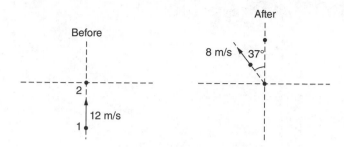

173. The diagram in the figure shows the top view of two identical steel balls on a horizontal table of negligible friction. The first ball moves with a speed of 12 m/s and the second ball is initially at rest. After the collision, the first ball moves with a speed of 8 m/s at an angle of 37° to the vertical. Which of the following diagrams best represents the approximate speed and direction of the second ball after the collision?

(A)

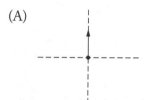

(B)

(C)

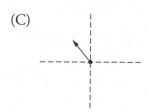

(D)

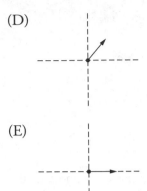

(E)

174. A known force **F** acts on an unknown mass for a known time Δt. From this information, you could determine the

(A) change in kinetic energy of the object
(B) change in velocity of the object
(C) acceleration of the object
(D) mass of the object
(E) change in momentum of the object

175. A block of mass m is moving to the right with a speed v_o on a horizontal surface of negligible friction when it explodes. The explosion causes the block to break into two pieces, each of which moves in the horizontal direction. One piece of mass $m/4$ moves to the left with a speed of $2v_o$. What is the velocity of the other piece?

(A) $2v_o$ to the right
(B) v_o to the right
(C) ¾ v_o to the right
(D) ½ v_o to the right
(E) ¼ v_o to the left

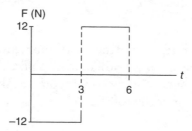

Questions 176–177. The graph shown indicates the force acting on a mass of 2 kg as a function of time.

176. For the time interval from $t = 0$ to $t = 6$ s, the change in momentum of the 2-kg mass is

(A) 48 kg m/s
(B) 24 kg m/s
(C) 12 kg m/s
(D) −12 kg m/s
(E) zero

177. If the object starts from rest, the speed at the end of the time interval from $t = 0$ to $t = 3$ s is

(A) zero
(B) 12 m/s
(C) 18 m/s
(D) 24 m/s
(E) 36 m/s

178. A 100-kg cannon sits at rest with a 1-kg cannonball in the barrel. The cannonball is fired with a speed of 50 m/s to the right, causing the cannon to recoil with a speed of 0.5 m/s to the left. The velocity of the center of mass of the cannon-cannonball system is

(A) zero
(B) 5 m/s to the right
(C) 5 m/s to the left
(D) 50 m/s to the right
(E) 50 m/s to the left

179. The vector shown represents the initial momentum of a moving object. The object collides with another object that is initially at rest. Which of the diagrams below could represent the momenta of the colliding objects after the collision?

(A)

(B)

(C)

(D)

(E)

Questions 180–181. A 20-kg boy runs at a speed of 3.0 m/s and jumps onto a 40-kg sled on frictionless ice that is initially at rest. The boy and the sled then move together for a short time.

180. The speed of the boy and sled after he jumps on it is

(A) 0.5 m/s
(B) 0.8 m/s
(C) 1.0 m/s
(D) 1.5 m/s
(E) 2.0 m/s

181. While the boy and sled are moving, he jumps off the back of the sled in such a way that the boy is at rest, and the sled continues to move forward. The speed of the sled after the boy jumps off is

(A) 1.5 m/s
(B) 2.0 m/s
(C) 3.0 m/s
(D) 4.5 m/s
(E) 6.0 m/s

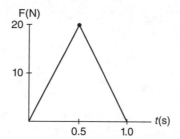

Questions 182–183

A cart of mass m_1 is initially moving with a speed of 4.0 m/s on a track toward a stationary cart of mass $m_2 = 2$ kg. After the collision, mass m_1 moves with a velocity of 1.5 m/s. The force vs. time graph is shown for the time during the collision, with the collision beginning at $t = 0$.

182. The impulse each cart applies to the other is most nearly

(A) 40 N s
(B) 20 N s
(C) 10 N s
(D) 5 N s
(E) 2 N s

183. The unknown mass m_1 is equal to

(A) 0.5 kg
(B) 1.5 kg
(C) 2.5 kg
(D) 4.0 kg
(E) 5.0 kg

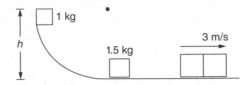

184. A 1.0-kg block is released from rest from a height *h* at the top of a fixed, curved ramp of negligible friction. The block slides down the ramp and collides with another block of mass 1.5-kg at rest at the bottom of the ramp. The two blocks stick together and move with a speed of 5 m/s. The height *h* from which the 1.0-kg block began is

(A) 0.8 m
(B) 1.2 m
(C) 1.8 m
(D) 2.8 m
(E) 7.8 m

185. A dart of mass *m* is fired into a wooden block of mass 4*m* that hangs from a string. The dart and block then rise to a maximum height *h*. An expression for the initial speed v_o of the dart before striking the block is

(A) $\sqrt{gh}$

(B) $\sqrt{2gh}$

(C) $\sqrt{50gh}$

(D) $\sqrt{100gh}$

(E) $\sqrt{250gh}$

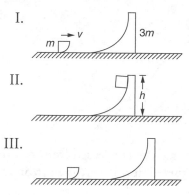

Questions 186–187. A small block of mass m slides on a horizontal frictionless surface toward a ramp of mass $3m$, which is also free to move on the surface. The small block slides up to a height h on the ramp with no friction (Figure I), then they move together (Figure II), and the small block slides back down the ramp to the horizontal surface (Figure III). Both the block and the ramp continue to slide on the horizontal surface after they separate.

186. Which of the following is true regarding the conservation laws throughout this process?

   (A) Kinetic energy is conserved from Figure I to Figure II.
   (B) Momentum is conserved from Figure I to Figure III.
   (C) Kinetic energy is conserved from Figure II to Figure III.
   (D) Potential energy is conserved from Figure I to Figure II.
   (E) Potential energy is conserved from Figure II to Figure III.

187. Which of the following is a true statement regarding Figure III?

   (A) The small block is moving to the left and the ramp is moving to the right.
   (B) The small block is moving to the right and the ramp is moving to the left.
   (C) The small block is moving to the right and the ramp is moving to the right.
   (D) The small block is moving to the left and the ramp is moving to the left.
   (E) The small block and the large block are moving with the same velocity.

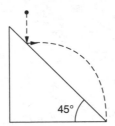

Questions 188–189. A rubber ball of mass m is released from rest from a height h onto a fixed, inclined plane angled at 45° to the horizontal. The ball collides with the surface elastically.

188. Which of the following diagrams best indicates the direction of the impulse vector **J** as it strikes the plane and the velocity vector **v** just after it strikes the plane?

    (A) → **J**
        → **v**

    (B) ↗ **J**
        ↗ **v**

    (C) ↗ **J**
        ↑ **v**

    (D) ↑ **J**
        ↗ **v**

    (E) ↗ **J**
        → **v**

189. The speed of the ball just after striking the surface is

    (A) $\sqrt{gh}$

    (B) $\sqrt{2gh}$

    (C) $\sqrt{5gh}$

    (D) $\sqrt{7gh}$

    (E) $\sqrt{10gh}$

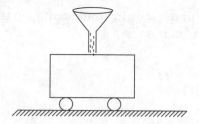

190. A 1,000-kg (empty mass) railroad car is rolling without friction on a horizontal track at a speed of 2.0 m/s. Sand is poured into the open top of the car for the time interval from $t = 0$ to $t = 4.0$ s. The mass of the sand poured into the car as a function of time is $m(t) = 60t^2$. The velocity of the car at a time of 4.0 s is most nearly

(A) 1 m/s
(B) 2 m/s
(C) 3 m/s
(D) 4 m/s
(E) 5 m/s

Questions 191–192. A remote controlled stunt car of mass 800 kg initially moving at 10 m/s is crashed into a rail car of mass m that is initially at rest. The cars stick together, and the speed v of both cars after the collision is given by $v = \dfrac{6}{t+1}$.

191. By considering the fact that the crash occurs at time $t = 0$, determine the mass m of the rail car.

(A) 288 kg
(B) 445 kg
(C) 533 kg
(D) 698 kg
(E) 800 kg

192. The magnitude of the resisting force acting on the cars as a function of time after the collision is

(A) $\dfrac{6m}{t+1}$

(B) $6m(t+1)$

(C) $6m(t+1)^2$

(D) $\dfrac{6m}{(t+1)^2}$

(E) $\dfrac{m(t+1)^2}{6}$

193. A force acts on a mass m according to the equation $F = 12t^3$. If the object starts from rest, the velocity of the object as a function of time is

(A) $36mt^3$

(B) $\dfrac{36m}{t^3}$

(C) $\dfrac{mt^3}{36}$

(D) $\dfrac{t^3}{3m}$

(E) $\dfrac{3t^4}{m}$

194. A dart in a long blow gun starts from rest and gains a momentum according to the equation $p = 3t^3 + 2t$ while moving through the barrel of the gun. The net force acting on the dart after 0.2 s is

(A) 1.2 N

(B) 2.4 N

(C) 6.0 N

(D) 12.2 N

(E) 16.1 N

195. A variable force acts on a mass causing it to accelerate. If a graph of this force vs. time is plotted, the change in momentum of the mass can be determined by finding the

(A) slope of the graph
(B) area under the graph
(C) y-intercept of the graph
(D) x-intercept of the graph
(E) change in slope of the graph

196. A moving object is changing its momentum during a time interval. If a graph of momentum vs. time is plotted, the net force acting on the mass at any time can be determined by finding the

(A) slope of line tangent to the graph at that time
(B) area under the graph
(C) y-intercept of the graph
(D) x-intercept of the graph
(E) change in slope of the graph from beginning to end

Free Response

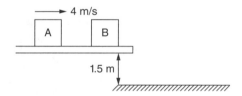

Questions 197–200. Two blocks rest on a smooth table that is 1.5 m high. Block A has a mass $m_A = 2$ kg and block B has a mass $m_B = 4$ kg. Block A is then given a velocity of 4 m/s toward block B, and they collide and stick together.

197. Determine the speed of the two blocks immediately after they collide inelastically.

198. Determine the horizontal distance the two blocks travel before striking the floor.

Similar to the previous questions, two blocks rest on a smooth table that is 1.5 m high. Block A has a mass $m_A = 2$ kg and block B has a mass $m_B = 4$ kg. Block A is then given a velocity of 4.0 m/s toward block B, and they collide *elastically*. Block A rebounds with a velocity of −1.0 m/s.

199. Determine the speed of block B immediately after they collide elastically.

200. Determine the horizontal distance block B travels before striking the floor.

CHAPTER 5

Circular and Rotational Motion

On all of the questions in this book, you may neglect air resistance and use $g = 10 \text{ m/s}^2$ unless otherwise noted.

201. A disk is rotating with the angular position of a point on the disk given by $\theta = 3 \text{ rad} - \left(2.5\dfrac{\text{rad}}{s^2}\right)t^2 + \left(4\dfrac{\text{rad}}{s^3}\right)t^3$. The angular velocity of the object at $t = 2$ s is

(A) 11 rad/s
(B) 22 rad/s
(C) 38 rad/s
(D) 45 rad/s
(E) Cannot be determined without the radius of the disk

202. An object begins rotating at $t = 0$ with an acceleration given by $\alpha = 2t - 2$. If the object has an initial velocity of -3 rad/s, when will the object come to rest?

(A) 1 s
(B) 3 s
(C) 5 s
(D) 7 s
(E) 9 s

203. A 0.5-kg ball is on the end of a 0.5-meter-long string and swung in a vertical circle. What is the minimum speed necessary to keep the ball moving in a circle at all points on the circle?

(A) 1.6 m/s
(B) 2.2 m/s
(C) 2.8 m/s
(D) 3.4 m/s
(E) 4.0 m/s

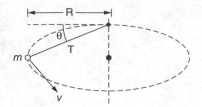

Questions 204–205. A ball of mass m and weight W on the end of a string is swung in a horizontal circle of radius R with a speed v. The string makes an angle θ below the horizontal as shown. The magnitude of the tension in the string is T.

204. Which of the following diagrams best shows the forces acting on the ball as it moves in a circle?

(A)

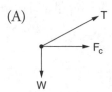

(B)

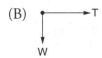

(C)

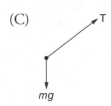

(D)

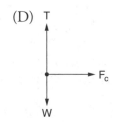

(E)

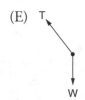

205. In terms of m, R, v, and θ, the magnitude of the tension T is

(A) $\dfrac{mv^2}{R}$

(B) $\dfrac{mv^2}{R\sin\theta}$

(C) $\dfrac{mv^2}{R\cos\theta}$

(D) $\dfrac{mv}{R\sin\theta}$

(E) $mvR\sin\theta$

206. A block of mass m is on a frictionless track with a vertical circular loop of radius R. As the block moves through the loop, the speed of the block at the top of the loop is v. The normal force acting on the block at the bottom of the loop as the block enters the loop is

(A) $4mg + \dfrac{mv^2}{R}$

(B) $5mg + \dfrac{mv^2}{R}$

(C) $mg + \dfrac{mv^2}{R}$

(D) mg

(E) $\dfrac{mv^2}{R}$

207. A car travels around a flat circular track with a 100-m radius at 15 m/s. The car begins increasing speed with a tangential acceleration function given by $a_t = 8t - 3$, where a is in m/s² and t is in seconds. After 2 s, the net acceleration of the car is

(A) 6.25 m/s²

(B) 9.75 m/s²

(C) 13.0 m/s²

(D) 14.4 m/s²

(E) 17.2 m/s²

Front view

Questions 208–209. A race car travels on a circular track that is banked at an angle θ from the horizontal, as shown.

208. The race car enters the curve at too great a speed and is about to slide. At the instant the car begins to slide, which of the following diagrams best shows the forces acting on the car as it moves on the banked track?

(A)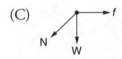

(B)

(C)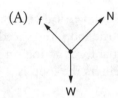

(D)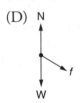

(E)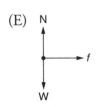

209. Which of the following statements is true of the forces acting on the car while on the circular track?

(A) The normal force the track exerts on the car provides the centripetal force.

(B) The weight of the car provides the centripetal force.

(C) The frictional force the track exerts on the car provides the centripetal force.

(D) The centripetal force is provided by a combination of the normal force and frictional force.

(E) There is no centripetal force in this case.

210. A uniform rod of mass M and length L is rotating about an axis at a distance $\dfrac{L}{4}$ from the end of the rod. The rotational inertia of the rod is

(A) $\dfrac{ML^2}{48}$

(B) $\dfrac{ML^2}{12}$

(C) $\dfrac{ML^2}{3}$

(D) $\dfrac{7ML^2}{48}$

(E) ML^2

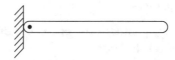

211. A uniform 1-kg, 0.5-m rod is attached to a wall at the left end and free to rotate. The rod is initially horizontal, as shown above. The initial angular acceleration of the rod is

(A) 12 rad/s²

(B) 15 rad/s²

(C) 18 rad/s²

(D) 21 rad/s²

(E) 24 rad/s²

Questions 212–213. A 3-kg object moves in a horizontal circle of radius 3 m with a constant speed of 2 m/s.

212. If the force that causes the object to move in the circle (on a level surface) is a frictional force, what is the coefficient of friction?

(A) 0.061
(B) 0.083
(C) 0.092
(D) 0.110
(E) 0.133

213. The angular momentum of the object is

(A) 18 kg m²/s
(B) 12 kg m²/s
(C) 9 kg m²/s
(D) 6 kg m²/s
(E) 4 kg m²/s

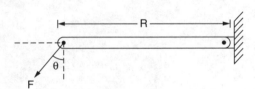

Questions 214–215. The diagram above shows a force **F** being applied at an angle θ to a rod that is pivoted at one end and is free to rotate without friction in a horizontal plane.

214. Which of the following equations represents the magnitude of the net torque τ acting on the rod?

(A) FR
(B) $FR\cos\theta$
(C) $FR\sin\theta$
(D) $FR\tan\theta$
(E) $\dfrac{FR}{\cos\theta}$

215. If the angle θ remains constant as the rod turns on its axis, and the rotational inertia of the rod is I, the angular acceleration of the rod is

(A) $\dfrac{FR}{I}$

(B) $\dfrac{I}{FR\cos\theta}$

(C) $\dfrac{FR\sin\theta}{I}$

(D) $\dfrac{FR\tan\theta}{I}$

(E) $\dfrac{FR\cos\theta}{I}$

216. A ballet dancer, while spinning at 20 rad/s, pulls her arms in so that her rotational inertia is reduced by a factor of 4. The ratio of her initial to final kinetic energy is

(A) ¼
(B) ½
(C) 1
(D) 2
(E) 4

Questions 217–218. A ball on the end of a string is swung in a circle of radius 2 m according to the equation $\theta = 4t^2 + 3t$, where θ is in radians and t is in seconds.

217. The angular acceleration of the ball is

(A) 6 rad/s²
(B) $4t^2 + 3t$ rad/s²
(C) $8t + 3$ rad/s²
(D) ¾ $t^3 + 3\,t^2$ rad/s²
(E) 8 rad/s²

218. The linear speed v of the ball at $t = 3$ s is

(A) 27 m/s
(B) 54 m/s
(C) 108 m/s
(D) 135 m/s
(E) 210 m/s

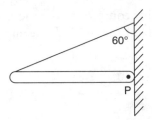

219. A uniform metal bar of mass M is attached to a pivot on the wall at point P, as shown above, and supported by a rope that makes an angle of $60°$ with the vertical wall. The tension in the rope is

(A) $Mg/4$
(B) $Mg/2$
(C) Mg
(D) $2Mg$
(E) $4Mg$

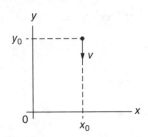

220. A particle of mass m moves with a constant speed v at a distance x_o parallel to the y-axis as shown. When the particle is in the position shown, the magnitude of its angular momentum relative to the origin is

(A) mvx_o
(B) mvy_o
(C) $mv\sqrt{x_o^2 + y_o^2}$
(D) $\dfrac{mv}{\sqrt{x_o^2 + y_o^2}}$
(E) zero

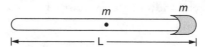

221. A uniform rod of length L and mass m has a rotational inertia of $1/12\ mL^2$ about its center. A particle, also of mass m, is attached to one end of the stick. The combined rotational inertia of the stick and particle about the center of the rod is

(A) $\dfrac{mL^2}{3}$

(B) $\dfrac{12mL^2}{13}$

(C) $\dfrac{13mL^2}{12}$

(D) $\dfrac{mL^2}{156}$

(E) $\dfrac{13mL^2}{156}$

Questions 222–223. A light rod of negligible mass is pivoted at point P a distance L from one end as shown. A mass m is attached to the left end of the rod at a distance of $3L$ from the pivot, and another mass $4m$ is attached to the other end a distance L from the pivot. The system begins from rest in the horizontal position.

222. The net torque acting on the system due to gravitational forces is

(A) $4mgL$ clockwise
(B) $3mgL$ clockwise
(C) $3mgL$ counterclockwise
(D) mgL counterclockwise
(E) mgL clockwise

223. The angular acceleration of the system when it is released from rest is

(A) zero

(B) $\dfrac{g}{5L}$

(C) $\dfrac{g}{4L}$

(D) $\dfrac{g}{13L}$

(E) $\dfrac{g}{L}$

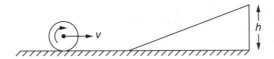

224. A hoop of radius R and mass m has a rotational inertia of mR^2. The hoop rolls without slipping along a horizontal floor with a constant speed v and then rolls up a long incline. The hoop can roll up the incline to a maximum vertical height of

(A) $\dfrac{v^2}{g}$

(B) $\dfrac{2v^2}{g}$

(C) $\dfrac{v^2}{2g}$

(D) $\dfrac{4v^2}{g}$

(E) $\dfrac{v^2}{4g}$

Z ○------ •------ ○ X

Y

225. A 3-kg ball on the end of a 0.25-m string is released from point X with a speed of 2 m/s as shown. The tension in the string when the ball is in position Y is

(A) 30 N
(B) 48 N
(C) 78 N
(D) 108 N
(E) 138 N

226. A variable force given by $\mathbf{F} = 2t^3 + \sin(\pi t)$, where $\mathbf{F}$ is in newtons and t is in seconds, is applied to a 2-meter-long bar at a 30° angle to the bar, as shown above. The torque produced by the force at $t = 1$ s is

(A) 2 N m
(B) 2.8 N m
(C) 3.5 N m
(D) 4.2 N m
(E) 4.9 N m

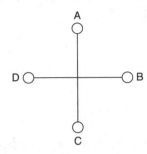

Questions 227–228. Two balls of equal mass are attached to each end of a rod that is spinning about its center in the vertical plane with a constant angular speed ω. Each ball is a radius r from the center of the rod. A bug holds on to one of the balls as the system rotates. Four points, A, B, C, and D, are marked at the quarter-circle points on the circle.

227. At which point would the bug need to apply the most adhesive force to remain on the ball?

(A) A
(B) B
(C) C
(D) D
(E) The bug would apply the same force at all points to remain on the ball.

228. The minimum force necessary the bug would have to apply to remain on the ball at point C is

(A) $m\omega r$
(B) $m\omega^2 r$
(C) mg
(D) $m\omega^2 r - mg$
(E) $m\omega^2 r + mg$

229. A pulley with a rotational inertia of 0.05 kg/m^2 is free to rotate about a center axle without friction. The pulley has a radius of 0.1 m and is subjected to a tangentially applied force $\mathbf{F} = 3t^2 + 2t$, with $\mathbf{F}$ in newtons and t in seconds. The pulley is initially at rest. At $t = 2$ s, the angular speed of the pulley is

(A) 8 rad/s
(B) 12 rad/s
(C) 16 rad/s
(D) 20 rad/s
(E) 24 rad/s

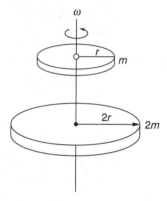

230. Two disks are fixed to a vertical axle that is rotating with a constant angular speed ω. The smaller disk has a mass m and a radius r, and the larger disk has a mass $2m$ and radius $2r$. The general equation for the rotational inertia of a disk of mass M and radius R is ½ MR^2. The ratio of the angular momentum of the larger disk to the smaller disk is

(A) 1/4
(B) 4/1
(C) 1/2
(D) 2/1
(E) 8/1

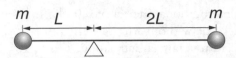

231. Two balls of mass m are attached to the ends of a massless rod, as shown above. A pivot is placed that is a distance L from the mass on the left and $2L$ from the mass on the right. When the rod is released to rotate, the magnitude of the initial linear acceleration of the mass on the right is

(A) $\dfrac{g}{5}$

(B) $\dfrac{2g}{5}$

(C) $\dfrac{3g}{5}$

(D) $\dfrac{4g}{5}$

(E) g

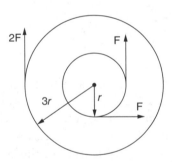

232. Two wheels are attached to each other and fixed so that they can only turn together. The smaller wheel has a radius of r and the larger wheel has a radius of $3r$. The two wheels can rotate together on a frictionless axle. Three forces act tangentially on the edge of the wheels as shown. The magnitude of the net torque acting on the system of wheels is

(A) Fr
(B) $2Fr$
(C) $3Fr$
(D) $4Fr$
(E) $6Fr$

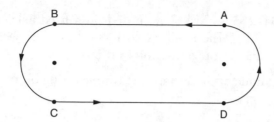

233. A speed skater races around a track in which the sides are equal
length and parallel and the curves are semicircular. The skater keeps
a constant speed throughout one entire lap. She starts at point A
and travels counterclockwise around the track for one lap. Which
of the following graphs best represents the magnitude of the skater's
acceleration as a function of time for one lap?

(A) a

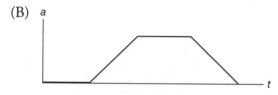

(B) a

(C) a

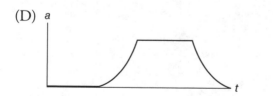

(D) a

(E) a

Questions 234–235. A disk is mounted on a fixed axle. The rotational inertia of the disk is I. The angular velocity of the disk is decreased from ω_o to ω_f during a time Δt due to friction in the axle.

234. The magnitude of the average net torque acting on the wheel is

(A) $\dfrac{(\omega_f - \omega_o)}{\Delta t}$

(B) $\dfrac{(\omega_f - \omega_o)^2}{\Delta t}$

(C) $\dfrac{I(\omega_f - \omega_o)}{\Delta t}$

(D) $\dfrac{I(\omega_f - \omega_o)^2}{\Delta t}$

(E) $\dfrac{I(\omega_f - \omega_o)}{\Delta t^2}$

235. The average power developed by the friction in the axle of the disk to bring it to a complete stop is

(A) $\dfrac{\omega_o}{\Delta t}$

(B) $\dfrac{(\omega_o)^2}{\Delta t}$

(C) $\dfrac{I(\omega_f - \omega_o)}{\Delta t}$

(D) $\dfrac{I(\omega_o)^2}{\Delta t}$

(E) $\dfrac{I(\omega_f - \omega_o)}{\Delta t^2}$

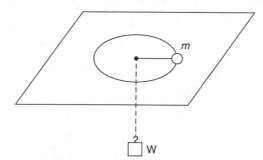

236. A string is pulled through a hole in a horizontal table. A puck of mass m is attached to one end of the string so that it can move in a circle of radius r on the smooth tabletop with a speed v, and a weight hangs from the other end under the table. If the weight is pulled down so that the length of the string is shortened to ¼ r while the puck is moving in a circle, the speed of the puck will

(A) decrease its speed to ¼ v
(B) decrease its speed to ½ v
(C) increase its speed to $2v$
(D) increase its speed to $4v$
(E) not change

237. A billiard ball of mass m and radius r rolls without slipping on a pool table with an angular speed ω. Which of the following relationships is true of the ball as it rolls?

(A) $v = r\omega$
(B) $v > r\omega$
(C) $v < r\omega$
(D) $v = 2r\omega$
(E) $v = ½ r\omega$

238. A billiard ball of mass m and radius r rolls and slips on a pool table with an angular speed ω. Which of the following relationships is true of the ball as it rolls and slips?

(A) $v = r\omega$
(B) $v > r\omega$
(C) $v < r\omega$
(D) $v = 2r\omega$
(E) $v = ½ r\omega$

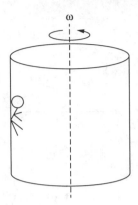

239. An amusement park ride consists of a cylindrical room with a 2-m radius that spins so fast that people can stick to the wall when the floor is lowered out from beneath them. The room accelerates from rest with a constant acceleration $\alpha = 5$ rad/s². If the coefficient of static friction between a person and the wall is 0.05, the minimum time at which the room is spinning fast enough for the people to stick to the wall is

(A) 1 s
(B) 2 s
(C) 3 s
(D) 4 s
(E) 5 s

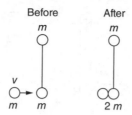

Before   After

240. Astronauts are conducting an experiment in a negligible gravity environment. Two spheres of mass m are attached to either end of a light rod. As the rod and spheres float motionless in space, an astronaut launches a piece of sticky clay, also of mass m, toward one of the spheres so that the clay strikes and sticks to the sphere perpendicular to the rod. Which of the following statements is true of the motion of the rod, clay, and spheres after the collision?

(A) Linear momentum is not conserved, but angular momentum is conserved.

(B) Angular momentum is not conserved, but linear momentum is conserved.

(C) Kinetic energy is conserved, but angular momentum is not conserved.

(D) Kinetic energy is conserved, but linear momentum is not conserved.

(E) Both linear momentum and angular momentum are conserved, but kinetic energy is not conserved.

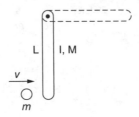

241. A rod of mass M, length L, and rotational inertia I hangs at rest from a frictionless axle as shown. A ball of mass m with a speed v strikes the rod perpendicularly at the end of the rod. As a result of the collision, the ball stops. The angular speed of the rod immediately after the collision is

(A) vL

(B) $\dfrac{v}{L}$

(C) $\dfrac{mv}{I}$

(D) $\dfrac{mvL}{I}$

(E) $\dfrac{mv}{IL}$

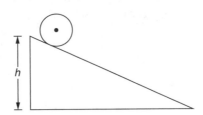

Questions 242–243
A hollow sphere of mass m and radius R begins from rest at a height h and rolls down a rough inclined plane. The rotational inertia of the hollow sphere is $2/3\ mR^2$.

242. Which of the following diagrams best represents the forces acting on the sphere as it rolls down the plane?

(A)

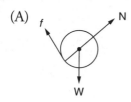

(B)

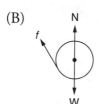

(C)

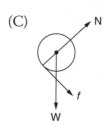

(D)

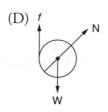

(E)

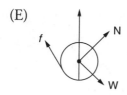

243. The speed of the sphere when it reaches the bottom of the plane is

(A) $\sqrt{\dfrac{8gh}{5}}$

(B) $\sqrt{\dfrac{6gh}{5}}$

(C) $\sqrt{\dfrac{5gh}{6}}$

(D) $\sqrt{\dfrac{7gh}{10}}$

(E) $\sqrt{\dfrac{gh}{2}}$

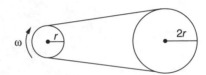

244. A belt is wrapped around two wheels as shown. The smaller wheel has a radius r, and the larger wheel has a radius $2r$. When the wheels turn, the belt does not slip on the wheels, and gives the smaller wheel an angular speed ω. The angular speed of the larger wheel is

(A) ω

(B) 2ω

(C) ½ ω

(D) ¼ ω

(E) 4ω

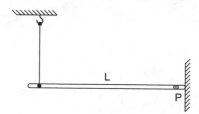

245. One end of a stick of length L, rotational inertia I, and mass m is pivoted on an axle with negligible friction at point P. The other end is tied to a string and held in a horizontal position. When the string is cut, the stick rotates counterclockwise. The angular speed ω of the stick when it reaches the bottom of its swing is

(A) $\dfrac{mgL}{I}$

(B) $\sqrt{\dfrac{mgL}{I}}$

(C) $\sqrt{\dfrac{2mgL}{I}}$

(D) $\sqrt{\dfrac{mgL}{2I}}$

(E) $\sqrt{\dfrac{4mgL}{I}}$

Free Response

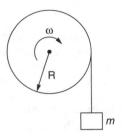

Questions 246–247. A mass m is hung on a string that is wrapped around a disk of radius R and mass M. The rotational inertia of this type of disk is found by the relationship $I = \frac{1}{2}mr^2$. The mass is released from rest and accelerates downward.

246. Determine the angular acceleration of the disk in terms of the given quantities and fundamental constants.

247. If the mass lowers by a distance h, find an expression for the speed of the mass in terms of given quantities and fundamental constants.

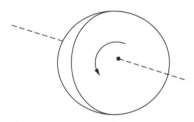

Questions 248–250. A hollow sphere has a rotational inertia given by $I = \frac{2}{3}MR^2$. The sphere is initially sliding without rolling along a rough surface with coefficients of friction $\mu_s = 0.5$ and $\mu_k = 0.3$. The sphere's mass and radius are 0.5 kg and 0.2 m, respectively.

248. The sphere will begin to roll when it loses half of its initial kinetic energy. If the sphere was moving initially at 8 m/s, how far will it move before it begins to roll?

249. The sphere is later rolling at a speed v. Derive an expression for the total kinetic energy of the sphere in terms of the speed v, mass M, and radius R.

250. When the sphere is rolling at 5 m/s, it then rolls up a 10°-inclined plane without losing energy to friction. How far up the incline will the sphere roll?

CHAPTER 6

Oscillations and Gravitation

On all of the questions in this book, you may neglect air resistance and use $g = 10 \text{ m/s}^2$ unless otherwise noted.

251. A physical pendulum is made of a uniform rod of length L and mass M. The period of the physical pendulum is

(A) $2\pi\sqrt{\dfrac{L}{g}}$

(B) $2\pi\sqrt{\dfrac{2L}{g}}$

(C) $2\pi\sqrt{\dfrac{L}{3g}}$

(D) $2\pi\sqrt{\dfrac{L}{2g}}$

(E) $2\pi\sqrt{\dfrac{2L}{3g}}$

252. A mass oscillates on the end of a spring that obeys Hooke's law. Which of the following statements is true?
(A) The amplitude of oscillation is equal to the potential energy of the spring.
(B) The kinetic energy of the oscillating mass is constant.
(C) The maximum potential energy occurs when the mass reaches the equilibrium position.
(D) The potential energy of the spring at the amplitude is equal to the kinetic energy at the equilibrium position.
(E) The kinetic energy of the spring at the amplitude is equal to the potential energy at the equilibrium position.

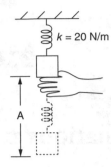

Questions 253–254

A mass of 1 kg is hung on a spring that is held at its unstretched length. The constant of the spring is 20 N/m. The mass is released from rest.

253. What is the distance the spring stretches from the point of release?

(A) $\dfrac{1}{2}$ m

(B) $\dfrac{1}{20}$ m

(C) $\dfrac{1}{4}$ m

(D) $\dfrac{1}{40}$ m

(E) 1 m

254. The period of the oscillation is

(A) $2\pi\sqrt{\dfrac{1}{40}}$ s

(B) $2\pi\sqrt{\dfrac{1}{20}}$ s

(C) $2\pi\sqrt{\dfrac{1}{400}}$ s

(D) $2\pi\sqrt{\dfrac{1}{200}}$ s

(E) $2\pi\sqrt{\dfrac{1}{10}}$ s

255. A superball is dropped from a height of 5.0 meters above a floor. The ball bounces off the floor in a perfectly elastic collision so that it rises to the same height with each bounce. The motion of the ball can be described as

(A) harmonic motion with a period of 2 s
(B) harmonic motion with a period of 1 s
(C) harmonic motion with a period of ½ s
(D) motion with a constant velocity
(E) motion with a constant momentum

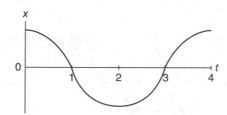

Questions 256–257
A position vs. time graph is shown above for an object in simple harmonic motion.

256. If the object is a simple pendulum with a 0.5-kg mass at the end of a string, what is the length of the pendulum?

(A) 4.1 m
(B) 4.4 m
(C) 4.7 m
(D) 5.0 m
(E) 5.3 m

257. Which of the following potential energy vs. time graphs best represents the motion of the object?

(A) *u*

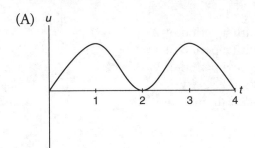

(B) *u*

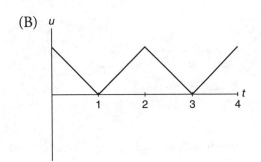

(C) *u*

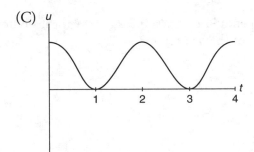

(D) *u*

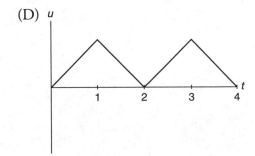

(E)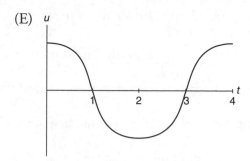

258. An object oscillates in simple harmonic motion along the x-axis according to the equation $x = 6\cos(4t)$. The period of oscillation of the object is

(A) ¼ s

(B) 4 s

(C) $\pi/4$ s

(D) $\pi/2$ s

(E) 4π s

259. A mass m oscillates on the end of a string of length L. The frequency of the pendulum is f. How would you increase the frequency of the pendulum to $2f$?

(A) Increase the length of the pendulum to $4L$

(B) Decrease the length of the pendulum to ¼ L

(C) Increase the length of the pendulum to $2L$

(D) Decrease the length of the pendulum to ½ L

(E) Decrease the mass of the pendulum to ½ m

260. A mass hangs from two parallel springs, each with the same spring constant k. Compared to the period T of the same mass oscillating on one of the springs, the period of oscillation of the mass with both springs connected to it is

(A) ¼ T

(B) ½ T

(C) T (unchanged)

(D) $2T$

(E) $4T$

261. Which of the following is generally true for an object in simple harmonic motion on a spring of constant k?

(A) The greater the spring constant k, the greater the amplitude of the motion.

(B) The greater the spring constant k, the greater the period of the motion.

(C) The greater the spring constant k, the greater the frequency of the motion.

(D) The lower the spring constant k, the greater the frequency of the motion.

(E) The lower the spring constant k, the greater the kinetic energy of the motion.

Questions 262–263

A mass m oscillates in simple harmonic motion along the x-axis on a spring of constant k.

262. Which of the following best represents the differential equation that describes the motion of the mass as it oscillates?

(A) $\dfrac{d^2x}{dt^2} = -\dfrac{k}{m}x$

(B) $\dfrac{dx}{dt} = -\dfrac{k}{m}x$

(C) $\dfrac{dx}{dt} = -\dfrac{m}{k}x$

(D) $\dfrac{d^2x}{dt^2} = -\dfrac{m}{k}x$

(E) $\dfrac{d^2x}{dt^2} = -\dfrac{dx}{dt}$

263. The position as a function of time can be expressed by the equation

(A) $x = x_o \cos kt$

(B) $x = x_o \cos \pi t$

(C) $x = x_o \cos \sqrt{\dfrac{k}{m}} t$

(D) $x = x_o \cos \sqrt{\dfrac{m}{k}} t$

(E) $x = x_o \cos \dfrac{k}{m} t$

Questions 264–266

A harmonic oscillator follows the equation $\dfrac{d^2 x}{dt^2} = -4x$. The spring constant k is 4 N/m.

264. The angular frequency ω of the harmonic motion is

(A) zero

(B) 2 rad/s

(C) 4 rad/s

(D) 8 rad/s

(E) 16 rad/s

265. The mass m oscillating on the spring is

(A) 1 kg

(B) 2 kg

(C) 4 kg

(D) 8 kg

(E) 16 kg

266. The period T of oscillation is

(A) zero

(B) $\pi/4$ s

(C) $\pi/2$ s

(D) π s

(E) 2π s

267. A pendulum of length L has a period of 2 s on Earth. A planetary explorer takes the same pendulum of length L to another planet where its period is 1 s. The gravitational acceleration on the surface of this planet is most nearly

(A) $8\,g$
(B) $4\,g$
(C) $2\,g$
(D) $\frac{1}{2}\,g$
(E) $\frac{1}{4}\,g$

268. A block of mass m is attached to a spring fixed to a wall. The mass oscillates on a frictionless horizontal surface with an amplitude x_0. The force constant of the spring is k. In terms of the given quantities, what is the maximum speed of the block?

(A) $\dfrac{k}{m}x_0$

(B) $\sqrt{\dfrac{k}{m}}\,x_0$

(C) $\sqrt{\dfrac{k}{m}}\ x_0$

(D) kmx_0

(E) $\dfrac{x_0}{m}k$

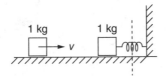

269. A block of mass 1.0 kg is sliding on a frictionless horizontal surface with a speed of 4.0 m/s when it collides inelastically with another 1.0-kg block attached to a spring. The spring compresses a distance of 0.5 m after the collision. The force constant k of the spring is

(A) 2 N/m
(B) 4 N/m
(C) 8 N/m
(D) 16 N/m
(E) 32 N/m

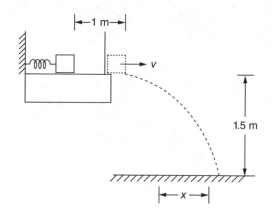

270. A block of mass 0.5 kg rests up against a compressed spring of force constant 5 N/m. The spring is released, and the block travels a distance of 1.0 m when the block leaves the spring at the edge of the horizontal frictionless table and is projected to the floor. The table is 1.5 m high. The horizontal distance from the table the block lands on the floor is

(A) 1.2 m
(B) 1.7 m
(C) 2.1 m
(D) 2.8 m
(E) 3.4 m

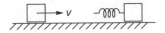

271. A mass moving with a velocity v travels toward another mass on a frictionless air track. The mass at rest has an ideal spring attached to it. The moving mass collides elastically with the mass at rest, compressing the spring, then bounces back. Which of the following graphs best represents the kinetic energy vs. time graph before, during, and after the collision?

(A)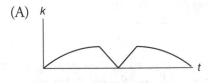

(B)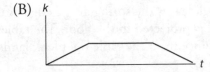

(C)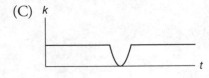

(D)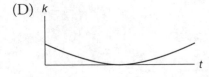

(E)

272. A satellite of mass m is in a circular orbit around a planet of mass M and radius R at an altitude equal to the radius of the planet. The total energy of the satellite is

(A) $-G\dfrac{mM}{R}$

(B) $-G\dfrac{mM}{2R}$

(C) $-G\dfrac{2mM}{R}$

(D) $-G\dfrac{4mM}{R}$

(E) $-G\dfrac{mM}{4R}$

273. A planet has a mass M and radius R. The work done against gravity in moving an object of mass m from the surface of the planet to an altitude equal to twice the radius of the planet is

(A) $-G\dfrac{mM}{3R}$

(B) $G\dfrac{mM}{3R}$

(C) $G\dfrac{mM}{2R}$

(D) $2G\dfrac{mM}{3R}$

(E) $-2G\dfrac{mM}{3R}$

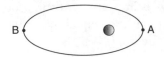

274. A satellite orbits the Earth in an elliptical orbit, with point A being close to the Earth and point B farther away. As the satellite moves from point A to point B, which of the following is true of the angular momentum and kinetic energy of the satellite?

	Angular Momentum	Kinetic Energy
(A)	Increases	Remains constant
(B)	Remains constant	Increases
(C)	Decreases	Remains constant
(D)	Remains constant	Decreases
(E)	Remains constant	Remains constant

275. A planet has a mass M and radius R. A second planet has the same density but twice the radius of the first. The ratio of the gravitational acceleration at the surface of the first planet to the second planet is

(A) ¼
(B) ½
(C) 1
(D) 2
(E) 4

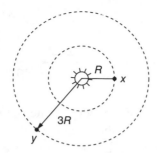

276. Two planets X and Y orbit a star. Planet X has a mass $3M$ and orbits the star at a distance R. Planet Y has a mass M and orbits the star at a distance $3R$. The ratio of the acceleration of planet X to planet Y around the star is

(A) 1/9
(B) 1/3
(C) 1
(D) 3
(E) 9

277. A satellite is in a stable circular orbit around the Earth at a radius R and speed v. At what radius would the satellite travel in a stable orbit with a speed $2v$?

(A) ¼ R
(B) ½ R
(C) R
(D) $2R$
(E) $4R$

278. A planet is in an elliptical orbit around a star such that the furthest distance the planet is from the star is three times the closest distance to the star. The ratio of the speed of the planet at the closest distance to the speed at the furthest distance is

(A) 1/9
(B) 1/3
(C) 1
(D) 3
(E) 9

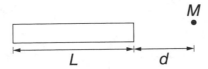

279. A small mass m is a distance d from the right end of uniform rod of mass M and length L, as shown above. The magnitude of the force of gravity between the rod and small mass is

(A) $G\dfrac{mM}{d^2}$

(B) $G\dfrac{mM}{L^2}$

(C) $G\dfrac{mM}{d(d+L)}$

(D) $4G\dfrac{mM}{(d+L)^2}$

(E) $2G\dfrac{mM}{dL}$

280. A planet orbits at a radius R around a star of mass M. The period of orbit of the planet is

(A) $\sqrt{\dfrac{4\pi^2 R^2}{GM}}$

(B) $\dfrac{4\pi^2 R^3}{GM}$

(C) $\sqrt{\dfrac{4\pi^2 R^3}{GM}}$

(D) $\sqrt{\dfrac{4\pi^2 R}{GM}}$

(E) $\dfrac{GM}{4\pi^2 R}$

281. A moon orbits a large planet in an elliptical orbit, with its closest approach at a distance a, and its farthest distance b. The speed of the moon at point b is v. The speed at point a is

(A) $\dfrac{av}{b}$

(B) $\dfrac{bv}{a}$

(C) $\dfrac{(a+b)v}{b}$

(D) $\dfrac{(b-a)v}{b}$

(E) $\dfrac{2bv}{a}$

Questions 282–283

Two masses are initially a very large distance apart. The masses are allowed to accelerate toward one another due to the gravitational force between them.

282. Which of the following best represents the potential energy U as a function of distance r as the masses move toward each other?

(A)

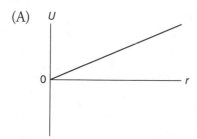

(B)

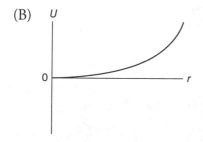

(C)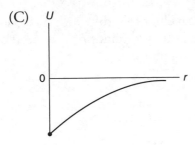

(D)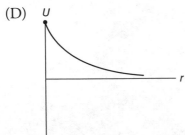

(E)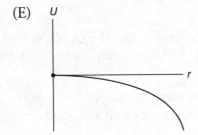

283. Which of the following best represents the potential energy U as a function of time t as the masses move toward each other?

(A)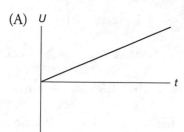

(B)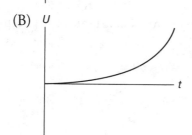

(C)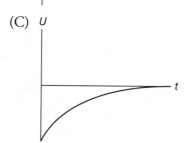

(D)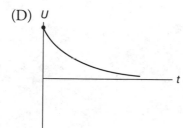

(E)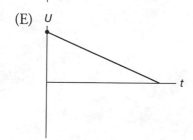

284. A satellite orbits the Earth in an elliptical orbit. Which of the following statements is true?

(A) The angular velocity of the satellite increases as it travels farther from the Earth.

(B) The acceleration of the satellite increases as it travels closer to the Earth.

(C) The angular momentum of the satellite increases as it travels closer to the Earth.

(D) The potential energy of the satellite is equal to its kinetic energy at all points in the orbit.

(E) The speed of the satellite must remain constant for it to remain in orbit around the Earth.

Questions 285–286

A satellite orbits a planet with a speed v in a circular orbit of radius R.

285. If the speed of the satellite is slightly increased, which of the following best represents the new orbit of the satellite?

(A)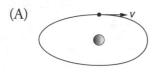

(B)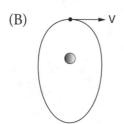

(C)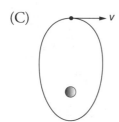

(D)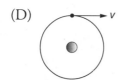

(E)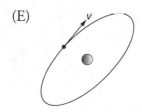

286. If the speed of the satellite is slightly decreased, which of the following best represents the new orbit of the satellite?

(A)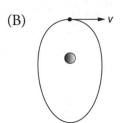

(B)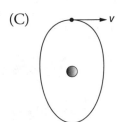

(C)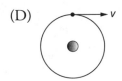

(D)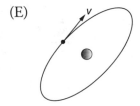

(E)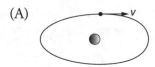

287. Two stars of equal mass M orbit around their center of mass, each with a speed v. The distance between the stars is R. Which of the following is an expression for the speed v of the stars?

(A) $\dfrac{GM}{R}$

(B) $\dfrac{GM}{R^2}$

(C) $\sqrt{\dfrac{GM}{R}}$

(D) $\sqrt{\dfrac{GM}{R^2}}$

(E) $\sqrt{\dfrac{GM}{2R}}$

288. A satellite of mass m travels in an elliptical orbit around a planet of mass M. The satellite has a speed v when it is closest to the planet at a distance r. Work is done by the engines of the satellite to change its orbit to a circular orbit when it is at this distance r. Which of the following statements is true of the transition from an elliptical orbit to a circular orbit?

(A) The work done by the satellite engines to change the orbit is equal to the change in kinetic energy of the satellite.

(B) The work done by the satellite engines to change the orbit is equal to the change in potential energy of the satellite.

(C) The work done by the satellite engines to change the orbit is equal to the change in angular momentum of the satellite.

(D) The work done by the satellite engines to change the orbit is equal to the change in speed of the satellite.

(E) The work done by the satellite engines to change the orbit is equal to the change in orbital radius of the satellite.

289. A satellite of mass m orbits the Earth with a potential energy U and a kinetic energy K. Which of the following statements would have to be true for the satellite to escape the Earth's gravity completely?

(A) The kinetic energy of the satellite would have to be equal to the potential energy between the Earth and the satellite.

(B) The potential energy between the Earth and the satellite would have to be greater than the kinetic energy of the satellite.

(C) The total energy of the satellite would have to be greater than the kinetic energy of the satellite.

(D) The kinetic energy of the satellite would have to be greater than the potential energy of the satellite.

(E) The total energy of the satellite would have to be equal to the potential energy of the satellite.

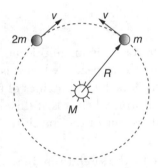

Questions 290–291

Two moons of mass m and $2m$ orbit a planet of mass M at the same radius R and speed v toward each other, as shown. The moons collide and stick together without destroying either moon.

290. The total momentum of the moons after the collision is

(A) mv

(B) $2mv$

(C) $3mv$

(D) $6mv$

(E) zero

291. The velocity of the two masses after the collision is

(A) v counterclockwise
(B) $v/2$ counterclockwise
(C) $v/2$ clockwise
(D) $v/3$ counterclockwise
(E) $v/3$ clockwise

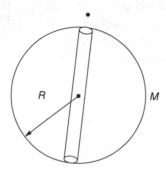

Questions 292–293

A tunnel is drilled through the diameter of a nonrotating planet of mass M and constant density, as shown. The radius of the planet is R. A small ball of mass m is dropped from rest into the hole at the surface of the planet.

292. The speed of the ball at the center of the planet is

(A) $\dfrac{GM}{R}$

(B) $\dfrac{GM}{R^2}$

(C) $\sqrt{\dfrac{2GM}{R}}$

(D) $\sqrt{\dfrac{2GM}{R^2}}$

(E) $\sqrt{\dfrac{GM}{2R}}$

293. Which of the following best describes the subsequent motion of the ball as it falls through the planet?

(A) The ball will come to rest at the center of the planet.

(B) The ball will travel through the planet and continue with a constant velocity after it leaves the planet.

(C) The ball will reverse the direction of its velocity at the center of the planet and return to the surface.

(D) The ball will travel completely through the planet and emerge on the other side, and then remain on the surface of the planet.

(E) The ball will oscillate about the center of the planet in harmonic motion with an amplitude R.

Free Response

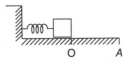

Questions 294–295

A mass m oscillates on an ideal spring of spring constant k on a frictionless, horizontal surface. The mass is pulled aside to a distance A from its equilibrium position and released.

294. In terms of the given quantities, at what distance from the equilibrium position is the potential energy of the mass equal to its kinetic energy?

295. In terms of the given quantities, what is a function for the velocity of the object if it begins at the maximum amplitude at time $t = 0$?

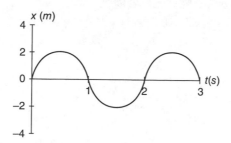

Questions 296–297

A mass oscillates in simple harmonic motion as shown by the position x vs. time t graph above.

296. If the oscillating object is a simple pendulum with a 2-kg mass, find the length of the pendulum.

297. Write the equation that represents the speed of the mass as a function of time.

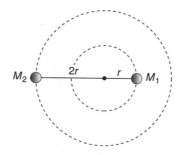

Questions 298–300

Two stars of unequal mass orbit each other about their common center of mass as shown. The star of mass M_1 orbits in a circle of radius r, and the star of mass M_2 orbits in a circle of radius $2r$.

298. Determine the ratio of masses M_1/M_2.

299. Determine the ratio of the acceleration a_1 of M_1 to the acceleration a_2 of M_2.

300. Determine the ratio of the period T_1 of M_1 to the period T_2 of M_2.

CHAPTER 7

Electric Force, Field, Potential, Gauss's Law

301. A positive charge is placed on a hollow spherical conducting shell of radius R. Which of the following statements is true?

(A) The charge is distributed evenly on the inside surface of the sphere.

(B) The charge is distributed evenly on the outside surface of the sphere.

(C) The charge is concentrated at the center of the sphere.

(D) The inside surface of the sphere is negatively charged.

(E) The charge is concentrated at the poles on the surface of the sphere.

302. A negative charge is placed on a solid conducting sphere of radius R. Which of the following statements is true?

(A) The electric field is zero everywhere inside the sphere.

(B) The electric field is zero just outside the surface of the sphere.

(C) The electric field is maximum at the center of the sphere.

(D) The electric field is directed radially outward outside the surface of the sphere.

(E) The electric field inside the sphere is equal and opposite to the electric field outside the surface of the sphere.

Questions 303–304

The shape shown is made of a solid conducting material of constant density. A positive charge is placed on the surface of the shape.

303. Which of the following diagrams best represents the distribution of charge on the surface of the shape?

(A)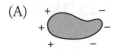

(B)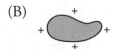

(C)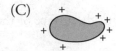

(D)

(E)

304. Which of the following statements is true?

    (A) The electric field must be uniform everywhere on the surface of the shape.

    (B) The electric field must be equal inside and outside the shape.

    (C) The electric potential must be uniform everywhere on the surface of the shape.

    (D) The charge must be equal both inside and outside the shape, but opposite in sign.

    (E) The charge must be equal both inside and outside the shape, having the same sign.

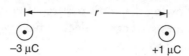

305. Two conducting spheres of equal radius are separated by a distance *r* as shown. A charge of −3 *μC* is placed on one of the spheres, and a charge of +1 *μC* is placed on the other sphere so that the force between them has a magnitude *F*. The two spheres are then connected by a conducting wire, and then the wire is removed. In terms of *F*, the new force between them is

(A) zero
(B) 3*F*, attractive
(C) 2*F*, repulsive
(D) ½ *F*, attractive
(E) 1/3 *F*, repulsive

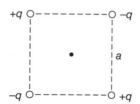

Questions 306–307
Four charges are arranged at the corners of a square of side *a* as shown.

306. Which of the following is true of the electric field and the electric potential at the center of the square?

	Electric Field	Electric Potential
(A)	zero	zero
(B)	$\dfrac{kQ}{a\sqrt{2}}$	zero
(C)	$\dfrac{kQ^2}{2a^2}$	$\dfrac{kQ}{2a}$
(D)	zero	$\dfrac{kQ}{\sqrt{2}a}$
(E)	$\dfrac{kQ^2}{2a}$	$\dfrac{kQ}{a\sqrt{2}}$

307. Which of the following diagrams best represents how you might rearrange the charges so that the electric field would point directly upward toward the top of the page?

(A)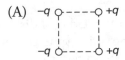

$-q$ ○----○ $+q$

$-q$ ○----○ $+q$

(B) $-q$ ○----○ $-q$

$+q$ ○----○ $+q$

(C) $+q$ ○----○ $+q$

$-q$ ○----○ $-q$

(D) $-q$ ○----○ $+q$

$+q$ ○----○ $-q$

(E) $+q$ ○----○ $-q$

$+q$ ○----○ $-q$

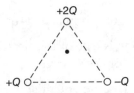

308. Three charges, $+Q$, $-Q$, and $+2Q$, are arranged in an equilateral triangle as shown. Which of the arrows below best represents the direction of the electric field at the center of the triangle?

(A) ↓

(B) ↑

(C) ↘

(D) ↙

(E) ↗

Questions 309–310

A positive charge Q is placed on a spherical shell of radius R.

309. Which of the following graphs best represents the electric field E as a function of distance r from the center of the sphere?

(A)
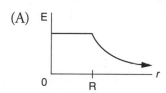

(B)
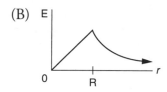

(C)
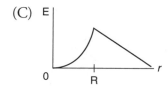

(D)
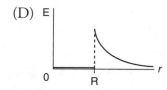

(E)
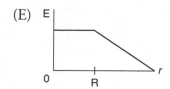

310. Which of the following graphs best represents the electric potential *V* as a function of distance *r* from the center of the sphere?

(A)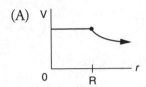

(B)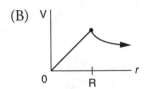

(C)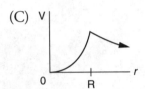

(D)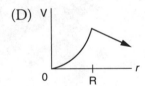

(E)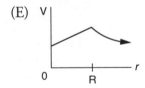

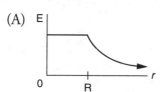

Questions 311–312

A nonconducting sphere of uniform charge density ρ contains a total charge $+Q$.

311. Which of the following graphs best represents the electric field E as a function of distance r from the center of the sphere?

(A)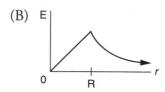

(B)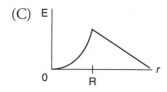

(C)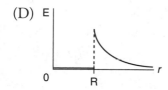

(D)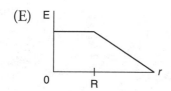

(E)

312. Which of the following graphs best represents the electric potential *V* as a function of distance *r* from the center of the sphere?

(A)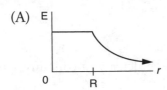

(B)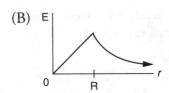

(C)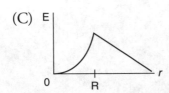

(D)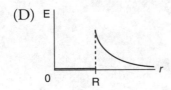

(E)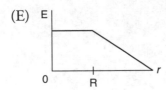

Questions 313–314
A nonconducting sphere does not have a uniform charge density, but the density ρ varies with the distance r from the center of the sphere according to the equation $\rho = \beta r$, where β is a positive constant.

313. The electric field inside the sphere ($r < R$) at a distance r from the center of the sphere is

(A) $\dfrac{\beta r^2}{12\varepsilon_o}$

(B) $\dfrac{\beta r}{2\varepsilon_o}$

(C) $\dfrac{\beta r^3}{3\varepsilon_o}$

(D) $\dfrac{\beta r^2}{2\varepsilon_o}$

(E) $\dfrac{\beta r^2}{4\varepsilon_o}$

314. The electric potential at the surface of the sphere is

(A) $\dfrac{\beta R^3}{4\varepsilon_o}$

(B) $\dfrac{\beta R}{2\varepsilon_o}$

(C) $\dfrac{\beta R^3}{3\varepsilon_o}$

(D) $\dfrac{\beta R^2}{2\varepsilon_o}$

(E) $\dfrac{\beta R^2}{4\varepsilon_o}$

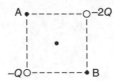

315. Two charges, $-Q$ and $-2Q$, are located at the corners of a square of side a as shown. Points A and B are at the opposite corners of the square. The work required to move a positive charge from point A to point B is

(A) negative
(B) positive
(C) dependent on the path from A to B
(D) equal to the electric potential between the charges
(E) zero

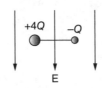

316. Two charges, $+4Q$ and $-Q$, are connected by an insulated rod and rest in a uniform electric field **E** as shown. Ignore the effects of gravity on the charges and rod. The rod and charges will experience

(A) a clockwise rotation and a downward acceleration
(B) a counterclockwise rotation and a downward acceleration
(C) a clockwise rotation and an upward acceleration
(D) a counterclockwise rotation and an upward acceleration
(E) no rotation, but a downward acceleration

Questions 317–318

A positive charge Q is placed at the center of a hollow conducting sphere.

317. The charge on the inside surface of the hollow sphere is

(A) $-Q$

(B) $+Q$

(C) $-2Q$

(D) $+2Q$

(E) zero

318. A grounding wire is connected to the sphere and then removed. The charge on the sphere is now

(A) $-Q$

(B) $+Q$

(C) $-2Q$

(D) $+2Q$

(E) zero

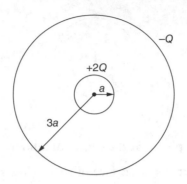

Questions 319–320
A solid conducting sphere of radius *a* is placed inside a conducting spherical shell of radius 3*a*, as shown. A charge +2*Q* is placed on the inner sphere, and a charge −*Q* is placed on the outer sphere.

319. Which of the following graphs best represents the electric field *E* as a function of the distance *r* from the center of the spheres?

(A) E

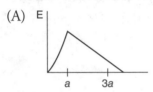

(B) E

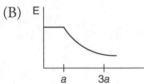

(C) E

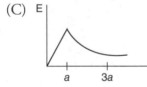

(D) E

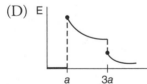

(E) E

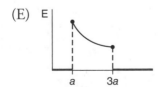

320. Which of the following graphs best represents the electric potential *V* as a function of the distance *r* from the center of the spheres?

(A)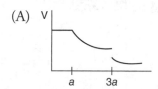

(B)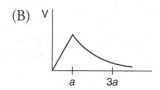

(C)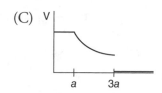

(D)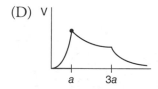

(E)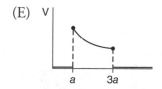

321. An irregularly shaped solid conductor has a positive charge placed on its surface. Which of the following statements is true of the conductor?

(A) The surface of the conductor is an equipotential surface.

(B) The electric field must be directed radially inward.

(C) The electric field is constant throughout the surface of the conductor.

(D) The surface charge density is constant throughout the surface of the conductor.

(E) Negative work is required to move a positive charge from one side of the conductor to the other.

322. The potential V as a function of distance r for a particular charge distribution is given by the equation $V = ar^{-1}$. The electric field as a function of distance r from the charge distribution is

(A) $1/3\ ar^{-3}$
(B) $2ar^{-1}$
(C) ar^{-2}
(D) $-a(\ln r)$
(E) $-ar^{-2}$

323. A positive charge of 4 μC is moved by an external force applied in the same direction as an electric field of magnitude 4,000 N/C. If the charge is moved a distance of 0.2 m, the work done by the external force is

(A) 200 μJ
(B) 800 μJ
(C) 1,600 μJ
(D) 3,200 μJ
(E) 6,400 μJ

Mass of oil droplet	3.2×10^{-7} kg
Charge on oil droplet	8.0×10^{-9} C
Electric field strength between the plates	200 N/C
Acceleration due to gravity	9.81 m/s^2

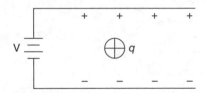

324. A charged oil droplet is located between two charged parallel plates as shown. The data table shows the measurements made by a student. Which of the following is true?

(A) The droplet will accelerate upward.
(B) The droplet will remain at rest.
(C) The droplet will move upward with a constant velocity.
(D) The droplet will move downward with a constant velocity.
(E) The droplet will accelerate downward.

325. Two conducting spheres, A and B, are separated by a large distance compared to their radii. Sphere A has a radius R, and sphere B has a radius $2R$. They each carry an equal charge $-Q$. The two spheres are then connected by a wire. In which direction will current flow in the wire?

(A) From A to B, since the potential is greater on the surface of sphere A.

(B) From B to A, since the potential is greater on the surface of sphere B.

(C) No current will flow between them, since the potential is the same for both spheres.

(D) No current will flow between them, since the charge is the same for both spheres.

(E) No current will flow between them, since the radius is not the same for both spheres.

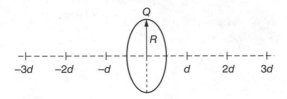

Questions 326–327
A positively charged ring of radius R is made of conducting material and has a charge Q distributed uniformly around it. The center of the ring is located at point 0 on the x-axis.

326. The potential V at a distance $3d$ from point 0 on the x-axis is

(A) $V = \dfrac{kQ}{9d^2}$

(B) $V = \dfrac{kQ}{3d^2}$

(C) $V = \dfrac{kQ}{R^2 + 9d^2}$

(D) $V = \sqrt{\dfrac{kQ}{R^2 + 9d^2}}$

(E) $\dfrac{kQ}{\sqrt{R^2 + 9d^2}}$

327. Which of the following graphs best represents the electric field E as a function of distance along the x-axis?

(A)

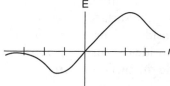

(B)

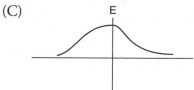

(C)

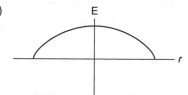

(D)

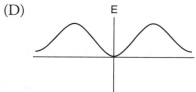

(E)

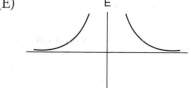

328. According to Gauss's law, the net electric flux passing through a closed surface is

(A) positive if the flux is entering the surface
(B) negative if the flux is exiting the surface
(C) positive if the net charge inside the surface is zero
(D) negative if the net charge inside the surface is zero
(E) zero if the net charge inside the surface is zero

329. According to Gauss's law, which of the following statements is true?

(A) It is possible to have a nonzero electric field but zero electric flux.
(B) It is possible to have a nonzero electric flux but zero electric field.
(C) It is possible to have a nonzero electric flux through a closed surface even if the enclosed charge in a surface is zero.
(D) If a surface is not closed (such as a sheet of paper), the flux through it must be zero.
(E) It is possible for charges located outside a closed surface to produce a net positive flux through the surface.

330. Electric potential

(A) is a vector quantity that depends on the direction of the electric field
(B) is a scalar quantity that depends on the magnitude and sign of charges in the vicinity
(C) is a scalar quantity that depends on the square of the distance from the charges in the vicinity
(D) is a vector quantity that depends on the sign of the charges in the vicinity
(E) is a vector quantity that must point from high to low potential

Questions 331–332

The two conducting spheres shown each have a charge Q on their surfaces. The larger sphere has a radius $4R$, and the smaller sphere has a radius R. The two spheres are far enough apart that their electric fields do not affect each other.

331. The ratio of the electric field near the surface of the larger sphere to the electric field near the surface of the smaller sphere is

(A) 16
(B) 4
(C) 2
(D) ¼
(E) 1/16

332. The ratio of the electric potential near the surface of the larger sphere to the electric potential near the surface of the smaller sphere is

(A) 4
(B) 2
(C) 1
(D) ½
(E) ¼

333. Which of the following statements is true of electric field and equipotential lines?

(A) The electric field vector always points in the same direction as the equipotential lines.
(B) The electric field always points in the opposite direction of the equipotential lines.
(C) The electric field always points perpendicular to the equipotential lines.
(D) The electric field is always equal to the equipotential lines.
(E) Equipotential lines always form a circle around electric field lines.

334. Electric field lines generally point from

    (A) low potential to high potential

    (B) high potential to low potential

    (C) negative charges to positive charges

    (D) negative potential to positive potential

    (E) low charge density to high charge density

335. Two oppositely charged parallel plates are shown in the figure. Which of the following diagrams best represents the equipotential lines between the plates?

    (A)

    (B)

    (C)

    (D)

    (E)

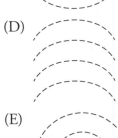

Questions 336–337
A nonconducting spherical charge distribution has a nonuniform positive charge density ρ. The center of the sphere is point 0; the radius of the sphere is a. The sphere is centered on the x-axis. A point inside the sphere lies on the x-axis at a distance x_1 from the center of the sphere. Another point, x_2, is outside the sphere on the x-axis.

336. The electric field at point x_2 can be determined by

   (A) using Gauss's law to determine the electric field from 0 to a, then using Gauss's law to determine the electric field from a to x_2, then finding the difference between the two electric fields

   (B) using Gauss's law to determine the electric field from 0 to a, then using Gauss's law to determine the electric field from a to x_2, then finding the sum of the two electric fields

   (C) integrating the electric potential outside the sphere from infinity to a, then integrating the electric potential inside the sphere from a to x_1, then finding the difference between the two potential integrals

   (D) integrating the electric potential outside the sphere from infinity to a, then integrating the electric potential inside the sphere from a to x_1, then finding the sum of the two potential integrals

   (E) determining the derivative of the potential function inside and outside the sphere, then finding the difference between the two derivatives

337. The electric potential at point x_1 can be determined by

  (A) determining the derivative of the electric field function inside
    and outside the sphere, then finding the difference between the
    two derivatives
  (B) determining the derivative of the electric field function inside
    and outside the sphere, then finding the sum of the two
    derivatives
  (C) integrating the derivative of the product of the electric field and
    potential functions, then finding their sum
  (D) integrating the electric field outside the sphere from infinity
    to a, then integrating the electric field inside the sphere from
    a to x_1, then finding the sum of the two potentials
  (E) integrating the electric field outside the sphere from infinity
    to a, then integrating the electric field inside the sphere from
    a to x_1, then finding the difference between the two potentials

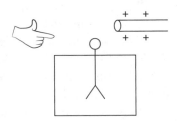

338. A simple electroscope consists of a metal knob at the top of a metal
rod, as shown. Two thin gold foil leaves hang at the bottom of the
rod. The rod and leaves are in an insulated container. A positively
charged rod is brought near but not touching the knob of the
electroscope, and then a student touches the knob with her finger.
Afterward, both the positive rod and her finger are removed. Which
of the following statements is true after she removes the rod and her
finger?

  (A) The knob is positively charged, and the leaves are negatively
    charged.
  (B) The knob is negatively charged, and the leaves are positively
    charged.
  (C) Both the knob and the leaves are negatively charged.
  (D) Both the knob and the leaves are positively charged.
  (E) Both the knob and the leaves are neutral.

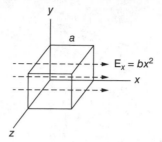

Questions 339–340

A cube has sides of length a. The cube rests so that one side rests on the x-axis as shown. An electric field is established in the x-direction according to the function $E_x = bx^2$, where b is a positive constant.

339. Which of the following statements is true?

(A) There is a net charge inside the cube.
(B) There is no net charge inside the cube.
(C) The flux passing through the cube is negative.
(D) The flux passing through the cube is zero.
(E) The flux diminishes while passing through the cube.

340. The charge inside the cube can be expressed by the equation

(A) $\varepsilon_o ba$
(B) $\varepsilon_o ba^2$
(C) $\varepsilon_o ba^3$
(D) $\varepsilon_o ba^4$
(E) $\varepsilon_o b^2 a^2$

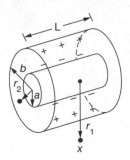

Questions 341–342

Two hollow coaxial cylinders are shown in the figure. The inner cylinder has a radius a and a charge $-Q$, and the outer cylinder has a radius b and a charge $+Q$. The length L of the cylinders is very long compared to the radii of the cylinders.

341. Point X is a distance r from the center of the cylinders. The electric field at point X outside the larger cylinder is

(A) $\dfrac{Q}{2\pi\varepsilon_o r_1 L}$

(B) $\dfrac{Q}{4\pi\varepsilon_o r_1 L}$

(C) $\dfrac{Q}{2\pi\varepsilon_o r_1^2 L}$

(D) $\dfrac{Q}{4\pi\varepsilon_o r_1^2 L}$

(E) zero

342. Point Y is halfway between the two cylinders at a distance of r_2 from the center of the cylinders. The electric field at r_2 is

(A) $\dfrac{Q}{2\pi\varepsilon_o r_2 L}$

(B) $\dfrac{Q}{4\pi\varepsilon_o r_2 L}$

(C) $\dfrac{Q}{2\pi\varepsilon_o r_2^2 L}$

(D) $\dfrac{Q}{4\pi\varepsilon_o r_2^2 L}$

(E) zero

343. Gauss's law is most convenient to use when calculating an electric field due to

(A) charges outside a closed surface
(B) charges inside a closed surface that has high symmetry
(C) charges inside a closed surface that has low symmetry
(D) a potential difference that is negative
(E) a potential difference that is positive

344. Gauss's law is convenient to use when the forces are produced by a distribution that

(A) is proportional to distance
(B) is negative
(C) follows the inverse square law
(D) is positive
(E) is described by a hyperbolic function

Free Response

Questions 345–347

Two positive charges, q_1 and q_2, have equal magnitudes Q and are placed on a line, as shown above.

345. What is the electric potential due to the two charges at the origin?

346. How much work is done bringing a positive third charge q_3 that has twice the magnitude of q_1 and placing this charge at the origin?

347. The third charge is removed, leaving the original two charges. The charges are released from rest. If q_1 has mass m and q_2 has mass $2m$, what is the speed of charge 1 when the charges are very far apart in terms of the given quantities and fundamental constants?

Questions 348–350. A charge of magnitude q is placed in the center of a spherical conducting shell of inner radius a to outer radius b, as shown below. It is not known if charge q is positive or negative. A plot of the electric flux as a function of distance from charge q is also shown below.

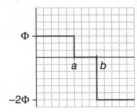
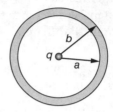

The flux from 0 to a is Φ, where $\Phi = 1 \times 10^6 \, \dfrac{\text{N} \cdot \text{m}^2}{\text{C}}$. The flux from a to b is zero, and the flux for distances b and larger is -2Φ.

348. What is the value of the point charge q?

349. What is the charge on the inner and outer surfaces of the spherical shell? What is the net charge?

350. An insulating sphere of radius R has charge $-2Q$ uniformly distributed throughout the shell. Derive an expression for the electric field inside the sphere.

CHAPTER 8

Electric Circuits,
Capacitors, Dielectrics

1.

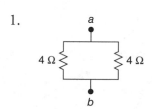

2.

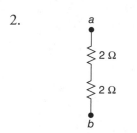

3.

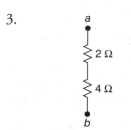

4.

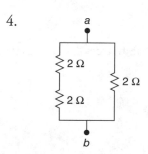

5.

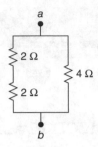

351. Which pair of the resistor arrangements shown have the same resistance between points *a* and *b*?

(A) 1 and 2
(B) 2 and 3
(C) 3 and 4
(D) 4 and 5
(E) 1 and 5

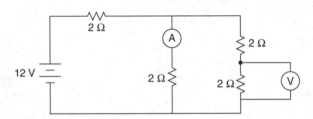

Questions 352–353

352. What is the reading on the voltmeter if the battery has no internal resistance?

(A) 0.5 V
(B) 2 V
(C) 2.4 V
(D) 4.8 V
(E) 12 V

353. What is the reading on the ammeter if the battery has no internal resistance?

(A) 1.2 A
(B) 2.4 A
(C) 3.6 A
(D) 4.8 A
(E) 6.0 A

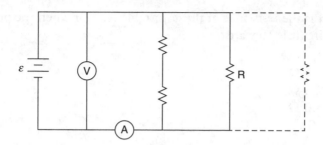

354. In the circuit shown, what effect would adding another resistor in parallel with the resistor labeled R have?

(A) The reading on the voltmeter would increase.
(B) The reading on the ammeter would increase.
(C) The reading on the voltmeter would decrease.
(D) The reading on the ammeter would decrease.
(E) The reading on the ammeter would not change.

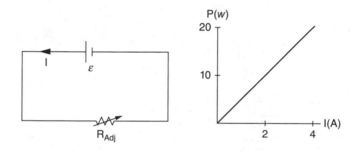

Questions 355–356
An adjustable resistor is connected to a battery of emf ε in a simple circuit. A graph of power vs. current in the battery is shown in the figure.

355. The emf ε of the battery is most nearly

(A) 5 V
(B) 10 V
(C) 20 V
(D) 40 V
(E) 60 V

356. What is the resistance of the adjustable resistor when the power in the circuit is 10 watts?

(A) 1.25 Ω
(B) 1.5 Ω
(C) 2.5 Ω
(D) 5.0 Ω
(E) 10 Ω

357. Five resistors are made of the same material. Which of the following has the highest resistance?

(A)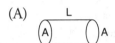

(B)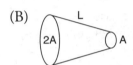

(C)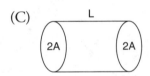

(D) $\frac{1}{2}$ A ⊂⎯⎯⎯L⎯⎯⎯⊃ $\frac{1}{2}$ A

(E) $\frac{1}{2}$ A ⊂⎯⎯⎯L⎯⎯⎯⊃ A

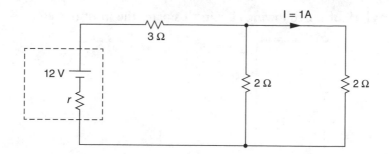

358. The circuit shown has a battery of emf ε and an unknown internal resistance. The internal resistance of the battery is

(A) 1 Ω
(B) 2 Ω
(C) 3 Ω
(D) 4 Ω
(E) 5 Ω

359. The current flowing in a wire as a function of time is given by the equation $I = 4t^3$. The charge that passes through the wire from 0 s to 2 s is

(A) 2 C
(B) 4 C
(C) 8 C
(D) 16 C
(E) 24 C

360. A 6-V battery with an internal resistance produces 1 A of current in the part of the circuit shown. A voltmeter connected across the battery will read

(A) 2 V
(B) 4 V
(C) 6 V
(D) 8 V
(E) 12 V

361. Which of the following circuits dissipates the most power?

(A)

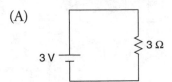

(B)

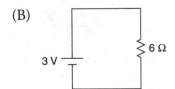

(C)

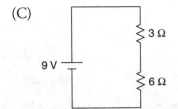

(D)

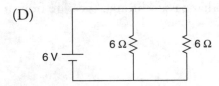

(E)

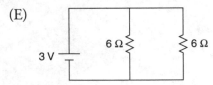

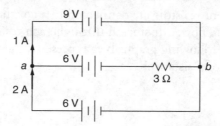

362. There are three batteries in the circuit shown. There may be other resistances not shown on the diagram. The potential difference between points *a* and *b* is

(A) 3 V
(B) 6 V
(C) 9 V
(D) 12 V
(E) 18 V

363. Several different resistors are connected to a constant voltage one at a time, and the power dissipated through each resistor is measured. Which of the following graphs best represents the power dissipated as a function of resistance?

(A)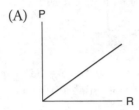

(B)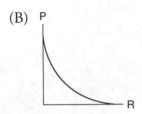

(C)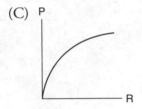

(D)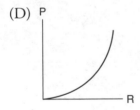

(E)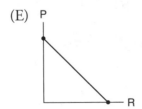

364. Each resistance in the five circuits below has a value of 2 Ω. Each circuit is connected to a 6-V battery. Which of the circuits would dissipate 9 watts of power?

(A)

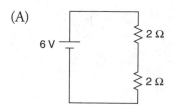

(B)

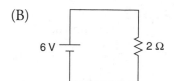

(C)

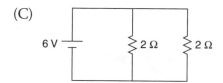

(D)

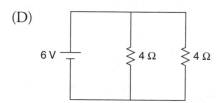

(E)

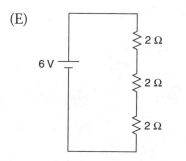

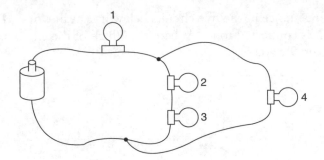

Questions 365–366
Four identical light bulbs are connected to a battery as shown.

365. Which bulb will burn the brightest?

(A) 1
(B) 2
(C) 3
(D) 4
(E) All will emit the same brightness.

366. If bulb 4 is removed, how will the brightness of each of the bulbs change, if at all?

(A) Bulb 2 will be less bright.
(B) Bulb 2 will be brighter.
(C) Bulb 3 will not change its brightness.
(D) Bulb 1 will not give off light.
(E) None of the bulbs will change their brightness.

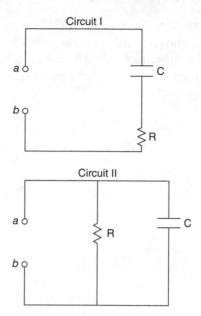

367. Circuit I and Circuit II shown each consist of a capacitor and a resistor. A battery is connected across *a* and *b*, and then removed. Which of the following statements is true of the circuits?

(A) Circuit I and Circuit II will both retain stored energy when the battery is removed.

(B) Neither Circuit I nor Circuit II will retain stored energy when the battery is removed.

(C) Only Circuit I will retain stored energy when the battery is removed.

(D) Only Circuit II will retain stored energy when the battery is removed.

(E) Current will continue to flow in both circuits after the battery is removed.

368. A parallel-plate capacitor has a capacitance *C*. A second parallel-plate capacitor has 4 times the area of the first, but ½ the separation distance between the plates. The capacitance of the second capacitor is

(A) $\dfrac{1}{8}C$

(B) $\dfrac{1}{4}C$

(C) $2\,C$

(D) $4\,C$

(E) $8\,C$

369. Two capacitors are connected in parallel. One of the capacitors has a capacitance C_o, and the other has a capacitance $2C_o$. A voltage V is applied across the capacitors. What is the ratio of the stored charge on the larger capacitor $2C_o$ to the charge stored on the smaller capacitor $2C_o$?

(A) ¼
(B) ½
(C) 2
(D) 4
(E) 8

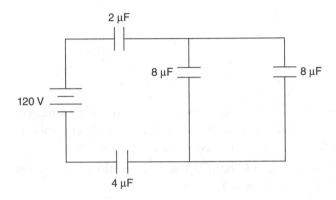

Questions 370–371

A circuit consisting of a battery and four capacitors is shown.

370. The equivalent capacitance of this circuit is

(A) 4/7 μF
(B) 7/4 μF
(C) 13/16 μF
(D) 16/13 μF
(E) 16/7 μF

371. The charge stored on the 2-μF capacitor is most nearly

(A) 22 μF
(B) 48 μF
(C) 148 μF
(D) 172 μF
(E) 202 μF

372. Kirchoff's junction rule states that the current entering a junction in a circuit must also exit that junction. This rule is an expression of

(A) conservation of charge
(B) conservation of energy
(C) Ohm's law
(D) Ampere's law
(E) Gauss's law

373. Two parallel conducting plates are connected to a battery and are separated by a distance d. If the separation distance is doubled to $2d$ while the battery remains connected to the plates, which of the following will occur?

(A) The capacitance is doubled.
(B) The charge on the plates is doubled.
(C) The voltage across the plates is doubled.
(D) The electric field between the plates is halved.
(E) The capacitance does not change.

374. A 10-μF capacitor is connected to a 12-V battery. The energy stored in the capacitor is

(A) 120 μJ
(B) 540 μJ
(C) 600 μJ
(D) 720 μJ
(E) 1,440 μJ

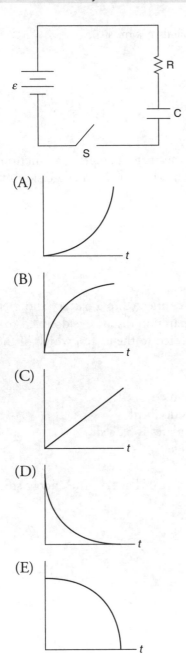

Questions 375–377
The capacitor in the circuit shown is initially uncharged when the switch S is closed at time $t = 0$. The graphs above could represent several quantities as a function of time for the circuit after the switch is closed.

375. Which of the graphs best represents the current in the circuit as a function of time?

(A) A
(B) B
(C) C
(D) D
(E) E

376. Which of the graphs best represents the voltage across the resistor as a function of time?

(A) A
(B) B
(C) C
(D) D
(E) E

377. Which of the graphs best represents the voltage across the capacitor as a function of time?

(A) A
(B) B
(C) C
(D) D
(E) E

378. Three 10-μF capacitors are connected in parallel with a 10-volt battery. The equivalent capacitance of the circuit is

(A) 3.3 μF
(B) 5 μF
(C) 10 μF
(D) 20 μF
(E) 30 μF

379. Three 9-μF capacitors are connected in series with a 9-volt battery. The charge on each capacitor is

(A) 1 μC
(B) 3 μC
(C) 6 μC
(D) 9 μC
(E) 27 μC

380. Three 6-μF capacitors are connected in series with a 6-volt battery. The energy stored on each capacitor is

(A) 1 μJ
(B) 3 μJ
(C) 4 μJ
(D) 6 μJ
(E) 12 μJ

381. A capacitor C_o is connected to a battery and stores charge. If the space between the capacitor plates is filled with oil, which of the following quantities increase?

(A) Capacitance and voltage across the plates
(B) Charge and voltage across the plates
(C) Capacitance and electric field between the plates
(D) Capacitance and charge on the plates
(E) Electric field between the plates and voltage across the plates

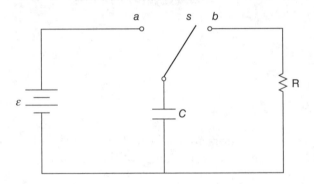

Questions 382–384
The circuit shows a capacitor, a battery, and a resistor. Switch S is first connected to point a to charge the capacitor, then a long time later switched to point b to discharge the capacitor through the resistor.

382. The time constant τ for discharging the capacitor through the resistor could be decreased (faster discharge) by

(A) placing another resistor in series with the first resistor
(B) placing another resistor in parallel with the first resistor
(C) placing another capacitor in parallel with the first capacitor
(D) placing another battery in series in the same direction with the first battery
(E) increasing both R and C

383. The maximum current through the resistor is

(A) $\varepsilon/2R$

(B) ε/R

(C) ε/RC

(D) $\varepsilon/2RC$

(E) $C\varepsilon/R$

384. Which of the graphs below best represents the current through the resistor as a function of time for a full charging and discharging cycle?

(A)

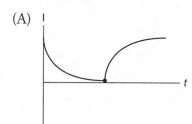

(B)

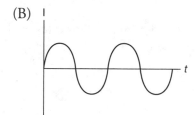

(C)

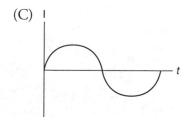

(D)

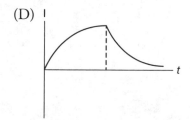

(E)

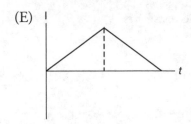

Questions 385–386

The equation for determining the capacitance of a capacitor of plate area A and separation d is $C = \dfrac{\varepsilon_o A}{d}$.

385. This equation can be derived from

(A) Ampere's law
(B) Faraday's law of induction
(C) Gauss's law for electrostatics
(D) Gauss's law for magnetism
(E) Ohm's law of circuits

386. If a dielectric of constant $\kappa = 4$ is placed between the plates of the capacitor and the separation between the plates is decreased to ½ d, the capacitance

(A) increases by a factor of 4
(B) decreases by a factor of 4
(C) increases by a factor of 8
(D) decreases by a factor of 8
(E) is unchanged

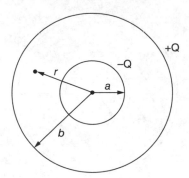

Questions 387–389

The spherical capacitor shown consists of a conducting shell of radius a inside a larger conducting shell of radius b. A charge $-Q$ is placed on the inner sphere and a charge $+Q$ is placed on the outer shell. The capacitance of the capacitor is C_o.

387. The magnitude of the electric field E at a distance r between the spheres is

(A) $\dfrac{Q}{4\pi\varepsilon_o r^2}$

(B) $\dfrac{Q}{4\pi\varepsilon_o r}$

(C) $\dfrac{Q}{4\pi\varepsilon_o a^2}$

(D) $\dfrac{Q}{4\pi\varepsilon_o b^2}$

(E) zero

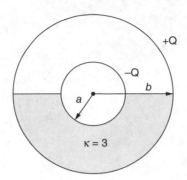

388. The bottom half of the space between the spheres is filled with oil of dielectric constant $\kappa = 3$, creating two capacitors connected to each other. Which of the following is true of the two capacitors?

(A) They are connected in series.
(B) They are connected in parallel.
(C) The total capacitance has not changed.
(D) The total capacitance of the spheres has decreased.
(E) The total capacitance is now zero.

389. With the bottom half of the space between the spheres having been filled with oil of dielectric constant $\kappa = 3$, the new capacitance of the spheres is

(A) zero
(B) C_o
(C) $2C_o$
(D) $3C_o$
(E) $4C_o$

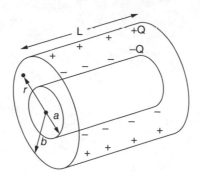

Questions 390–392

The cylindrical capacitor shown consists of a conducting shell of radius a inside a larger conducting shell of radius b. A charge $-Q$ is placed on the inner sphere and a charge $+Q$ is placed on the outer shell. The length of the capacitor is L, which is very long compared to a and b. The capacitance of the capacitor is C_o.

390. The magnitude of the electric field E at a distance r between the cylinders is

(A) $\dfrac{Q}{4\pi\varepsilon_o r^2}$

(B) $\dfrac{Q}{\pi\varepsilon_o rL}$

(C) $\dfrac{Q}{2\pi\varepsilon_o rL}$

(D) $\dfrac{Q}{2\pi\varepsilon_o L^2}$

(E) zero

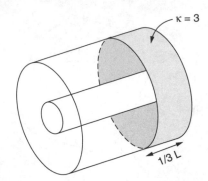

391. One-third of the length of the space between the cylinders is filled with oil of dielectric constant $\kappa = 3$, creating two capacitors connected to each other. Which of the following is true of the two capacitors?

(A) They are connected in series.
(B) They are connected in parallel.
(C) The total capacitance has not changed.
(D) The total capacitance of the spheres has decreased.
(E) The total capacitance is now zero.

392. With one-third of the space between the cylinders having been filled with oil of dielectric constant $\kappa = 3$, the new capacitance of the spheres is

(A) zero
(B) C_o
(C) $1/3\ C_o$
(D) $5/3\ C_o$
(E) $4C_o$

393. A battery of voltage V_o is attached to two parallel conducting plates. Charge is distributed on the plates, and then the battery is removed. A dielectric is then inserted between the plates, filling the space. Which of the following decreases after the battery is removed and the dielectric is inserted to fill the space between the plates?

(A) Capacitance
(B) Charge on the plates
(C) Net electric field between the plates
(D) Area of the plates
(E) Separation distance between the plates

Free Response

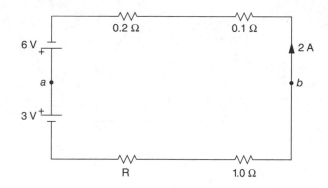

Questions 394–396

The circuit shown includes an unknown resistance R. The current in the circuit is 2 A.

394. What is the value of the resistance R?

395. What will a voltmeter read if it is connected from point a to point b?

396. How much energy is dissipated in the 1.0-ohm resistor in a time of 30 s?

Questions 397–400

A capacitor C is fully charged when it is connected in a circuit to a resistance R. As the capacitor discharges, the equation for the charge q on the capacitor as a function of time t is $q(t) = 6e^{\frac{-t}{4}}$, where charge is in coulombs.

397. What is the maximum charge on the capacitor before discharging?

398. Write an expression for current as a function of time as the capacitor discharges.

399. What does the number 4 in the denominator of the exponent of e represent?

400. Show that the product of resistance and capacitance has the SI units of time.

CHAPTER 9

Magnetic Fields and Forces

401. A straight wire carries a current I as shown. The magnetic field **B** at a point a distance r above the wire is

(A) $2\pi rI$ directed into the page

(B) $\mu_o I$ directed out of the page

(C) $\dfrac{\mu_o I}{2\pi r}$ directed into the page

(D) $\dfrac{\mu_o I}{2\pi r}$ directed out of the page

(E) zero

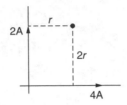

Questions 402–403

Two wires carry currents 2A and 4A in the directions shown. Point P is a distance r from the wire carrying 2A, and a distance $2r$ from the wire carrying 4A.

402. Which of the following statements is true?

(A) The magnetic field produced at point P by the wire carrying 2A is greater than the magnetic field produced at point P by the wire carrying 4A, but opposite in direction.

(B) The magnetic field produced at point P by the wire carrying 2A is less than the magnetic field produced at point P by the wire carrying 4A, and in the same direction.

(C) The magnetic field produced at point P by the wire carrying 2A is equal to the magnetic field produced at point P by the wire carrying 4A, but opposite in direction.

(D) The magnetic field produced at point P by the wire carrying 2A is equal to the magnetic field produced at point P by the wire carrying 4A, and in the same direction.

(E) The magnetic field produced at point P by the wire carrying 2A is greater than the magnetic field produced at point P by the wire carrying 4A, and in the same direction.

403. The magnitude of the resultant magnetic field at point P due to the current in the two wires is

(A) zero

(B) $\dfrac{\mu_o(2A)}{2\pi r}$

(C) $\dfrac{\mu_o(2A)}{\pi r}$

(D) $\dfrac{\mu_o(4A)}{2\pi r}$

(E) $\dfrac{\mu_o(6A)}{4\pi r}$

Questions 404–405

Two wires are parallel to each other, one carrying twice the current as the other. The two currents flow in the same direction.

404. Which of the following is true of the forces the wires exert on each other?

(A) The wire with the larger current exerts a greater force on the other wire.

(B) The wire with the smaller current exerts a greater force on the other wire.

(C) The wires exert equal and opposite forces on each other.

(D) The wires exert equal forces on each other, but in the same direction.

(E) The net force between the wires is zero.

405. The direction of the force between the wires is

(A) repulsive

(B) attractive

(C) zero

(D) into the page

(E) out of the page

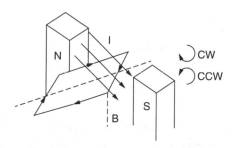

406. An electric motor consists of a current-carrying loop of wire mounted to an axle and turned at a slight angle in a magnetic field as shown. The wire loop will

(A) experience a torque and turn clockwise

(B) experience a torque and turn counterclockwise

(C) accelerate upward out of the magnetic field

(D) accelerate downward out of the magnetic field

(E) not experience a force or torque

407. A current is passed through an analog ammeter and the needle moves to indicate the current flowing through the circuit. Which of the following best explains how an analog ammeter works?
   (A) Current is passed through the needle placed in a magnetic field, and the needle is attracted to the high side of the scale.
   (B) The needle is a magnet and is attracted to a magnet on the high side of the scale.
   (C) The needle gathers an electrostatic charge from the current and is attracted to an electrostatic charge on the high side of the scale.
   (D) Current is passed through a spring coil of wire placed in a magnetic field, and the coil rotates, moving the needle proportionally to the current in the coil.
   (E) Current flows through the needle, making it heavier, and it falls to the high side of the scale.

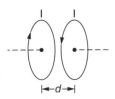

Questions 408–410
Two wire loops of equal radius are placed parallel to each other a distance d apart. Each carries a current I_o, but the currents are in opposite directions.

408. Which of the following statements is true of the force between the loops?
   (A) The loops exert a repulsive force on each other.
   (B) The loops exert an attractive force on each other.
   (C) The loops exert a force on each other in such a way that they will accelerate up toward the top of the page.
   (D) The loops exert a force on each other in such a way that they will accelerate down toward the bottom of the page.
   (E) The loops do not apply a force to each other.

409. Which of the following could be done to increase the force between the loops by a factor of 4?

(A) Double the current in one of the loops
(B) Reduce the current in one loop by half
(C) Reduce the current in both loops by half
(D) Double the distance between them
(E) Double the current in both of the loops

410. The direction of the net magnetic field at the center of the loop on the right is

(A) directed into the page
(B) directed out of the page
(C) directed to the right
(D) directed to the left
(E) zero

411. A wire in the plane of the page carries a current directed to the right as shown. The wire is placed in a magnetic field that is directed into the plane of the page. The force the magnetic field applies to the wire is

(A) directed into the page
(B) directed out of the page
(C) directed to the top of the page
(D) directed to the bottom of the page
(E) zero

412. A loop of wire in the plane of the page carries a clockwise current I and is placed in a magnetic field that is directed into the page as shown. Which of the following will happen as a result of the wire loop being in the magnetic field?

 (A) The wire loop will rotate clockwise.
 (B) The wire loop will rotate counterclockwise.
 (C) The wire loop will flip on a horizontal axis through its center.
 (D) The wire loop will expand in size.
 (E) The wire loop will contract in size.

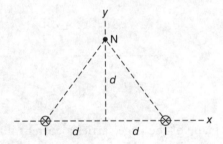

Questions 413–414
Two long parallel wires are separated by a distance $2d$ as shown. Each wire carries a current I, both directed into the page. Point P lies halfway between the two wires on the x-axis, and point N lies a distance d on the y-axis.

413. The resultant magnetic field at point P is

 (A) zero

 (B) $\dfrac{\mu_o I}{2\pi d}$

 (C) $\dfrac{\mu_o I}{\pi d}$

 (D) $\dfrac{\mu_o (2I)}{\pi d}$

 (E) $\dfrac{\mu_o I}{2\pi d^2}$

414. The direction of the resultant magnetic field at point N is best represented by which of the arrows below?

(A) ↓

(B) ↑

(C) ↘

(D) ←

(E) →

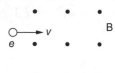

Questions 415–417

An electron enters a magnetic field that is directed out of the page as shown. The velocity of the electron is to the right.

415. The force the magnetic field exerts on the electron when it enters the magnetic field is

(A) directed into the page

(B) directed out of the page

(C) directed to the top of the page

(D) directed to the bottom of the page

(E) zero

416. The resulting path of the electron after entering the magnetic field is a

(A) straight line

(B) circle

(C) spiral

(D) parabola

(E) hyperbola

417. The work done by the magnetic field on the electron for one complete revolution at a radius r is

(A) $qvBr$

(B) qvB/r

(C) qv/Br

(D) Br/qv

(E) zero

Questions 418–419
The velocity **v** of a positive charge is directed out of the page as shown, and experiences a magnetic force **F** at an angle to the horizontal due to traveling through a magnetic field **B**.

418. Which of the arrows below best represents the direction of the magnetic field **B** that applies the force **F** to the positive charge?

   (A) ↓
   (B) ↑
   (C) ↘
   (D) ↖
   (E) →

419. The magnetic field is rotated so that the angle between the velocity **v** and the magnetic field **B** is 30°. The resulting path of the electron in this magnetic field is a

   (A) straight line
   (B) circle
   (C) spiral
   (D) parabola
   (E) hyperbola

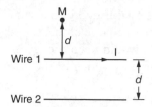

420. Two wires, 1 and 2, are separated by a distance d as shown. Point M is located at a distance d above wire 1. When there is only current flowing in wire 1 and none in wire 2, the magnitude of the magnetic field at point M is B_1. If a current is established in wire 2 so that both wires now have equal currents I, with both directed to the right, the magnetic field at point M is

(A) ½ B_1
(B) 2/3 B_1
(C) ¾ B_1
(D) 3/2 B_1
(E) zero

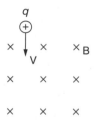

Questions 421–422
A positive charge $q = 2 \times 10^{-6}$ C enters a region of magnetic field $B = 0.2$ T directed into the page with a speed $v = 2 \times 10^6$ m/s directed down to the bottom of the page.

421. The magnitude and direction of the magnetic force acting on the positive charge is

(A) 0.2 N to the right
(B) 0.4 N to the left
(C) 0.8 N to the right
(D) 1.0 N to the left
(E) 4.0 N to the right

422. An electric field E is established in the same region as the magnetic field just as the positive charge enters the region. The direction of the electric field that would keep the charge moving in a straight line is best represented by which of the arrows below?

(A) ↓

(B) ↑

(C) ↘

(D) ←

(E) →

Questions 423–424

A negative charge $q = 4 \times 10^{-6}$ C enters a region of magnetic field $B = 0.5$ T directed into the page with a speed $v = 8 \times 10^6$ m/s directed to the right. An electric field also exists in the same region, causing the negative charge to follow a straight path.

423. Which of the following arrows best represents the direction of the electric field?

(A) ↓

(B) ↑

(C) ↘

(D) ←

(E) →

424. The magnitude of the electric field E that would cause the negative charge to follow a straight path is

(A) 2×10^6 N/C

(B) 4×10^6 N/C

(C) 8×10^6 N/C

(D) 2×10^7 N/C

(E) 4×10^7 N/C

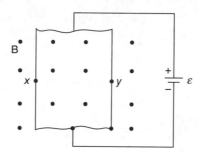

425. A thin sheet of copper is placed in a uniform magnetic field. A battery is connected to the top and bottom ends of the copper sheet, so that conventional current flows from the top to the bottom of the sheet. Points X and Y are on the left and right sides of the sheet, respectively. Which of the following statements is true?

(A) Point X is at a higher potential than point Y.
(B) Point Y is at a higher potential than point X.
(C) Point X and point Y are at equal potential.
(D) Point X is at zero potential, and point Y has a positive potential.
(E) Point Y is at zero potential, and point X has a negative potential.

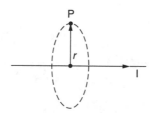

Questions 426–427
A wire carries a current I. Point P is a perpendicular distance r from the wire. An imaginary circle of radius r is drawn around the wire.

426. Which of the following is a correct application of Ampere's law that can be used to solve for the magnetic field B at point P?

(A) $\dfrac{B}{2\pi r} = \mu_o I$

(B) $\dfrac{B}{4\pi r^2} = \mu_o I$

(C) $B(2\pi r) = \mu_o I$

(D) $B(\pi r^2) = \mu_o I$

(E) $\dfrac{B}{2\pi r} = \dfrac{\mu_o I}{2r}$

427. Which of the graphs below best represents the magnetic field B as a function of distance from the wire r?

(A)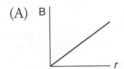

(B)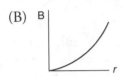

(C)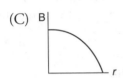

(D)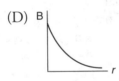

(E)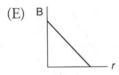

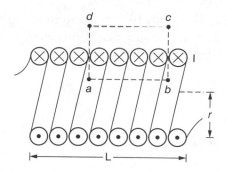

Questions 428–430

A cross section of a solenoid of length L and radius r is shown. A current I is passed through the solenoid so that the current comes out toward you on the bottom and into the page on the top. An imaginary square of side x is drawn on the figure.

428. The magnetic field in the region just outside the solenoid at a distance d from the center of the solenoid is

(A) zero

(B) $\dfrac{\mu_o I}{2\pi d}$

(C) $\dfrac{\mu_o I}{\pi d}$

(D) $\dfrac{\mu_o (2I)}{\pi d}$

(E) $\dfrac{\mu_o I}{2\pi d^2}$

429. The direction of the magnetic field inside the solenoid is best represented by which of the arrows below?

(A) ↓

(B) ↑

(C) ↘

(D) ←

(E) →

430. Ampere's law can correctly be applied to the imaginary square path *abcd* to determine the magnetic field produced by the solenoid in which of the following equations?

(A) $\int_{c}^{d} B \cdot dl = \mu_o I$

(B) $\int_{a}^{b} B \cdot dl = \mu_o I_{enc}$

(C) $\int_{b}^{c} B \cdot dl = \mu_o I_{enc}$

(D) $\int_{a}^{a} B \cdot dl = \mu_o I_{enc}$

(E) $\int_{b}^{b} B \cdot dl = \mu_o I_{enc}$

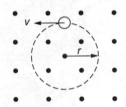

Questions 431–433
A negatively charged particle of mass *m* and charge *q* in a uniform magnetic field *B* travels in a circular path of radius *r*.

431. In terms of the other given quantities, the charge-to-mass ratio q/m of the particle is

(A) $\dfrac{Bv}{r}$

(B) $\dfrac{r}{Bv}$

(C) $\dfrac{rv}{B}$

(D) rvB

(E) $\dfrac{v}{rB}$

432. The work done by the magnetic field after two full revolutions of the charge is

(A) zero

(B) $-qvB/rm$

(C) qvm/Br

(D) $-mBr/qv$

(E) $-mqvBr$

433. Which of the following graphs best represents the radius r as a function of magnetic field B for a constant speed?

(A)

(B)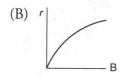

(C)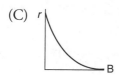

(D)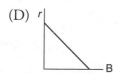

(E)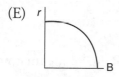

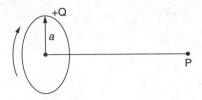

Questions 434–436

A ring of radius r has a positive charge $+Q$ distributed uniformly around its circumference. The ring begins to rotate clockwise about the x-axis with a constant speed v, with the charge Q rotating with the ring. The period of rotation is T. Point P is on the x-axis a distance d from the center of the ring.

434. The current produced by the rotation is

(A) $\dfrac{Q}{2\pi T}$

(B) $\dfrac{Q}{2\pi r T}$

(C) $\dfrac{2\pi r}{T}$

(D) $\dfrac{Q}{T}$

(E) zero

435. The direction of the magnetic field at the center of the loop is

(A) ↓

(B) ↑

(C) ↘

(D) ←

(E) →

436. The direction of the magnetic field at point P due to the rotating ring is

(A) ↓

(B) ↑

(C) ↘

(D) ←

(E) →

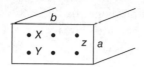

Questions 437–439

A very long conducting slab of copper of height a and width b carries a current I throughout its cross-sectional area. The current density j is constant throughout the slab and is directed out of the page through the facing area of the slab. Points X and Y are marked on the facing area of the slab.

437. The current density j can be expressed by the expression

(A) $\dfrac{I}{a^2}$

(B) $\dfrac{I}{b^2}$

(C) $\dfrac{I}{(ab)^2}$

(D) $\dfrac{I}{ab}$

(E) $\dfrac{I}{a+b}$

438. Which of the following diagrams best represents the integration path taken to apply Ampere's law to determine the magnetic field at points X or Y inside the slab?

(A)

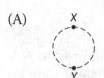

(B)

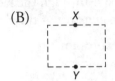

(C)

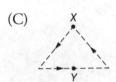

(D)

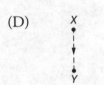

(E)

439. Which of the following best represents the direction of the magnetic field vectors at points X and Y?

(A) 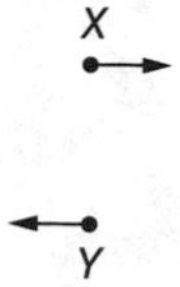   X
      •→

      ←•
      Y

(B) 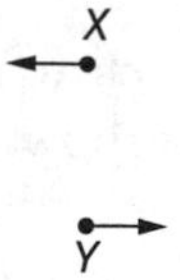   X
      ←•

      •→
      Y

(C)   X
      ↙•

      •↗
      Y

(D)   X
      •↘

      ↖•
      Y

(E)   ↑
      •X

      •Y
      ↓

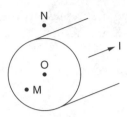

Questions 440–441
A long cylinder made of conducting material carries a total current *I* parallel to the length of the cylinder and directed into the page, as shown. The current density is uniform throughout the cross-sectional area of the cylinder. Point M is inside the cylinder and point N is outside the cylinder in the positions shown.

440. Which of the following arrows best represents the direction of the magnetic field vector at point M?

(A) ↓

(B) ↑

(C) ↘

(D) ↖

(E) →

441. Which of the following arrows best represents the direction of the magnetic field vector at point N?

(A) ↓

(B) ↑

(C) ↘

(D) ←

(E) →

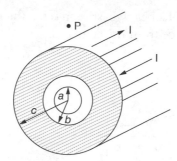

Questions 442–443

A long coaxial cable consists of a solid cylindrical conductor of radius a surrounded by a hollow coaxial conductor of inner radius b and outer radius c. The two conductors each carry a uniformly distributed current I but in opposite directions. Point P is outside the larger cylinder at a distance d from the center of the cylinders.

442. The magnetic field B at point P is

(A) zero

(B) $\dfrac{\mu_o I}{2\pi d}$

(C) $\dfrac{\mu_o I}{\pi d}$

(D) $\dfrac{\mu_o (2I)}{\pi d}$

(E) $\dfrac{\mu_o I}{2\pi d^2}$

443. Which of the graphs below best represents the magnetic field B as a function of distance from the center r?

(A)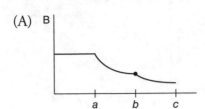

(B)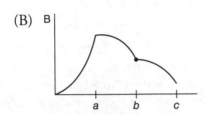

(C)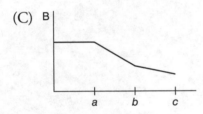

(D)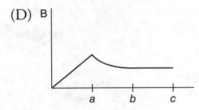

(E)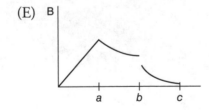

444. A stationary compass placed above a charge moving with a speed v deflects its needle so that it aligns perpendicular to the velocity of the charge. If the compass also moves at the speed v along with the charge, the compass will

(A) deflect 90° relative to the velocity of the charge
(B) deflect 60° relative to the velocity of the charge
(C) deflect 45° relative to the velocity of the charge
(D) deflect 180° relative to the velocity of the charge
(E) not deflect

Free Response

Questions 445–447
A solid conducting cylinder of radius a has a current I distributed uniformly throughout its cross-sectional area as shown.

445. Determine the magnetic field at a distance r greater than a.

446. Determine the magnetic field at a distance r less than a.

447. On the axes below, sketch the graph that best represents the magnetic field B as a function of distance r from the center of the cylinder.

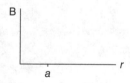

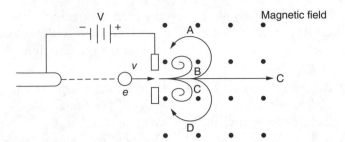

Questions 448–450

An electron of mass m and charge q is accelerated from rest through a potential difference V toward a positively charged plate. The electron has a speed v when it enters a magnetic field B directed out of the page in the region just beyond the positive plate.

448. What is the potential difference V necessary to give the electron a speed v as it reaches the positive plate?

449. On the diagram above, sketch the path that best indicates the electron's motion in the magnetic field.

450. Determine the radius of orbit for the electron.

CHAPTER 10

Electromagnetic Induction, Inductance, and Maxwell's Equations

451. Which of the following will induce a current in a loop of wire?

(A) A magnetic field passes through the loop.
(B) A magnetic flux passes through the loop.
(C) A magnetic field is created outside the loop.
(D) A magnetic flux is changing through the loop.
(E) A magnetic flux is greater than the loop.

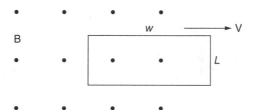

Questions 452–453

A rectangular loop of wire of width w and length L has a resistance R and lies in the plane of the page. A magnetic field of strength B is directed out of the page as shown. The loop of wire moves to the right with a constant speed v.

452. What is the induced current in the loop?

(A) BLv/R^2
(B) BLv/wR^2
(C) $BLwv/R$
(D) BLv/R
(E) Zero

453. The direction of the induced current in the loop is
   (A) out of the page
   (B) into the page
   (C) clockwise
   (D) counterclockwise
   (E) no direction, since the induced current is zero

454. In each of the diagrams below, a bar magnet and a loop of wire are aligned so that the magnet can pass through the loop. Which of the following situations would NOT induce a current in the loop?

(A)

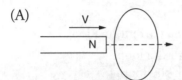

(B)

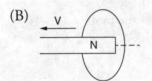

(C)

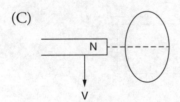

(D)

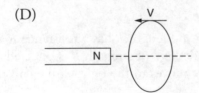

(E)

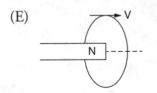

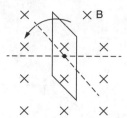

Questions 455–456

A square loop of conducting wire lies in a plane that is perpendicular to a magnetic field $B = 0.3$ T, which is directed into the page. The square has an area of 0.4 m² and is turned a quarter of a turn in a time of 0.2 s in such a way that it becomes parallel to the magnetic field lines (that is, the magnetic field lines no longer pass through the loop).

455. During the quarter turn, the change in magnetic flux through the loop is

   (A) 0.006 T m²
   (B) 0.012 T m²
   (C) 0.024 T m²
   (D) 0.036 T m²
   (E) 0.048 T m²

456. The average emf ε induced in the loop during the quarter turn is

   (A) 0.006 V
   (B) 0.012 V
   (C) 0.024 V
   (D) 0.036 V
   (E) 0.048 V

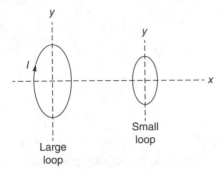

457. A large wire loop and a small wire loop are parallel to each other and centered on the *x*-axis as shown. The large loop carries a current *I*. Which of the following procedures will NOT induce a current in the smaller loop?

(A) Changing the current in the larger loop at a constant rate
(B) Rotating the smaller loop about the *y*-axis
(C) Moving the larger loop toward the smaller loop at a constant velocity
(D) Increasing the area of the smaller loop during a time interval
(E) Rotating the smaller loop about the *x*-axis

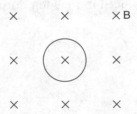

458. A magnetic field directed into the page increases at a constant rate. The changing magnetic field passes perpendicularly through a wire loop of radius *r*. Which of the following statements is true of the induced current in the loop?

(A) The induced current in the loop is zero.
(B) The induced current in the loop is clockwise.
(C) The induced current in the loop is counterclockwise.
(D) The induced current in the loop is directed out of the page.
(E) The induced current in the loop is directed into the page.

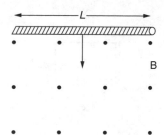

459. A thick wire of length L falls perpendicularly through a magnetic field that is directed out of the page. Which of the following graphs best represents the induced potential difference across the ends of the wire as a function of falling velocity?

(A) ε

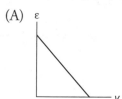

(B) ε

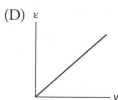

(C) ε

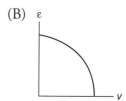

(D) ε

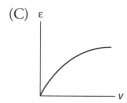

(E) ε

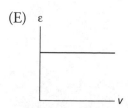

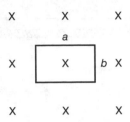

460. A rectangular loop of wire has a length a and width b and rests in a magnetic field that is directed into the page as shown. The resistance of the wire is R. The magnetic field is constantly changed so as to induce a current in the loop. The rate at which the magnetic field must change to produce the current I can be expressed as

(A) $\dfrac{Iab}{R}$

(B) $\dfrac{Ia}{bR}$

(C) $\dfrac{IR}{ab}$

(D) $\dfrac{ab}{IR}$

(E) $\dfrac{Ib}{bR}$

L

× × ×

× × ×

↓
V

× × ×

× × ×

Questions 461–463

The top view of rails of width L is shown. A bar of length L lies perpendicular to the rails and slides without friction with a speed v. A magnetic field B is directed into the page throughout the area of the rails.

461. The direction of the induced current in the bar is

(A) to the left

(B) to the right

(C) into the page

(D) out of the page

(E) zero

462. The magnetic force **F** acting on the bar as it slides is

(A) $\dfrac{BLv}{R}$

(B) $\dfrac{BL^2v}{R}$

(C) $\dfrac{B^2L^2v}{R}$

(D) $\dfrac{B^2L^2v}{R^2}$

(E) zero

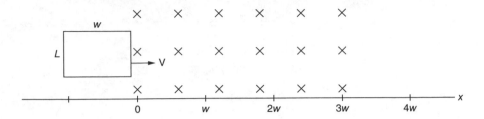

Questions 463–464

A rectangular loop of wire of length L and width w is mounted on a frictionless cart and passes through a constant magnetic field B with a speed v. The magnetic field is directed into the page and exists in a region with a width $2w$.

463. Which of the following graphs best represents the magnetic flux Φ through the loop as a function of distance x?

(A)

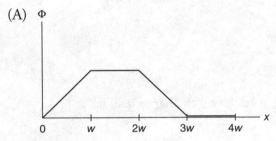

(B)

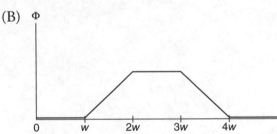

(C)

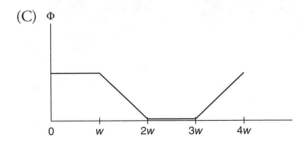

(D) Φ

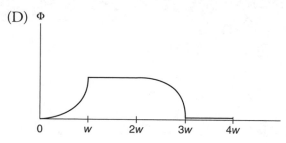

(E) Φ

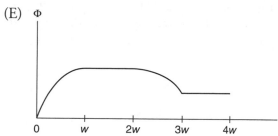

464. In reality, the speed of the loop may not remain constant. Which of the following statements is true of the speed of the loop as it passes through the magnetic field?

(A) The speed will decrease due to a negative magnetic force acting on the bar.

(B) The speed will increase due to a positive magnetic force acting on the bar.

(C) The speed will decrease because the magnetic flux is increasing.

(D) The speed will increase because the magnetic flux is decreasing.

(E) The speed of the bar will not change.

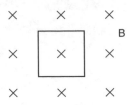

465. A square loop of side 0.2 m and resistance 0.5 Ω is placed in a magnetic field of 0.1 T directed into the page. The magnetic field decreases to zero at a constant rate during a time of 4 s. The magnitude and direction of the induced current in the loop is

(A) 0.0004 A
(B) 0.004 A
(C) 0.002 A
(D) 0.05 A
(E) 0.15 A

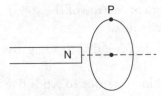

466. The north pole of a bar magnet is pushed through a conducting loop of wire so that it just crosses the plane of the loop, and then is pulled back out of the loop. The current induced in the wire passing through point P at the top of the loop is

(A) first into the page away from you, then out of the page toward you
(B) first out of the page toward you, then into the page away from you
(C) down toward the bottom of the page, then up toward the top of the page
(D) up toward the top of the page, then down toward the bottom of the page
(E) always in the same direction as the motion of the magnet

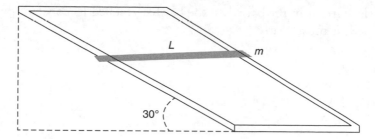

Questions 467–470

A bar of mass 0.2 kg and length $L = 0.3$ m slides down a ramp made of two frictionless rails. The ramp forms an angle of 30° with the horizontal.

467. The acceleration of the bar as it slides down the ramp is most nearly

(A) zero
(B) 2 m/s^2
(C) 5 m/s^2
(D) 7 m/s^2
(E) 10 m/s^2

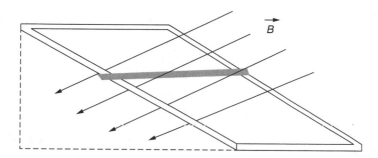

A magnetic field $B = 0.3$ T is established in a direction that passes through the rails perpendicularly to the plane of the ramp as shown. A current is induced in the bar as it slides down the rails.

468. Which of the following statements is true regarding the forces and motion involved?

(A) The only force acting on the bar as it slides is gravity.
(B) The only force acting on the bar as it slides is a magnetic force.
(C) Both a magnetic force and a component of the gravitational force act on the bar as it slides down the rails.
(D) The magnetic field changes as the bar slides down the rails.
(E) The magnetic flux is constant as the bar slides down the rails.

469. The current in the bar when the bar has reached its constant final speed is most nearly

(A) 1 A
(B) 2 A
(C) 3 A
(D) 5 A
(E) 10 A

470. The bar in the previous questions is now at rest at the bottom of the rails. The same magnetic field is now rotated so that it is directed straight downward toward the bottom of the page through the circuit formed by the rails and bar. The total length of the rails is 0.6 m. The magnetic flux Φ through the ramp surface is most nearly

(A) 0.078 T m^2
(B) 0.099 T m^2
(C) 0.11 T m^2
(D) 0.18 T m^2
(E) zero

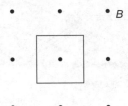

Questions 471–472
A square conducting loop of wire of side s and resistance R is placed in a magnetic field B, which is directed out of the page as shown. The field increases with time t according to the equation $B = k + Ct$, where k and C are positive constants.

471. The rate of change of magnetic flux with respect to time is

(A) $s(k + Ct)$
(B) $s^2(k + Ct)$
(C) $s^2(Ct)$
(D) s^2C
(E) $2sk$

472. The induced current I in the square loop is

(A) $s(k + Ct)/R$
(B) $s^2(k + Ct)/R$
(C) $s^2(Ct)/R$
(D) s^2C/R
(E) $2sk/R$

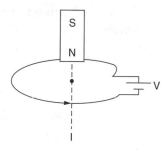

473. A loop of wire is connected to a battery and carries a current I, as shown in the figure. The north pole of a magnet is placed near the center of the loop. The force the magnet applies to the current loop is

(A) zero
(B) directed up toward the top of the page
(C) directed down toward the bottom of the page
(D) directed out of the page
(E) directed into the page

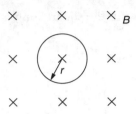

474. A circular loop of wire of radius r is placed in a magnetic field B that is varying with time. The induced emf ε in the loop is given by the equation $\varepsilon = k\pi r^2 t^{3/2}$, where k is a positive constant. The magnetic field B can be expressed as

(A) $\dfrac{3}{2}kt^{\frac{1}{2}}$

(B) $\dfrac{3}{2}kt^{\frac{3}{2}}$

(C) $\dfrac{2}{3}kt^{\frac{3}{2}}$

(D) $\dfrac{2}{3}kt^{\frac{5}{2}}$

(E) $\dfrac{4}{3}kt^{\frac{3}{2}}$

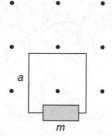

475. A mass m is attached to the bottom of a square conducting loop of side a as shown. The mass of the loop is negligible. The loop carries a current that causes the loop and mass to be suspended vertically in a magnetic field B, which is directed out of the page. The amount of current necessary to keep the loop and mass suspended in the field is

(A) $\dfrac{mg}{aB}$

(B) $\dfrac{aB}{mg}$

(C) $\dfrac{mg}{a^2B}$

(D) $\dfrac{a^2B}{mg}$

(E) $\dfrac{mg}{B}$

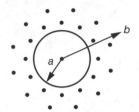

Questions 476–477

A magnetic field occupies a circular region of space of radius r. A conducting circular loop of wire of radius b and resistance R is placed in the magnetic field, which is directed out of the page as shown. The field decreases with time t according to the equation $B = B_o - kt$, where k is a positive constant.

476. The magnitude of the current induced in the loop of wire is

(A) $\dfrac{b\pi r^2}{R}$

(B) $\dfrac{k\pi r^2}{R}$

(C) $\dfrac{\pi b^3}{R}$

(D) $\dfrac{\pi b^2}{R}$

(E) zero

477. The induced current will reverse direction at a time equal to

(A) $\dfrac{2B_0}{k}$

(B) $\dfrac{B_0}{k}$

(C) $\dfrac{B_0}{R}$

(D) $\dfrac{B_0}{kR}$

(E) The current will never reverse direction.

Questions 478–479

A conducting loop of wire of area A is placed so that its plane is perpendicular to a magnetic field B. The magnetic field decreases according to the equation $B = 4e^{-2t}$.

478. The magnetic flux Φ as a function of time t is

(A) $4Ae^{-3t}$

(B) $8Ae^{-t}$

(C) $4Ae^{-2t}$

(D) $16Ae^{-2t}$

(E) $16Ae^{-4t}$

479. The induced current in the loop is

(A) $\dfrac{4Ae^{-3t}}{R}$

(B) $\dfrac{8Ae^{-t}}{R}$

(C) $\dfrac{8Ae^{-2t}}{R}$

(D) $\dfrac{16Ae^{-2t}}{R}$

(E) $\dfrac{16Ae^{-4t}}{R}$

480. Which of the following expressions could be used to determine the energy dissipated through the loop from $t = 0$ to $t =$ infinity?

(A) $\displaystyle\int_{0}^{\infty} IR\,dt$

(B) $\displaystyle\int_{0}^{\infty} \varepsilon R\,dt$

(C) $\displaystyle\int_{0}^{\infty} IR^2\,dt$

(D) $\displaystyle\int_{0}^{\infty} I^2 R^2\,dt$

(E) $\displaystyle\int_{0}^{\infty} I^2 R\,dt$

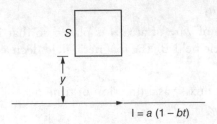

Questions 481–482
A long, straight wire carries a current that varies with time according to the equation $I = a(1 - bt)$, where a and b are positive constants. A square conducting loop of side s is placed a distance y above the long wire.

481. When $bt > 1$, the direction of the magnetic field inside the square loop is

  (A) out of the page
  (B) into the page
  (C) toward the top of the page
  (D) toward the bottom of the page
  (E) toward the left

482. Which of the following expressions could be used to determine the flux through the square loop as a function of time?

  (A) Bs^2

  (B) $B(y + s)^2$

  (C) $\displaystyle\int_0^{y+s} \mathbf{B} \cdot d\mathbf{A}$

  (D) $\displaystyle\int_y^{y+s} \mathbf{B} \cdot d\mathbf{A}$

  (E) $\displaystyle\int_s^{y+s} \mathbf{B} \cdot d\mathbf{A}$

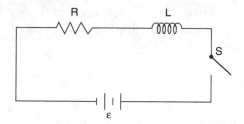

Questions 483–484
An inductance-resistance (LR) circuit is shown. The switch is closed at time $t = 0$.

483. Which of the following graphs best represents the potential difference V_R across the resistance R as a function of time?

(A) V_R

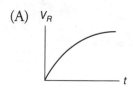

(B) V_R

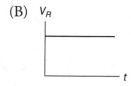

(C) V_R

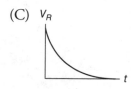

(D) V_R

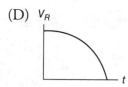

(E) V_R

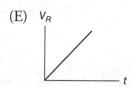

484. Which of the following graphs best represents the potential difference V_L across the inductor L as a function of time?

(A) V_L

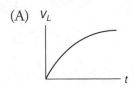

(B) V_L

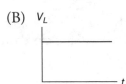

(C) V_L

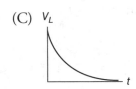

(D) V_L

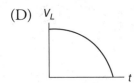

(E) V_L

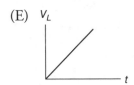

485. The ratio L/R has units of
  (A) volts
  (B) amperes
  (C) seconds
  (D) henrys
  (E) ohms

486. A time-dependent current is described by the equation $I = 3t^2$. The current passes through a 0.5-H inductor. The back emf ε_L across the inductor at a time of 2 s is

(A) −2 V
(B) −3 V
(C) −6 V
(D) −12 V
(E) −24 V

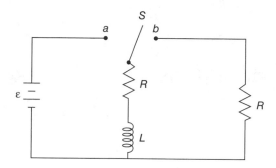

Questions 487–488
The circuit shown includes a battery of emf ε, a switch S, two resistors R, and an inductor L.

487. What is the differential equation that best describes the behavior of the circuit after the switch is connected to a?

(A) $\varepsilon - IR - L\dfrac{dI}{dt} = 0$

(B) $\varepsilon - \dfrac{dI}{dt}R - L\dfrac{d^2I}{dt^2} = 0$

(C) $\varepsilon - \dfrac{dI}{dt}R = 0$

(D) $\varepsilon - L\dfrac{d^2I}{dt^2} = 0$

(E) $\varepsilon - IR - L\dfrac{dI}{dt} = 2R$

488. After a long time, the switch is connected to *b*. What is the differential equation that best describes the behavior of the circuit after the switch is connected to *b*?

(A) $\varepsilon - IR - L\dfrac{dI}{dt} = 0$

(B) $\varepsilon - \dfrac{dI}{dt}R - L\dfrac{d^2 I}{dt^2} = 0$

(C) $\varepsilon - 2IR - L\dfrac{dI}{dt} = 0$

(D) $-2IR - L\dfrac{dI}{dt} = 0$

(E) $\varepsilon - \dfrac{dI}{dt}2R - L\dfrac{d^2 I}{dt^2} = 0$

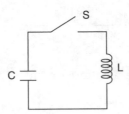

489. An ideal circuit consists of a capacitor *C* and inductor *L*. The capacitor is fully charged. The switch is closed at time $t = 0$. Which of the following statements is true of the behavior of the circuit after the switch is closed?

(A) The capacitor will discharge through the inductor, and the current will decrease to zero.

(B) The capacitor will discharge through the inductor, transferring potential energy to kinetic energy.

(C) The capacitor will discharge through the inductor, transferring energy to the inductor, and then the inductor will recharge the capacitor.

(D) The capacitor will discharge through the inductor, and the inductor will store the charge.

(E) The capacitor will not discharge through the inductor, so there will be no current.

490. Which of the Maxwell's equations below indicates that there are no magnetic monopoles?

(A) $\int E \cdot dA = \dfrac{q_{enc}}{\varepsilon_o}$

(B) $\int B \cdot dA = 0$

(C) $\int B \cdot dl = \mu_o I_{enc}$

(D) $\varepsilon = \int E \cdot dl = \dfrac{-d\Phi}{dt}$

(E) $\int g \cdot dA = -4\pi GM$

491. Which of the Maxwell's equations below relates electric flux to charge enclosed in a closed surface?

(A) $\int E \cdot dA = \dfrac{q_{enc}}{\varepsilon_o}$

(B) $\int B \cdot dA = 0$

(C) $\int B \cdot dl = \mu_o I_{enc}$

(D) $\varepsilon = \int E \cdot dl = \dfrac{-d\Phi}{dt}$

(E) $\int g \cdot dA = -4\pi GM$

492. Which of the Maxwell's equations below relates current to magnetic field?

(A) $\int E \cdot dA = \dfrac{q_{enc}}{\varepsilon_o}$

(B) $\int B \cdot dA = 0$

(C) $\int B \cdot dl = \mu_o I_{enc}$

(D) $\varepsilon = \int E \cdot dl = \dfrac{-d\Phi}{dt}$

(E) $\int g \cdot dA = -4\pi GM$

493. Which of the Maxwell's equations below relates the electric field produced to a changing magnetic flux?

(A) $\int E \cdot dA = \dfrac{q_{enc}}{\varepsilon_o}$

(B) $\int B \cdot dA = 0$

(C) $\int B \cdot dl = \mu_o I_{enc}$

(D) $\varepsilon = \int E \cdot dl = \dfrac{-d\Phi}{dt}$

(E) $\int g \cdot dA = -4\pi GM$

494. Which of the Maxwell's equations below relates the gravitational field to mass?

(A) $\int E \cdot dA = \dfrac{q_{enc}}{\varepsilon_o}$

(B) $\int B \cdot dA = 0$

(C) $\int B \cdot dl = \mu_o I_{enc}$

(D) $\varepsilon = \int E \cdot dl = \dfrac{-d\Phi}{dt}$

(E) $\int g \cdot dA = -4\pi GM$

Free Response

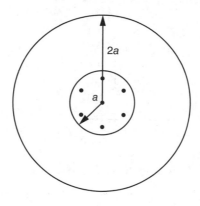

Questions 495–497

A circular region of radius a has a magnetic field B passing through it in an outward direction and perpendicular to the page. A circular conducting loop of radius a is placed in the magnetic field, and a conducting loop of radius $2a$ is placed around the magnetic field. The magnetic field is increasing at a rate dB/dt. Both loops have a resistance R.

495. On the diagram above, indicate the direction of the current I in the smaller loop.

496. In terms of the given quantities, determine the induced current I_1 in the smaller loop.

497. In terms of the given quantities, determine the induced current I_2 in the larger loop.

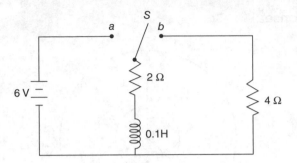

Questions 498–500

The switch S in the LR circuit shown has been open for a long time.

498. When the switch is connected to a, what is the voltage across the inductor L?

499. After a long time, what is the current through the 2-ohm resistor?

500. After the switch has been connected to a for a long time, what is the energy stored in the inductor?

ANSWERS

Chapter 1: Kinematics

1. (A) The time of fall must first be found. Using $y = y_0 + v_{0y}t - \frac{1}{2}gt^2$ with $y_0 = h$, $y = 0$, and $v_{0y} = 0$, $t = \sqrt{\frac{2h}{g}}$, the horizontal velocity is constant; thus, $x = v_0 t = v_0 \sqrt{\frac{2h}{g}}$.

2. (A) The vertical acceleration is constant, so the vertical velocity increases linearly with time.

3. (D) Horizontal velocity remains constant (v_0). Vertical velocity can be calculated with $v_y^2 = v_{0y}^2 - 2g\Delta y$, where v_{0y} is zero and $\Delta y = -h$. Thus, the vertical velocity (magnitude) is $v_y = \sqrt{2gh}$. The speed in total is the magnitude of the vector sum of the horizontal and vertical velocities, found using the Pythagorean theorem: $v^2 = v_0^2 + v_{0y}^2 = v_0^2 + 2gh$, yielding $v = \sqrt{v_0^2 + 2gh}$.

4. (D) If x is the total distance (100 m) traveled, then

$$x = 100 = \frac{1}{2}a(2)^2 + v \times (11 - 2)$$

where v is the speed after the 2-second acceleration. v can be found with the 2-second acceleration as $v = v_0 + at = a(2) = 2a$. Substituting, we get

$$100 = \frac{1}{2}a(2)^2 + 9v = 2a + 9(2a) = 20a$$

so $a = 100/20 = 5$ m/s^2.

5. (B) The velocity function must be found by integration because the acceleration is not constant:

$$v(t) = \int 5t^{1.5}\,dt = \frac{5}{2.5}t^{2.5} + C$$

Because the initial velocity would be zero, the constant of integration (C) is zero. To find the distance covered, the velocity function can be integrated over the 2-second interval:

$$x(2) = \int_0^2 2t^{2.5}\,dt = 6.5 \text{ m}$$

6. (C) $a = \dfrac{2y}{t^2} = \dfrac{2(1.2 \text{ m})}{(1.5 \text{ s})^2} = 1.1 \text{ s}$

7. (A) The package moves upward with the same speed as the helicopter (+3 m/s), rises to its maximum height, then falls back downward. When the package once again reaches the height from which the rope broke, it will be traveling at 3 m/s downward. The speed v_f at which the package strikes the ground is

$$v_f = \sqrt{2ax + v_i^2} = \sqrt{2\left(10 \ \dfrac{\text{m}}{\text{s}^2}\right)(8 \text{ m}) + \left(3 \ \dfrac{\text{m}}{\text{s}}\right)^2} = 13 \ \dfrac{\text{m}}{\text{s}}$$

8. (B) The time of fall is $t = \sqrt{\dfrac{2y}{g}} = \sqrt{\dfrac{2(1.0 \text{ m})}{10 \text{ m/s}^2}} = 0.44$ s.

$$x = v_x t = \left(5 \ \dfrac{\text{m}}{\text{s}}\right)(0.44 \text{ s}) = 2.3 \text{ m}$$

9. (E) The horizontal range (100 m) is described by $x = 100 = v_0 \cos(60)t = \dfrac{v_0 t}{2}$ (no acceleration horizontally). The vertical velocity can be described by

$-v_0 \sin(60) = v_0 \sin(60) - 9.8t$. Solving each equation for t and equating them yields

$\dfrac{200}{v_0} = \dfrac{\sqrt{3}v_0}{9.8}$. Cross multiplying to solve yields $v_0 = 33.6$ m/s.

10. (B) The cart moves with constant velocity on the level part of the track, then has negative acceleration (negative slope) as it rolls up the hill, then positive acceleration (positive slope) when it rolls down the hill, and then continues on the level track with the same velocity as it initially was moving.

11. (C) The speed of the particle is found using the Pythagorean theorem after determining the horizontal and vertical components of the velocity.

$$v_x = v_{ix} + a_x t = 3 \dfrac{\text{m}}{\text{s}} + \left(6 \dfrac{\text{m}}{\text{s}^2}\right)(4 \text{ s}) = 27 \dfrac{\text{m}}{\text{s}}$$

$$v_y = v_{iy} + a_y t = 0 + \left(4 \dfrac{\text{m}}{\text{s}^2}\right)(4 \text{ s}) = 16 \dfrac{\text{m}}{\text{s}}$$

$$v = \sqrt{v_x^2 + v_y^2} = \sqrt{(27 \text{ m/s})^2 + (16 \text{ m/s})^2} = 31 \dfrac{\text{m}}{\text{s}}$$

12. (D) The total displacement is found by applying the Pythagorean theorem after determining the horizontal and vertical components of the displacement.

$$x = x_i + v_{ix}t + \frac{1}{2}a_x t^2 = 0 + \left(3\frac{m}{s}\right)(4\ s) + \frac{1}{2}\left(6\frac{m}{s^2}\right)(4\ s)^2 = 60\ m$$

$$y = y_i + v_{iy}t + \frac{1}{2}a_y t^2 = 0 + 0 + \frac{1}{2}\left(4\frac{m}{s^2}\right)(4\ s)^2 = 32\ m$$

$$r = \sqrt{x^2 + y^2} = \sqrt{(60\ m)^2 + (32\ m)^2} = 68\ m$$

13. (A) The acceleration due to gravity can be found by

$$y = v_{0y}t + \frac{1}{2}gt^2$$

$$g = \frac{2(y - v_{0y}t)}{t^2} = \frac{2\left[6\ m - \left(2\frac{m}{s}\right)(2\ s)\right]}{(2\ s)^2} = 1\frac{m}{s^2}$$

Note: This solution is using a coordinate system where the initial position is 0 m and the downward direction is positive.

14. (B) The graph crosses the time axis at 8 s and 36 s, indicating velocity of zero at these times.

15. (B) The graph crosses the time axis at 8 s and 36 s, indicating velocity of zero at these times and going from positive velocity to negative velocity, thus turning around and changing direction.

16. (B) The initial horizontal velocity $v_x = v_o$, and the time of fall is $t = \sqrt{\frac{2y}{g}} = \sqrt{\frac{2D\sin\theta}{g}}$. The vertical velocity at time t is $v_y = gt = g\left(\sqrt{\frac{2D\sin\theta}{g}}\right)$. Using the Pythagorean theorem to find the speed of the ball, we get

$$v_f = \sqrt{v_x^2 + v_y^2}$$

$$v_f = (v_o^2 + 2D\sin\theta g)^{\frac{1}{2}}$$

17. (D) First we calculate the time it takes for the projectile to reach maximum height, where the vertical velocity is zero:

$$v_{iy} = gt$$

$$t_{top} = \frac{v_{iy}}{g} = \frac{40\,\dfrac{\text{m}}{\text{s}}\sin 60°}{g} = 3.5 \text{ s}$$

The time it takes for the projectile to reach its original height is twice this time: $2ty = 7.0$ s. The time it takes for the projectile to fall the additional 20 m is

$$t = \sqrt{\frac{2y}{g}} = \sqrt{\frac{2(20 \text{ m})}{10 \text{ m/s}^2}} = 2.0 \text{ s}. \text{ The total time of flight is } 7.0 \text{ s} + 2.0 \text{ s} = 9.0 \text{ s}.$$

18. (E) The speed is found by separating the variables:

$$a = \frac{dv}{dt} = -kv$$

$$-\int k\,dt = \int_{v_o}^{v} \frac{dv}{v}$$

$$-kt = \ln v]_{v_o}^{v}$$

$$v = v_o e^{-kt}$$

19. (B) The initial velocity of the filters is zero; then they begin falling at the acceleration due to gravity, but the air resistance decreases the acceleration until the velocity is constant. In other words, the slope (acceleration) of the graph decreases as it falls.

20. (B) Using the velocity equation from Question 18, $k = -1 \text{ s}^{-1}$, and $v = 0.5v_0$, the time that half the initial velocity is reached can be found:

$$0.5v_0 = v_0 e^{-t}$$
$$\ln 0.5 = -t$$
$$t = -\ln 0.5 = -(\ln 1 - \ln 2) = \ln 2$$

The velocity equation can then be integrated from $t = 0$ to $t = \ln 2$ using the initial velocity of 12 m/s to find the displacement over this time interval:

$$\Delta x = \int_{0}^{\ln 2} \left(12\,\frac{\text{m}}{\text{s}}\right) e^{-t}\,dt = (-1 \text{ s})\left(12\,\frac{\text{m}}{\text{s}}\right) e^{-t}\Bigg|_{0}^{\ln 2}$$

$$= -(12 \text{ m})(e^{-\ln 2} - e^0) = -(12 \text{ m})\left(\frac{1}{2} - 1\right) = 6 \text{ m}$$

21. (E) Since the velocity function is $v = \left(v_o^2 + \dfrac{Ct^2}{m} \right)$, the velocity is never zero, even at $t = 0$.

22. (D) The acceleration is the derivative of the velocity function with respect to time.

$$a = \frac{dv}{dt} = \frac{d}{dt}\left(v_o^2 + \frac{Ct^2}{m} \right) = \left(0 + \frac{2Ct}{m} \right) = \left(\frac{2Ct}{m} \right)$$

23. (E) Since the area under the graph for Car Q is greater than the area under the graph for Car P, at 10 s, Car Q has more displacement than Car P.

24. (D) The area under each graph is the same at $t = 20$ seconds. Displacement is the area under the velocity graph.

25. (C) For the positions to be the same, there must be a net displacement of zero. The area from $t = 3$ to $t = 4$ hours is $\Delta x = \dfrac{1}{2}(1\ \text{hr})\left(-20\,\dfrac{\text{km}}{\text{hr}} \right) = -10$ km. By calculation or inspection of symmetry, the area from $t = 2$ to $t = 3$ hours is $+10$ km.

26. (B) The velocity function can be found by integrating the acceleration function:

$$v = \int -8t\,dt = -4t^2 + C = -4t^2 + 16\,\frac{\text{m}}{\text{s}}$$

Using the initial velocity of 16 m/s at $t = 0$ seconds, to find when the car momentarily stops, set the velocity function equal to 0 m/s:

$$0 = -4t^2 + 16\,\frac{\text{m}}{\text{s}}$$
$$t^2 = 4\ \text{s}^2$$
$$t = \sqrt{4} = 2\ \text{s}$$

27. (C) The car accelerates positively in the first time interval, then moves with a constant velocity ($a = 0$) during the second time interval, then accelerates negatively during the third time interval, and then again has zero acceleration during the fourth time interval. The position vs. time graph would curve upward, then have a constant slope, then curve downward, and the velocity vs. time graph would have a constant slope, zero slope, and then a constant negative slope to show this motion.

28. (C) Since the plane's engines can make it move up to 200 km/h, without wind it could travel 100 km in a half hour. Since the crosswind would add distance to the flight, it would take more than a half hour for the plane to travel 100 km.

29. (E) The acceleration of the object would have to remove the x-component of the velocity and add a vertically upward component, so the acceleration would have to be directed up and to the left to cancel the horizontal motion and add an upward vertical motion.

30. (C) The velocity is the time integral of acceleration, and the position is the integral of velocity.

$$v = \int a \, dt = \int 4t^2 \, dt = \frac{4}{3} t^3$$

$$x = \int v \, dt = \int \frac{4}{3} t^3 \, dt = \frac{1}{3} t^4$$

At $t = 3$ s, $\frac{1}{3}(3 \text{ s})^4 = 27$ m

31. (B) The time of flight for the ball and the rock is the same: $t = \sqrt{\dfrac{2y}{g}} = \sqrt{\dfrac{2(80 \text{ m})}{10 \text{ m/s}^2}} = 4$ s. The horizontal distance the projected rock travels is 40 m. The horizontal speed is $v_x = \dfrac{x}{t} = \dfrac{40 \text{ m}}{4 \text{ s}} = 10 \dfrac{\text{m}}{\text{s}}$.

32. (C) Acceleration is the derivative of velocity with respect to time, so the derivative of the velocity with respect to time is 3.8 m/s².

33. (C) The average velocity is the difference in position divided by the time interval:

$$x(0) = 2 \times 0^3 - 3 \times 0^2 + 4 \times 0 = 0 \text{ m}, \quad x(4) = 2 \times 4^3 - 3 \times 4^2 + 4 \times 4 = 96 \text{ m}$$

$$v_{\text{avg}} = \frac{96 \text{ m} - 0 \text{ m}}{4 \text{ s}} = 24 \text{ m/s}$$

As an alternative, the same result is found by differentiating the position function to obtain the velocity function and then applying the mean value theorem for integrals.

34. (E) When the ball is dropped, it has a vertical velocity (free fall) and a horizontal velocity equal to the velocity of the train. It will follow a parabolic path as it falls, and the total speed can be found by combining the horizontal and vertical velocities using the Pythagorean theorem.

35. (B) At the top of its flight, the velocity of the ball is zero, since it's turning around to come back down. Gravity continually causes the acceleration, so the ball's acceleration is g everywhere during its flight.

36. (B) Let the initial velocity of the dart be v. Then the vertical component of the initial velocity is $v \sin\theta = v \sin 45 = \dfrac{\sqrt{2}}{2}v$. Since the general equation relating the maximum height of the dart is $v = \sqrt{2gh}$, then $\dfrac{\sqrt{2}}{2}v = \sqrt{2gh}$, giving a height of $2h$ for the initial speed v. So the new height is 2 m.

37. (C) The velocity at point A is horizontal and constant and equal to the initial horizontal velocity of the projectile.

38. (E) The acceleration everywhere on the flight path is g, which is always directed downward.

39. (A) In the first time interval, the position vs. time graph curves upward, indicating a positive acceleration, depicted on the velocity vs. time graph as a line with a constant positive slope. The constant slope in the second interval indicates a constant velocity, producing a horizontal line on the velocity vs. time graph. Then the position vs. time graph shows the object slowing down with a negative acceleration, indicated by a line with a negative slope on the velocity vs. time graph and zero velocity in the last interval.

40. (B) The acceleration is the derivative of the velocity with respect to time:

$$a = \frac{dv}{dt} = \frac{d}{dt}\left(16t - \frac{1}{2}t^4\right) = 16 - 2t^3$$

41. (C) At terminal velocity, acceleration is zero. We set the equation for acceleration equal to zero, solve for time, then substitute that time back into the equation for velocity:

$a = 0 = 16 - 2t^3$, which gives $t = 2$ s. Then substituting $t = 2$ s into $v = 16t - \frac{1}{2}t^4$ gives $v = 24$ m/s.

42. (B) Since the horizontal distance x is proportional to horizontal velocity v_x for the same amount of time of fall (same vertical height), the student would have to jump twice as fast to land twice as far away.

43. (D) The distance an object falls can be found by $y = \frac{1}{2}gt^2$. Rearranging for g, we get

$$g = \frac{2y}{t^2} = \frac{2(2 \text{ m})}{(1 \text{ s})^2} = 4\frac{\text{m}}{\text{s}^2}$$

44. (A) The average speed of the car is equal to the total distance divided by the total time:

$$v_{avg} = \frac{\Delta x}{\Delta t} = \frac{500 \text{ m}}{90 \text{ s}} = 5.6\frac{\text{m}}{\text{s}}$$

45. (C) The object accelerates at a constant rate, positively in the first interval, then negatively in the second interval. The net result is that whatever speed it gained in the first interval, it lost in the second interval. The displacement is not zero, since the object continued gaining velocity throughout the trip.

46. The equation $v = v_0 + at$ can be used for each 5-second interval, working backward to find v_0. Each acceleration occurs over a 5-second interval:

$$\text{At } t = 10 \text{ s, } v_0 = v - at = 0 - \left(-5\frac{\text{m}}{\text{s}^2}\right) \times 5 \text{ s} = 25 \text{ m/s.}$$

$$\text{At } t = 5 \text{ s, } v_0 = v - at = 25\frac{\text{m}}{\text{s}} - (0) \times 5 \text{ s} = 25 \text{ m/s.}$$

$$\text{At } t = 0 \text{ s, } v_0 = v - at = 25\frac{\text{m}}{\text{s}} - \left(5\frac{\text{m}}{\text{s}^2}\right) \times 5 \text{ s} = 0 \text{ m/s.}$$

Alternatively, the velocity change is the area (integral) under the acceleration-time graph. From $t = 0$ to $t = 15$ seconds, the area is zero, so there is no net velocity change from $t = 0$ to $t = 15$ s.

47. For the elevator to be moving down, the velocity must be negative. In the solution to Question 46, velocities in the first three time intervals are shown to be positive. In the final 5 seconds ($t = 15$ to $t = 20$ s), the acceleration is zero (from the graph); thus, the velocity does not change from $t = 15$ to $t = 20$ s, and as given, the velocity at $t = 15$ s is 0 m/s. Therefore, the elevator is never moving down, let alone moving down and slowing down (to be slowing down, the acceleration and velocity must have opposite signs).

48. The velocity is given at $t = 15$ seconds as 0 m/s. Acceleration is the slope of velocity, and these slopes are used to sketch the graph below.

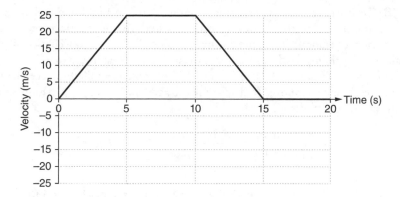

49. Since the horizontal velocity is $v_x = 6$ m/s, the horizontal displacement is $x = v_x t = 6t$. Then

$$v_y = \frac{dy}{dt} = \frac{d}{dt}[2(6t)^2] = 72t$$

50. The horizontal acceleration is zero (constant velocity), so the only acceleration is vertically upward. Imagine a projectile following a parabolic path, in which the acceleration due to gravity is vertical.

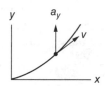

Chapter 2: Dynamics: Newton's Laws of Motion

51. (D) A ball moving in a circle has a centripetal force acting on it. A space probe does not need a net force to travel at a constant velocity, but it will continue due to its inertia. An object changing any component of its velocity is accelerating, so there must be a net force acting on it.

52. (C) Newton's third law states that the objects apply equal and opposite forces to each other, although the resulting accelerations will not be the same for each.

53. (A) The law of inertia states that the object must be moving with a constant velocity, and Graph (A) indicates constant velocity.

54. (B) Treat the two blocks as a single system. The normal force is determined by summing forces in the vertical direction, where the net vertical force is zero (no vertical acceleration). Thus, the downward force of $(4 \text{ kg} + 2 \text{ kg})(10 \text{ m/s}^2) = 60 \text{ N}$ is balanced by the upward normal force of 60 N. The maximum static friction is $f_s = \mu_s F_N = 0.2(60) \text{ N} = 12 \text{ N}$. Because 18 N of force is applied to accelerate the system, the system will move. To determine the acceleration, apply Newton's second law in the horizontal direction:

$$a = \frac{F_{net}}{m} = \frac{18 \text{ N} - \mu_k F_N}{2 \text{ kg} + 4 \text{ kg}} = \frac{18 \text{ N} - 0.1(60 \text{ N})}{6 \text{ kg}} = 2 \text{ m/s}^2$$

55. (E) Because the blocks are no longer accelerating, the net force on the system, and each block, is zero. Apply Newton's second law to the 2-kg block:

$$F_{net} = 0$$
$$F_{cord} - f_k = 0$$
$$k\Delta x - \mu_k F_N = 0$$

$$\Delta x = \frac{\mu_k F_N}{k} = \frac{0.1(2 \text{ kg})\left(10\dfrac{\text{m}}{\text{s}^2}\right)}{4\dfrac{\text{N}}{\text{m}}} = 0.5 \text{ m}$$

56. (D) Since the pulley has no mass, the net force accelerating the system of blocks is the weight of the 2-kg block, which is 20 N. The combined mass of the system that is being accelerated is 3 kg, so the acceleration of the system is

$$a = \frac{F_{net}}{m} = \frac{20 \text{ N}}{3 \text{ kg}} = 6.7 \ \frac{\text{m}}{\text{s}^2} \ \text{or} \ \frac{2}{3}g$$

57. (A) Since the initial velocity of the 2-kg block is zero, the speed after descending a distance D can be found by

$$v = \sqrt{2aD} = \sqrt{2\left(\frac{2}{3}g\right)D} = \sqrt{\frac{4D}{3}}$$

58. (B) The horizontal component of tension in the slanted cord must equal the tension in the horizontal cord, so the tension in the slanted cord must be greater than the tension in the horizontal cord.

59. (C) The horizontal component of tension in the slanted cord T_v must equal the tension in the horizontal cord. The tension in the horizontal cord = $T_v \cos 60° =$ ½ T_v.

60. (A) The initial velocity is c when time $t = 0$.

61. (B) The net force is given by Newton's second law:

$$F_{net} = ma = m\frac{dv}{dt} = m(3bt^2) = 3mbT^2$$

62. (B) For an object moving with constant acceleration, the distance traveled along the plane is proportional to the square of the time. Equivalently, the distance between each second increases with the odd integers: 1, 3, 5, 7. . . . So if the block travels 1 m in the first second, it will travel 3 m in the next second.

63. (C) Since the particle is following a parabolic path (imagine a projectile moving under the influence of gravity), the horizontal velocity is constant, and the only acceleration is vertical. Since the particle's path is curving upward, there must be a vertical force and acceleration.

64. (D) For the blocks to be set into motion, the applied force F must equal the maximum static frictional force:

$$F = f_s$$

$$6t = \mu_s F_N = (0.4)(3 \text{ kg} + 2 \text{ kg} + 1 \text{ kg})\left(10\frac{\text{m}}{\text{s}^2}\right)$$

$$t = 4 \text{ s}$$

65. (C) To find the contact force on the 3-kg block, the applied force F and acceleration of the system must first be found at $t = 6$ s: $F = 6t = 36$ N. To find acceleration, apply Newton's second law to the system:

$$a = \frac{F_{net}}{m} = \frac{F - \mu_k F_N}{m} = \frac{36 \text{ N} - (0.2)(6 \text{ kg})\left(10\frac{\text{m}}{\text{s}^2}\right)}{6 \text{ kg}} = 4\frac{\text{m}}{\text{s}^2}$$

Apply Newton's second law to the 3-kg block to find the unknown contact force that the 2-kg block exerts on the 3-kg block:

$$F_{net} = ma$$
$$F - f_k - F_{contact} = (3 \text{ kg})a$$
$$F_{contact} = 36 \text{ N} - (0.2)(3 \text{ kg})\left(10\frac{\text{m}}{\text{s}^2}\right) - (3 \text{ kg})\left(4\frac{\text{m}}{\text{s}^2}\right) = 18 \text{ N}$$

66. (D) The force acting on the puck removes the horizontal motion of the puck and adds an acceleration in the vertical direction, so the force must be directed upward and to the left.

67. (E) Since the block is sliding at a constant velocity, the frictional force directed up the incline must equal the component of the weight along the incline, $f = mg\sin\theta$. The coefficient of friction is $\mu = \frac{f}{N}$, where N is the normal force and is equal and opposite to the component of the weight that points downward and perpendicular to the plane, that is $N = mg\cos\theta$. Substituting into our equation for the coefficient of friction, we get

$$\mu = \frac{f}{N} = \frac{mg\sin\theta}{mg\cos\theta} = \tan\theta = \tan 30° = 0.6$$

68. (B) The net force is zero when the acceleration is zero.

$$v_y = \frac{dy}{dt} = \frac{d}{dt}[8t - 4t^2 + t^3] = 8 - 8t + 3t^2$$

$$a_y = \frac{dv_y}{dt} = \frac{d}{dt}[8 - 8t + 3t^2] = -8 + 6t$$

The acceleration and net force are zero when $t = 4/3$ s.

69. (D) Because the incline is a constant incline (angle doesn't vary), the kinetic friction is constant (normal force doesn't change, and kinetic friction is independent of speed). Air resistance increases with speed, so the air resistance is increasing.

70. (E) The acceleration must be found first. Using kinematics, we get

$$a = \frac{v^2}{2\Delta x} = \frac{\left(7.1\frac{m}{s}\right)^2}{2(10\ m)} = 2.52\frac{m}{s^2}$$

Applying Newton's second law to the elevator, the tension T is found:

$$F_{net} = ma$$
$$T - mg = ma$$
$$T = ma + mg = m(a + g) = (800\ kg)\left(2.52\frac{m}{s^2} + 10\frac{m}{s^2}\right) = 10{,}016\ N$$

71. (B) The net force acting on the elevator is still 2,000 N, which produces a downward acceleration of 2.5 m/s². The final velocity is zero, which gives an initial velocity of

$$v_i = \sqrt{2ah} = \sqrt{2\left(10\frac{m}{s^2}\right)(10\ m)} = 7\frac{m}{s}$$

72. (D) The vertical component of F_A must be greater than the vertical component of FB, since it must support more of the weight W due to F_A's larger angle to the horizontal.

73. (D) The free-body diagram for the block appears below.

The weight W is found by $W = mg$, and the component of the weight W parallel to the surface is $mg\sin(\theta)$ and accelerates the block downhill. The component of the weight perpendicular to the surface is $mg\cos(\theta)$ and is equal to the normal force N (by Newton's second law, the forces perpendicular to the surface would sum to zero). The coefficient of kinetic friction can be found by applying Newton's second law parallel to the incline (in the direction of motion), with downhill as the positive direction (by choice):

$$F_{net} = ma = 0$$
$$mg \sin\theta - \mu_k mg \cos\theta = 0$$
$$\mu_k = \frac{\sin\theta}{\cos\theta} = \tan(30) = 0.57$$

74. (C) The coefficient of kinetic friction, 0.57, was found in Question 73. The applied force is directed up the incline, as stated in the question, and thus the kinetic friction is acting downhill (opposite the slide). Apply Newton's second law along the incline, with uphill as the positive direction (by convenience or choice):

$$F_{net} = ma = 0$$
$$F_{app} - f_k - mg \sin\theta = 0$$
$$F_{app} = f_k + mg \sin\theta = \mu_k mg \cos\theta + mg \sin\theta$$
$$F_{app} = (0.57)(1 \text{ kg})\left(10\frac{\text{m}}{\text{s}^2}\right)\cos(30) + (1 \text{ kg})\left(10\frac{\text{m}}{\text{s}^2}\right)\sin(30) = 9.9 \text{ N}$$

75. (D) The acceleration must be found by differentiating the velocity function:

$$a(t) = v'(t) = 4t - 3$$

The acceleration at $t = 4$ s is then $a(4) = 4(4) - 3 = 13$ m/s². By Newton's second law, $F_{net} = ma = (2 \text{ kg})(13 \text{ m/s}^2) = 26$ N.

76. (C) Both blocks accelerate at the same acceleration, but the string only has to accelerate the 2-kg block, which represents 1/3 of the total mass. So the tension in the string only has to apply 1/3 F to accelerate the small block.

77. (B) The upward vertical component of the force is $F\sin\theta$, and this component of the force lightens the normal force, producing a normal force of $mg - F\sin\theta$. The frictional force is then

$$f = \mu N = \mu(mg - F\sin\theta)$$

78. (E) Because the ropes are of negligible mass, the tension within an individual rope will not vary. Because the block is uniform, each rope will support an equal amount of the block's weight, equal to 1/3 (three supporting ropes) of the total weight of the block, or $3T = W$.

79. (C) There are two forces acting on the stone: the given resistive force $F = cv$, which acts opposite to the direction of motion (down), and the force of gravity $F_g = mg$, acting in the downward direction. Choosing the upward direction to be positive and applying Newton's second law,

$$a = \frac{F_{net}}{m} = \frac{-cv - mg}{m} = -\frac{cv}{m} - g$$

80. (A) The net force accelerating the system is the weight of block m, which is mg. The weight of block m accelerates masses totaling $5m$. So

$$a = \frac{F_{net}}{m} = \frac{mg}{5m} = \frac{1}{5}g$$

81. (B) The net force is now $mg - \frac{1}{2} mg = \frac{1}{2} mg$. The acceleration is

$$a = \frac{F_{net}}{m} = \frac{\frac{1}{2}mg}{5m} = \frac{1}{10}g$$

82. (C) The acceleration is produced by the component of the weight that is directed down the incline, $mg\sin\theta$.

$$F_{net} = mg\sin\theta = ma$$

$$a = g\sin\theta = g\left(\frac{3}{5}\right) = 6 \frac{m}{s^2}$$

83. (D) The normal force is equal and opposite to the component of the weight that is perpendicular to the plane, $N = mg\cos\theta = (10 \text{ N})(4/5) = 8 \text{ N}$.

84. (E) The net force acting on the projectile is the weight of the projectile, which is always directed downward.

85. (A) The net force acting on the projectile now consists of the gravitational force (straight down) and the air resistance, which is always opposite to motion. The instantaneous velocity is always tangent to the path, so it's at the top of the parabola in this instance horizontally to the right. The air resistance is therefore opposite the velocity, or horizontally to the left. The net force therefore must be somewhere between horizontally left (due to air resistance) and vertically downward (due to the gravitational force).

86. (C) The acceleration is the derivative of velocity with respect to time, and velocity is the derivative of position with respect to time.

$$v_x = \frac{dx}{dt} = \frac{d}{dt}[2t^2 - 3t^3] = 4t - 9t^2$$

$$a_x = \frac{dv_x}{dt} = \frac{d}{dt}[4t - 9t^2] = 4 - 18t$$

At $t = 1$ s, $F_{net} = ma = m(4 - 18t) = -14$ N

87. (B) The force becomes negative after $4 - 18t = 0$, when $t = 0.22$ s.

88. (A) The position function can be found by integrating each term:

$$\mathbf{r} = \int 4t^3 \, dt \, \mathbf{i} + \int 6t^2 \, dt \, \mathbf{j} = t^4 \mathbf{i} + 2t^3 \mathbf{j} + C$$

The constant of integration is found using the initial condition at time 0 for position, or

$$\mathbf{r} = t^4 \mathbf{i} + 2t^3 \mathbf{j} + 2\mathbf{i} - 3\mathbf{j} = (t^4 + 2)\mathbf{i} + (2t^3 - 3)\mathbf{j}$$

The position at 1 second is then

$$\mathbf{r} = (1^4 + 2)\mathbf{i} + (2 \times 1^3 - 3)\mathbf{j} = 3\mathbf{i} - \mathbf{j}$$

The acceleration is the derivative of the velocity with respect to time:

$$\mathbf{a} = \frac{dv}{dt} = \frac{d}{dt}[4t^3 \mathbf{i} + 6t^2 \mathbf{j}] = 12t^2 \mathbf{i} + 12t\mathbf{j}$$

89. (C) Newton's second law states that

$$F_{net} = ma = (0.5 \text{ kg})(12\mathbf{i} + 12\mathbf{j}) = 6\mathbf{i} + 6\mathbf{j}$$

at $t = 1$ s. The magnitude of the net force is then

$$F_{net} = \sqrt{F_x^2 + F_y^2} = \sqrt{6^2 + 6^2} = 8.5 \text{ N}.$$

90. (D) If the net force is directed perpendicular to the velocity (such as on an object in circular motion), then the force cannot change the speed of the object, only the direction of its velocity.

91. (D) The filter begins from rest ($v = 0$) and begins with a high acceleration, indicated by the high slope at the beginning of the fall. As the filter accelerates, its acceleration decreases due to the increasing resistive force of the air. Eventually, the speed of the filter is constant (terminal velocity).

92. (E) The maximum frictional force that can act on the 2-kg block is

$$f = \mu mg = (0.2)(2 \text{ kg})\left(10 \ \frac{\text{m}}{\text{s}^2}\right) = 4 \text{ N}$$

This frictional force corresponds to a maximum acceleration of the 2-kg block (so that it does not slip off):

$$a = \frac{F_{net}}{m} = \frac{4 \text{ N}}{2 \text{ kg}} = 2 \frac{\text{m}}{\text{s}^2}$$

So the force acting on the 4-kg block cannot accelerate the system (6 kg) by more than 2 m/s².

$$F_{net} = ma = (6 \text{ kg})\left(2 \frac{\text{m}}{\text{s}^2}\right) = 12 \text{ N}$$

93. (B) The maximum acceleration the frictional force can tolerate is 2 m/s². If the 4-kg block is accelerating at 3 m/s², the 2-kg block will appear to accelerate to the left at 1 m/s² *relative to the 4-kg block*. We could also say that the 2-kg block is accelerating at 2 m/s² to the right relative to the table top.

94. The normal force the table exerts on the system is equal to the weight of the system: $2mg + 2mg + 4mg = 8mg$.

95. The net force that accelerates the system is $3mg$. The acceleration of the system then is

$$a = \frac{F_{net}}{m} = \frac{3mg}{5m} = \frac{3}{5}g$$

96. The acceleration of the system is 3/5 g. The tension in the string is accelerating a total mass of $4m$. The tension in the string is

$$T = ma = 4m\left(\frac{3}{5}g\right) = \frac{12}{5}mg$$

97. Less than $8mg$. While the system is accelerating, the tension in the strings must be less than the corresponding weights. Thus, the effect is that the tensions decrease the normal force acting on the stand as the system accelerates when compared with the system at rest, in which the normal force is simply the sum of the weights.

98. The tension in the string must be 10 N, since it supports the hanging 10 N weight in equilibrium.

99. Since the tension in the string is 10 N, the sum of the frictional force and component of the weight that is perpendicular to the plane ($mg\sin\theta$) must equal 10 N.

$$f + mg\sin\theta = 10 \text{ N}$$

$$f = 10 \text{ N} - (10 \text{ N})\sin 37° = 4 \text{ N}$$

100. The net force acting on the block on the incline is $mg\sin\theta - f$. The acceleration of the block on the incline is

$$a = \frac{mg\sin\theta - f}{m} = \frac{(10 \text{ N})\sin 37° - 4 \text{ N}}{1 \text{ kg}} = 2\frac{\text{m}}{\text{s}^2}$$

The velocity at the bottom of the incline is

$$v = \sqrt{2aD} = \sqrt{2\left(2\frac{\text{m}}{\text{s}^2}\right)(5 \text{ m})} = 4.5\frac{\text{m}}{\text{s}}$$

Chapter 3: Work, Energy, Power, and Conservation of Energy

101. (C) The work done from 0 to 4 m is equal to the area under the graph, $4 \text{ J} + 2 \text{ J} = 6 \text{ J}$.

102. (C) The change in kinetic energy from 0 to 5 s is equal to the work done during this time. The area under the graph from 0 to 4 m is 6 J, and the area from 4 m to 5 m is $-\frac{1}{2}$ J, giving a change of kinetic energy of $6 \text{ J} - \frac{1}{2} \text{ J} = 5.5 \text{ J}$.

103. (D) Average power for nonconstant forces and/or velocities is found by the integral

$$P = \frac{W}{t} = \frac{1}{t}\int_0^t F \times v \, dt = \frac{1}{t}\int_0^t T \times 2t^{\frac{3}{2}} \, dt = \frac{1}{t} 2Tt^{\frac{5}{2}}\left(\frac{2}{5}\right) = \frac{4}{5}Tt^{\frac{3}{2}}$$

104. (D) The general equation for potential energy is $U = mgh$. Both masses have a potential energy, but one is rising and one is descending. So the change in potential energy of the system is

$$m_A gD - m_B gD = (m_A - m_B)gD$$

105. (A) According to the law of conservation of energy, the change in potential energy equals the change in kinetic energy:

$$\frac{1}{2}(m_A + m_B)v^2 = (m_A - m_B)gD$$

Solve for the speed v:

$$v = \sqrt{\frac{(m_A - m_B)}{(m_A + m_B)}gD}$$

106. (E) The work done on the object is equal to the change in kinetic energy of the object. The work done can be estimated by the area under each graph. The least area under the graph corresponds to the least change in kinetic energy.

107. (C) The kinetic energy of the particle is given by $K = \frac{1}{2}mv^2$, where v is found by the derivative of position x with respect to time:

$$v = \frac{dx}{dt} = \frac{d}{dt}\left[2t^{\frac{5}{2}}\right] = 5t^{\frac{3}{2}}$$

Then the kinetic energy is

$$K = \frac{1}{2}mv^2 = \frac{1}{2}m\left(5t^{\frac{3}{2}}\right)^2 = \frac{5}{2}mt^3$$

108. (B) Work is found by

$$W = \int_0^t F \times v\, dt = \int_0^3 (2.5 \text{ N}) \times (2)(1 - e^{-2t})\, dt = 5\left(t + \frac{1}{2}e^{-2t}\right)\Big|_0^3 = 12.5 \text{ J}$$

109. (E) The work done by gravity will be equal to the opposite of the potential energy change, or $W = -\Delta U = -(0 - mgh) = mgh$, where h is the height of the projectile at point P. Use $v_y^2 = v_{o,y}^2 - 2gh$ to determine h:

$$h = \frac{v_y^2 - v_{0,y}^2}{-2g} = \frac{0 - \left(20\,\frac{m}{s}\sin 37°\right)^2}{-2\left(10\,\frac{m}{s^2}\right)} = 7.2 \text{ m}$$

The work done by gravity is then $W = mgh = (2 \text{ kg})\left(10\,\frac{m}{s^2}\right)(7.2 \text{ m}) = 144 \text{ J}$

110. (C) The initial energy of the projectile is entirely kinetic, or

$$K = \frac{1}{2}mv^2 = \frac{1}{2}(2 \text{ kg})\left(20\,\frac{m}{s}\right)^2 = 400 \text{ J}$$

Because 20 J of energy is lost to air resistance, the final energy is 400 J – 120 J = 280 J.

111. (D) The height h of the pendulum from which it starts above the lowest point of the swing is

$$h = L - L\cos 30°$$

By conservation of energy,

$$mgh = mg(L - L\cos 30) = \frac{1}{2}mv^2$$

$$v = \sqrt{2g(L - L\cos 30°)}$$

112. (D) The change in kinetic energy corresponds to the net work done on the weight, 15 N – 10 N = 5 N upward. If the question had asked for the work done against gravity only, you would use only the 10-N force.

113. (B) Because the particle is at rest, the total energy of the system is given by the potential energy function at $x = 0$ and is $U(0) = 4(0)^2 - 2(0) + 3 = 3$ J. To find the other location where the particle is at rest, set $U(x) = 3$ J and solve for x:

$$3 = 4x^2 - 2x + 3$$
$$0 = 4x^2 - 2x$$
$$0 = x(4x - 2)$$
$$x = 0 \quad \text{or} \quad x = 0.5 \text{ m}$$

114. (C) The force is equal to the negative derivative of U with respect to time:

$$F = -\frac{dU}{dx} = -\frac{d}{dx}[4x^2 - 2x + 3] = -8x - 2 = -8\left(\frac{1}{4}\text{ m}\right) - 2 = -4\text{ N, or a magnitude}$$

of 4 N.

115. (B) The total energy is the sum of potential and kinetic energy. At $x = 0$, $U(0) = 4(0)^2 - 2(0) + 3 = 3$ J, so $K = 10$ J $- 3$ J $= 7$ J. Using kinetic energy to solve for speed,

$$K = \frac{1}{2}mv^2$$

$$7\text{ J} = \frac{1}{2}(2\text{ kg})v^2$$

$$v = 2.6\frac{\text{m}}{\text{s}}$$

116. (B) The mass of the ball is $m = \dfrac{U}{gh} = \dfrac{30\text{ J}}{\left(10\dfrac{\text{m}}{\text{s}^2}\right)(5\text{ m})} = 0.6$ kg. Conservation of

energy gives

$$mgh + \frac{1}{2}mv^2 = mgh_{\text{max}}$$

$$h_{\text{max}} = \frac{mgh + \dfrac{1}{2}mv^2}{mg} = \frac{(0.6\text{ kg})\left(10\dfrac{\text{m}}{\text{s}^2}\right)(5\text{ m}) + 20\text{ J}}{(0.6\text{ kg})\left(10\dfrac{\text{m}}{\text{s}^2}\right)} = 8.3\text{ m}$$

117. (C) Work is found by integrating the force function over the displacement:

$$W = \int_0^1 4dx + \int_0^3 4y^3 dy = 4x\,|_0^1 + y^4\,|_0^3 = (4 - 0) + (3^4 - 0) = 85\text{ J}$$

118. (B) The particle moves from $(0, 0)$ to $(1, 3)$, so it undergoes a vertical displacement of 3 m. The work by gravity is $W = -\Delta U = -\left[(2\text{ kg})\left(10\dfrac{\text{m}}{\text{s}^2}\right)(3\text{ m}) - 0\right] = -60$ J.

119. (B) The force is given by the negative of the derivative (slope) of the U vs. x graph, which is constant between $x = 3$ and $x = 4$.

120. (D) The particle does not have enough energy to reach point P. From the graph, the potential energy at $x = 2$ m is -1 J, and the prompt gives the kinetic energy as 3 J. Therefore, the total energy is 2 J. At $x = 1$ m, the potential energy is 0 J; therefore, all energy is kinetic, or 2 J.

121. (B) The potential energy function is equal to the negative integral of the force over the position x:

$$U(x) = -\int F(x)dx$$
$$= -\int (-3x^2 - 2x - 4)dx = x^3 + x^2 + 4x = 2^3 + 2^2 + 4(2) = 20 \text{ J}$$

122. (E) $F = -dU/dx = -4x - 1$, so the force is linearly related to the position x, with a negative slope.

123. (A) The net work done depends on the change in potential energy Δmgh, which depends on the mass of the object and the height between P and Q.

124. (A) Only the horizontal component of the force gives the block a horizontal displacement and thus does work on the block. The horizontal component of the force is $F\sin\theta$, and it is applied through a horizontal distance x. So, $W = Fx\sin\theta$.

125. (D) Since the block is moving with a constant speed, the frictional force must be equal to the horizontal component of the applied force. The coefficient of friction is equal to the frictional force divided by the normal force. The normal force is the sum of the vertical component of the applied force and the weight of the block.

$$\mu = \frac{f}{N} = \frac{F\sin\theta}{F\cos\theta + mg}$$

126. (A) The electrostatic force would be perpendicular to the velocity, so there is no component of force along the direction of motion, and the work done is zero.

127. (B) Between x_o and $3x_o$, the potential energy of the particle decreases by $2U_o$, which must have been converted to kinetic energy.

128. (D) From Question 127, it is seen that the potential energy decreases by $2U_0$, which then becomes an increase in kinetic energy. Because the particle now starts with 2 J of kinetic energy, the kinetic energy at $3x_0$ is $2 + 2U_0$, or

$$K = \frac{1}{2}mv^2 = 2U_0 + 2 \text{ J, giving } v = 2\sqrt{\frac{U_0 + 1}{m}}.$$

129. (A) The maximum compression of the spring is found by conservation of energy $U_g = U_s$ yields $mgh = \frac{1}{2}kx^2$ yields $x = 0.14$ m. Conservation of energy then can find the speed of the block when the spring is compressed half the distance, but gravitational potential energy cannot be neglected:

$$mgh = \frac{1}{2}mv^2 + mg\left(\frac{x}{2}\right) + \frac{1}{2}k\left(\frac{x}{2}\right)^2 \text{ yields } v = 2.5 \text{ J}$$

130. (C) If gravity does +100 J in moving the block downward from a height h, it must do −100 J of work as it slides back up to a height h, since gravity is a conservative force.

131. (C) The time of fall needs to be found to get the initial velocity. The time of fall is $t = \sqrt{\frac{2y}{g}} = \sqrt{\frac{2(45 \text{ m})}{10 \text{ m/s}^2}} = 3$ s. The initial horizontal velocity is thus $v_x = \frac{x}{t} = \frac{60 \text{ m}}{3 \text{ s}} = 20$ m/s. The total energy is the sum of potential and kinetic energies:

$$U + K = mgh + \frac{1}{2}mv^2 = (5 \text{ kg})\left(10\frac{\text{m}}{\text{s}^2}\right)(45 \text{ m}) + \frac{1}{2}(5 \text{ kg})\left(20\frac{\text{m}}{\text{s}}\right)^2 = 3,250 \text{ J}$$

132. (A) Using conservation of energy,

$$mgh + \frac{1}{2}mv_x^2 = \frac{1}{2}mv^2$$

$$(5 \text{ kg})\left(10\frac{\text{m}}{\text{s}^2}\right)(45 \text{ m}) + \frac{1}{2}(5 \text{ kg})\left(20\frac{\text{m}}{\text{s}}\right)^2 = \frac{1}{2}(5 \text{ kg})v^2$$

$$v = 12 \text{ m/s}$$

133. (A) The kinetic energy is high at the beginning, then decreases to zero at the top of the path of the ball, and then increases as the ball falls.

134. (B) The potential energy graph would be the inverse of the kinetic energy graph, starting low near the ground at the beginning of the flight, increasing with height as it rises, then decreasing as it falls back to the ground.

135. (D) The drop in height of the block is $h = R − R\cos\theta$. The kinetic energy at θ is equal to the drop in potential energy:

$$K = mg(R − R\cos\theta)$$

136. (D) The speed of the block at θ can be found by setting the equation for kinetic energy equal to the equation for potential energy:

$$K = \frac{1}{2}mv^2 = mg(R - R\cos\theta), \text{ giving } v = \sqrt{2g(R - R\cos\theta)}$$

137. (D) At a point halfway down the ramp, $\theta = 45°$. Using conservation of energy (from the top),

$$h = R\sin 45°$$

$$mgh = mgR\sin 45° = \frac{1}{2}mv^2$$

$$v = \sqrt{2gR\sin 45°}$$

138. (D) The energy expended by the machine is

$$E = \int_0^{10} P\,dt = \int_0^{10} (4t^3 + 3t^2 - 2)\,dt = [t^4 + t^3 - 2t]_0^{10} = 10,080 \text{ J}$$

139. (B) Work for nonconstant forces is found from integrating

$$F = \int F\,dx = \int_{0.25}^{0.5} (3x^2 + 2x)\,dx = (x^3 + x^2)\Big|_{0.25}^{0.5}$$

$$= [(0.5)^3 + (0.5)^2] - [(0.25)^3 + (0.25)^2] = 0.297 \text{ J}$$

140. (C) Since the crate is moving at a constant speed, the applied force must be equal and opposite to the frictional force.

$$F = f = \mu mg$$

The rate at which work is done is power:

$$P = fv = \mu mgv$$

141. (D) The height above the bottom of the swing is $h = L - L\cos\theta$. The potential energy at this height is

$$mgh = mg(L - L\cos\theta)$$

This potential energy is converted to kinetic energy according to conservation of energy:

$$mgh = mg(L - L\cos\theta) = \frac{1}{2}mv^2$$

The speed v at the bottom of the swing is $\sqrt{2g(L - L\cos\theta)}$.

142. (A) The potential energy at the top of the ramp is mgr. All of this potential energy is dissipated by friction when it comes to rest at the end of the surface.

143. (B) The kinetic energy just after it strikes the floor is equal to the potential energy at the height of 4 m.

$$mgh = \frac{1}{2}mv^2$$

$$v = \sqrt{2gh} = \sqrt{2\left(10\frac{m}{s^2}\right)(4 \text{ m})} = 9\frac{m}{s}$$

144. (B) If there were no energy lost, the ball would rebound at 12 m/s and rise to a height h after the bounce:

$$mgh = \frac{1}{2}mv^2$$

$$h = \frac{v^2}{2g} = \frac{\left(12\frac{m}{s}\right)^2}{2\left(10\frac{m}{s^2}\right)} = 7.2 \text{ m}$$

The potential energy associated with this height is

$$mgh = (1 \text{ kg})\left(10\frac{m}{s^2}\right)(7.2 \text{ m}) = 72 \text{ J}$$

But the ball only rises to 4 m, so

$$mgh = (1 \text{ kg})\left(10\frac{m}{s^2}\right)(4 \text{ m}) = 40 \text{ J}$$

The fraction of energy lost is

$$\frac{72 \text{ J} - 40 \text{ J}}{72 \text{ J}} = 0.44$$

145. Work is found through integrating the force function:

$$W = \int F dx = \int_0^{1.5} 4x^3 dx = x^4 \Big|_0^{1.5} = 5.1 \text{ J}$$

146. The block will have 5.1 J of energy when it leaves the spring. Because kinetic energy is proportional to speed squared, when the spring is traveling half its maximum spring (speed when leaving the spring), the mass will have $(1/2)^2 = 1/4$ the total energy, or $5.1/4 = 1.275$ J of energy. Thus, 5.1 J $- 1.275$ J $= 3.825$ J of work was done by friction (in the negative direction). Because the frictional force is constant, $W = Fd$, and

$$Fd = \mu_k F_n d = (0.2)(5 \text{ kg})\left(10\frac{\text{m}}{\text{s}^2}\right)d = 3.825 \text{ J, giving } d = 2.6 \text{ m}.$$

147. The spring will lose energy due to friction found by $W = Fd = \mu_s F_n d = (0.2)(5 \text{ kg})\left(10\frac{\text{m}}{\text{s}^2}\right)(1.5 \text{ m}) = 15$ J. Because this is greater than the total energy available, the mass will stop sliding before leaving the spring.

148. The potential energy, as well as total energy, is maximum at $x = 2$ m.

149. When the displacement is -1 m, the potential energy is 0.5 J. Since the total energy is 3.0 J, the kinetic energy must be 2.5 J.

150. The kinetic energy is 3.0 J, since the potential energy is zero at $x = 0$. So,

$$K = \frac{1}{2}mv^2 = 3.0 \text{ J}$$

$$\frac{1}{2}(2 \text{ kg})v^2 = 3.0 \text{ J}$$

$$v = \sqrt{3} \text{ m/s}$$

Chapter 4: Impulse, Linear Momentum, and Conservation of Linear Momentum

151. (C) In elastic collisions, both momentum and energy are conserved. This is only possible in a collision of equal-massed carts, where one cart is initially at rest, if the moving cart comes to rest following the collision.

152. (C) By definition, a perfectly elastic collision conserves both momentum and kinetic energy.

153. (A) The area under the graph represents the impulse acting on the 2.0-kg mass. The area under the graph from 0 s to 2 s is 4 N s, the impulse from 2 s to 4 s is 8 N s, and the impulse from 4 s to 6 s is 4 N s. The total impulse then on the 2.0-kg mass is 16 N s. The impulse equals the change of momentum of the 2.0-kg mass and thus is 16 kg·m/s. Because the momentum change came from the collision with the 4.0-kg mass, the 4.0-kg mass must have a momentum change of −16 kg·m/s.

154. (C) The impulse was determined to be −16 kg·m/s. Because impulse J equals change in momentum, $\Delta v = \dfrac{J}{m} = \dfrac{-16 \text{ kg m/s}}{4 \text{ kg}} = -4$ m/s. Given the initial velocity of 4 m/s, the final velocity is 4 m/s + −4 m/s = 0 m/s.

155. (D) The horizontal component of the momentum of the ball when it strikes the wall is $mv\cos\theta$. The horizontal component of the momentum of the ball after the collision is $-mv\cos\theta$, giving a change of momentum of $-mv\cos\theta - (-mv\cos\theta) = 2mv\cos\theta$.

156. (A) Because the blocks have different masses, their respective accelerations will be different, but the impulse applied to each mass and the product of each mass and its corresponding velocity (momentum) will be the same.

157. (B) The total energy can be found from the initial potential energy $E = U = mgh = (1 \text{ kg})\left(10\dfrac{\text{m}}{\text{s}^2}\right)(1.8 \text{ m}) = 18$ J. The energy after the collision is therefore 18 J − 5 J = 13 J. The energies immediately before and after the collision are kinetic, so setting total energies equal to kinetic energy will determine the speeds before and after the collision. $E = \dfrac{1}{2}mv^2$ yields $v = \sqrt{\dfrac{2E}{m}} = \sqrt{\dfrac{2(18 \text{ J})}{1 \text{ kg}}} = $ −6 m/s (negative because the ball is moving downward) before the collision and $v = \sqrt{\dfrac{2(13 \text{ J})}{1 \text{ kg}}} = 5.1$ m/s after. Impulse equals change of momentum, so $J = \Delta mv = (1 \text{ kg})\left[5.1\dfrac{\text{m}}{\text{s}} - \left(-6\dfrac{\text{m}}{\text{s}}\right)\right] = 11.1 \text{ kg}\dfrac{\text{m}}{\text{s}}$.

158. (A) The impulse was found to be 11.1 kg·m/s. With an average force of 24 N, $t = \dfrac{J}{F} = \dfrac{11.1 \text{ kg m/s}}{24 \text{ N}} = 0.46$ s

159. (E) The velocity of the center of mass would be unchanged by the collision. Using information from before the collision, there is only velocity in the y-direction:

$$v_{cm} = \frac{\sum m_i v_i}{\sum m_i} = \frac{(1 \text{ kg})\left(-16\frac{\text{m}}{\text{s}}\right)+(2 \text{ kg})\left(0\frac{\text{m}}{\text{s}}\right)}{(1 \text{ kg}+2 \text{ kg})} = -5.33\frac{\text{m}}{\text{s}}$$

160. (B) Because momentum is conserved, the momentum of the 2-kg ball after the collision can be determined by conservation of momentum. In the x-direction, the total momentum before the collision is zero. Thus, p_{2x} must be $-9 \text{ kg} \cdot \text{m/s}$. The total momentum before the collision in the y-direction is -16; thus, p_{2y} must be $-16 \text{ kg} \cdot \text{m/s}$. The horizontal component of the velocity of the 2-kg ball after the collision is $v_x = \dfrac{p_x}{m} = \dfrac{-9\dfrac{\text{kg m}}{\text{s}}}{2 \text{ kg}} = -4.5\dfrac{\text{m}}{\text{s}}$. Similarly, the vertical component of the velocity is $v_y = \dfrac{p_y}{m} = \dfrac{-16\dfrac{\text{kg m}}{\text{s}}}{2 \text{ kg}} = -8\dfrac{\text{m}}{\text{s}}$. This places the velocity vector in the third quadrant. The angle beneath the horizontal is $\theta = \tan^{-1}\left(\dfrac{-8\dfrac{\text{kg m}}{\text{s}}}{-4.5\dfrac{\text{kg m}}{\text{s}}}\right) = 61°$.

The magnitude of the velocity is $v = \sqrt{v_x^2 + v_y^2} = \sqrt{\left(-4.5\dfrac{\text{m}}{\text{s}}\right)^2 + \left(-8\dfrac{\text{m}}{\text{s}}\right)^2} = 9.2\dfrac{\text{m}}{\text{s}}$.

161. (A) The work done on the ball changes the kinetic energy of the ball, or $W = \dfrac{1}{2}mv_f^2$. Multiplying both sides by 2 m yields $2Wm = m^2 v_f^2$, or $mv_f = \sqrt{2Wm}$. Because the change in momentum equals impulse, $J = mv_f - 0 = \sqrt{2(70 \text{ J})(0.3 \text{ kg})} = 6.5 \text{ N s}$.

162. (A) Conservation of momentum must be applied to determine the final velocity of the 2-kg block. $(m_1 + m_2)v_i = m_1 v_{1,f} + m_2 v_{2,f}$ yields

$$v_{2,f} = \frac{(m_1 + m_2)v_i - m_1 v_{1,f}}{m_2} = \frac{(1 \text{ kg}+2 \text{ kg})\left(4\frac{\text{m}}{\text{s}}\right) - (1 \text{ kg})\left(-2\frac{\text{m}}{\text{s}}\right)}{(2 \text{ kg})} = 7\frac{\text{m}}{\text{s}}$$

The kinetic energy before the explosion is

$$K = \frac{1}{2}(m_1 + m_2)v_i^2 = \frac{1}{2}(1 \text{ kg} + 2 \text{ kg})\left(4\frac{\text{m}}{\text{s}}\right)^2 = 24 \text{ J}$$

The kinetic energy after the explosion is

$$K = \frac{1}{2}m_1 v_{1,f}^2 + \frac{1}{2}m_2 v_{2,f}^2 = \frac{1}{2}(1 \text{ kg})\left(-2\frac{\text{m}}{\text{s}}\right)^2 + \frac{1}{2}(2 \text{ kg})\left(7\frac{\text{m}}{\text{s}}\right)^2 = 51 \text{ J}$$

The ratio of initial to final energies is then 24/51.

163. (C) The x- and y-components of the momentum of $2m$ are equal and opposite to the x- and y-components of the momenta of the other two masses. So the momentum of mass $2m$ after the explosion is

$$2mv' = \sqrt{(mv)^2 + (mv)^2}, \text{ giving } v' = \frac{\sqrt{2}}{2}v$$

164. (D) The momentum vector of mass $2m$ must be equal and opposite to the resultant momentum of the two smaller masses. The resultant momentum of the two smaller masses is down and to the left, so the resultant momentum of $2m$ must be up and to the right.

165. (C) The momentum of the center of mass of the system is equal to the vector sum of the individual momenta of the blocks:

$$-2mv + mv = 3mv_{CM}$$

$$v_{CM} = \frac{1}{3}(2 \text{ kg} + 1 \text{ kg})v$$

166. (A) Conservation of momentum can be applied to the dart being fired from the block to determine the velocity of the block after the dart is fired: $0 = mv_0 + Mv_b$ yields $v_b = -\frac{mv_0}{M}$, where v_b is the velocity of the block after the dart is fired.

167. (A) Conservation of energy applied to the block with an initial speed v_b and final height h can be used to determine how high the block will swing:

$$K = U_g$$

$$\frac{1}{2}Mv_b^2 = Mgh$$

$$\frac{1}{2}\left(-\frac{m}{M}v_0\right)^2 = gh$$

$$h = \frac{m^2 v_0^2}{2M^2 g}$$

168. (B) The horizontal components of the momenta before the collision are equal and opposite, so there is only vertical momentum after the collision.

$$2mv_o \sin 30° = 2mv'$$

$$v' = \frac{1}{2}v_o$$

169. (B) Momentum is conserved in an elastic collision. The symmetry of the path of each piece of clay shows that there is no momentum in the horizontal direction, and the net momentum before the collision is in the negative y-direction. If **(B)** were true, the momentum after the collision would be in the positive y-direction and thus momentum would not be conserved.

170. (A) By conservation of momentum,

$$mv = (m + 2m)v_{CM}$$

$$v_{CM} = \left(\frac{m}{m + 2m}\right)v$$

171. (C) The magnitude of the momentum before the collision is $p = mv =$ $(0.5 \text{ kg})\left(10\frac{\text{m}}{\text{s}}\right) = 5\frac{\text{kg m}}{\text{s}}$. The horizontal component is $p_x = \left(5\frac{\text{kg m}}{\text{s}}\right)\cos 60° =$ $2.5\frac{\text{kg m}}{\text{s}}$. The vertical component of velocity is $p_y = -\left(5\frac{\text{kg m}}{\text{s}}\right)\sin 60° = -4.3\frac{\text{kg m}}{\text{s}}$.

In unit-vector notation, the momentum is $\vec{p} = (2.5\vec{i} - 4.3\vec{j})\frac{\text{kg m}}{\text{s}}$.

172. (B) The impulse is equal to the change in momentum. The final momentum is found similarly as to in Question 171:

$$\vec{p} = (0.5 \text{ kg})\left(8\frac{\text{m}}{\text{s}}\right)\cos 60°\hat{i} + (0.5 \text{ kg})\left(8\frac{\text{m}}{\text{s}}\right)\sin 60°\vec{j} = (2\vec{i} + 3.5\vec{j})\frac{\text{kg m}}{\text{s}}.$$ The

impulse is then

$$\vec{J} = \Delta\vec{p} = (2\vec{i} + 3.5\vec{j})\frac{\text{kg m}}{\text{s}} - (2.5\vec{i} - 4.3\vec{j})\frac{\text{kg m}}{\text{s}} = (-0.5\vec{i} + 7.8\vec{j})\frac{\text{kg m}}{\text{s}}$$

173. (D) Since there is no x-component of momentum before the collision, the momentum of ball 1 must have a positive x-component of momentum after the collision as well as a positive y-component of momentum to be added to the y-component of momentum of ball 2. So the momentum of ball 1 must point upward and to the right.

174. (E) The product $F\Delta t$ is impulse and is equal to the change in momentum of the object on which it acts.

175. (A) Momentum is conserved:

$$mv_o = -\frac{m}{4}(2v_o) + \frac{3mv'}{4}$$

$v' = 2v_o$ to the right

176. (E) The impulse is equal to the area under the force vs. time graph, which is −36 N s from 0 to 3 s, then + 36 N s from 3 s to 6 s, giving a net impulse of zero. Impulse is equal to the change in momentum of the mass, so the change in momentum is also zero.

177. (C) The area under the graph from 0 to 3 s represents the change in momentum of the mass.

$$-36 \text{ N s} = m\Delta v = (2 \text{ kg})v_3$$

$$v_3 = 18\frac{\text{m}}{\text{s}}$$

178. (A) Since the momentum of the center of mass of the cannon and cannonball is zero before they are fired, the momentum of the center of mass must remain stationary after the cannon is fired.

179. (E) The vector sum of the choices must be equal in magnitude and direction of the given vector. The resultant of answer (E) lies between the vectors shown and in the direction of the original given vector.

180. (C) The boy and the sled collide inelastically.

$$m_B v_B = (m_B + m_S)v'$$

$$(20 \text{ kg})\left(3\frac{\text{m}}{\text{s}}\right) = (20 \text{ kg} + 40 \text{ kg})v'$$

$$v' = 1.0 \frac{\text{m}}{\text{s}}$$

181. (A) Momentum is conserved before and after the boy jumps off the sled:

$$(m_B + m_S)v' = m_s v_s$$

$$(60 \text{ kg})\left(1\frac{\text{m}}{\text{s}}\right) = (40 \text{ kg})v'_s$$

$$v'_s = 1.5\frac{\text{m}}{\text{s}}$$

182. (C) The impulse J is the area under the triangle:

$$J = Area = \frac{1}{2}(20 \text{ N})(1 \text{ s}) = 10 \text{ N s}$$

183. (D) The impulse is equal to the change in momentum of the mass:

$$10 \text{ N s} = m_1\left(4\frac{\text{m}}{\text{s}}\right) - m_1\left(1.5\frac{\text{m}}{\text{s}}\right)$$

$$m_1 = 4 \text{ kg}$$

184. (E) The speed the 1-kg block was moving just before striking the 1.5-kg block can be found by applying conservation of momentum.

$$m_1 v_1 = (m_1 + m_2)v'$$

$$(1 \text{ kg})v_1 = (1 \text{ kg} + 1.5 \text{ kg})\left(5\frac{\text{m}}{\text{s}}\right)$$

$$v_1 = 12.5\frac{\text{m}}{\text{s}}$$

Apply conservation of energy to the top and bottom of the ramp before the collision:

$$m_1 gh = \frac{1}{2} m_1 v_1^2$$

$$h = \frac{v_1^2}{2g} = \frac{\left(12.5 \dfrac{m}{s}\right)^2}{2\left(10 \dfrac{m}{s^2}\right)} = 7.8 \text{ m}$$

185. (C) Momentum is conserved before and after the dart strikes the block:

$$m_1 v_o = (m_1 + m_2)v'$$

$$1v_o = (1+4)v'$$

$$v' = \frac{1}{5} v_o$$

Apply conservation of energy after the collision:

$$(m_1 + m_2)gh = \frac{1}{2}(m_1 + m_2)v'^2$$

$$5mgh = \frac{1}{2}(5m)\left(\frac{1}{5}v_o\right)^2$$

$$v_o = \sqrt{50gh}$$

186. (B) Since there is no friction, or other external forces, the momentum in Figure I is equal to the momentum in Figure III, as if the blocks collided elastically in between.

187. (A) Any time a smaller mass collides with a larger mass in what is essentially an elastic collision between Figure I and Figure III, the smaller block will reverse its direction of motion.

188. (E) The impulse vector **J** is applied perpendicularly to the surface of the ramp (up and to the right) and the velocity rebounds from the surface at the same angle to the normal in which it struck the surface, which causes the velocity vector **v** to be directed to the right.

189. (B) Since the collision with the plane is elastic, the speed with which it rebounds is equal to the speed it strikes the plane. Setting the potential energy at height h equal to the kinetic energy just before or after striking the plane gives

$$mgh = \frac{1}{2}mv^2$$

$$v = \sqrt{2gh}$$

190. (A) The mass of the sand at $t = 4$ s is $60(4s)^2 = 960$ kg. Conservation of momentum after 4 s gives

$$m_o v_o = (m_o + m_s)v'$$

$$(1{,}000 \text{ kg})\left(2\frac{\text{m}}{\text{s}}\right) = (1{,}960 \text{ kg})v'$$

$$v' = 1\frac{\text{m}}{\text{s}}$$

191. (C) Applying conservation of momentum just after the collision gives

$$m_1 v_o = (m_1 + m_2)v'$$

$$(800 \text{ kg})\left(10\frac{\text{m}}{\text{s}}\right) = (800 \text{ kg} + m)\left(\frac{6}{0+1}\right)$$

$$m = 533 \text{ kg}$$

192. (D) The resisting force is proportional to the acceleration of each car during the collision.

$$v = \frac{6}{t+1}$$

$$a = \frac{dv}{dt} = \frac{d}{dt}\left(\frac{6}{t+1}\right) = \frac{d}{dt}[6(t+1)^{-1}] = -6(t+1)^{-2}$$

$$F_{\text{net}} = ma = \frac{6m}{(t+1)^2}$$

193. (E) $a = \dfrac{F}{m} = \dfrac{12t^3}{m}$. The velocity as a function of time is the time integral of acceleration:

$$v = \int a\,dt = \int \frac{12t^3}{m}\,dt = \frac{12t^4}{4m} = \frac{3t^4}{m}$$

194. (B) The net force acting on the dart is equal to the derivative of momentum with respect to time.

$$F_{net} = \frac{dp}{dt} = \frac{d}{dt}(3t^3 + 2t) = 9t^2 + 2 = 9(0.2 \text{ s})^2 + 2 = 2.4 \text{ N}$$

195. (B) The change in momentum of the object is equal to the impulse given to the object, which can be represented by the area under a force vs. time graph.

196. (A) The force acting on an object to change its momentum p is given by the derivative $F = dp/dt$, which represents the slope of a momentum vs. time graph.

197. Momentum is conserved:

$$m_A v_A = (m_A + m_B)v'$$

$$(2 \text{ kg})\left(4\,\frac{\text{m}}{\text{s}}\right) = (2 \text{ kg} + 4 \text{ kg})v'$$

$$v' = \frac{4}{3}\,\frac{\text{m}}{\text{s}}$$

198. The time of fall is $t = \sqrt{\dfrac{2y}{g}} = \sqrt{\dfrac{2(1.5 \text{ m})}{10 \text{ m/s}^2}} = 0.55 \text{ s}$

$$x = v_x t = \left(\frac{4}{3}\,\frac{\text{m}}{\text{s}}\right)(0.55 \text{ s}) = 0.7 \text{ m}$$

199. Momentum is conserved:

$$m_A v_A = m_A v'_A + m_B v'_B$$

$$(2 \text{ kg})\left(4\,\frac{\text{m}}{\text{s}}\right) = (2 \text{ kg})\left(4\,\frac{\text{m}}{\text{s}}\right) + (4 \text{ kg})v'_B$$

$$v'_B = 2.5\,\frac{\text{m}}{\text{s}}$$

200. The time of fall is $t = \sqrt{\dfrac{2y}{g}} = \sqrt{\dfrac{2(1.5 \text{ m})}{10 \text{ m/s}^2}} = 0.55$ s

$$x = v_x t = \left(2.5 \,\dfrac{\text{m}}{\text{s}}\right)(0.55 \text{ s}) = 1.4 \text{ m}$$

Chapter 5: Circular and Rotational Motion

201. (C) Angular velocity is the derivative of the angular position function. At $t = 2$ s,

$$\omega = \dfrac{d\theta}{dt} = 0 - \left(2.5\dfrac{\text{rad}}{\text{s}^2}\right)(2t) + \left(4\dfrac{\text{rad}}{\text{s}^3}\right)(3t^2) = -\left(2.5\dfrac{\text{rad}}{\text{s}^2}\right)(2 \times 2\text{s}) +$$

$$\left(4\dfrac{\text{rad}}{\text{s}^3}\right)(3 \times (2 \text{ s})^2 = 38 \text{ rad/s}.$$

202. (B) Angular velocity is the integral of acceleration: $\omega = \displaystyle\int (2t - 2)\,dt = t^2 - 2t + C$. With the initial velocity of -3 rad/s, $\omega = t^2 - 2t - 3$. To find when the velocity is zero, set the function equal to 0 and solve by factoring: $0 = t^2 - 2t - 3 = (t - 3)(t + 1)$ or $t = -1$, $t = 3$ s. The negative solution is not in the domain of the problem.

203. (B) At the top of the circular path, gravity can provide the force necessary to maintain circular motion. Thus, if the tension is zero at the top of the path, applying Newton's second law gives

$$F_{\text{net}} = ma_c$$

$$mg = m\dfrac{v^2}{r}$$

$$v = \sqrt{gr} = \sqrt{\left(10 \,\dfrac{\text{m}}{\text{s}^2}\right)(0.5 \text{ m})} = 2.2 \,\dfrac{\text{m}}{\text{s}}$$

204. (C) There are only two forces acting on the ball, its weight W, directed downward, and the tension T in the string, which is directed up and at an angle.

205. (C) The horizontal component of the tension provides the centripetal force.

$$T\cos\theta = \dfrac{mv^2}{R}. \text{ Solving for T gives } T = \dfrac{mv^2}{R\cos\theta}.$$

206. (B) The speed of the block at the bottom of the circle can be found with conservation of energy:

$$U_{top} + K_{top} = K_{bottom}$$

$$mgh + \frac{1}{2}mv^2 = \frac{1}{2}mv_{bottom}^2$$

$$v_{bottom}^2 = 2gh + v^2 = 2g(2R) + v^2 = 4gR + v^2$$

The normal force can be found by applying Newton's second law:

$$F_{net} = \frac{mv^2}{R}$$

$$F_N - mg = \frac{m(4gR + v^2)}{R} = 4mg + \frac{mv^2}{R}$$

$$F_N = 5mg + \frac{mv^2}{R}$$

207. (D) The tangential acceleration of the car is easily found with the given function $a_t = 8t - 3 = 8(2) - 3 = 13 \frac{m}{s^2}$. The car is moving in a circle, so the centripetal acceleration is also needed, which depends on speed. The speed can be found by integrating the tangential acceleration $v = 15\frac{m}{s} + \int_0^2 (8t - 3)dt = 15 + (4t^2 - 3t)\big|_0^2 = 15 + 4 \times 2^2 - 3 \times 2 - (0) = 25\frac{m}{s}$. Centripetal acceleration is then

$$a_c = \frac{v^2}{r} = \frac{\left(25 \frac{m}{s}\right)^2}{100 \text{ m}} = 6.25 \text{ m/s}^2.$$ The centripetal acceleration and tangential acceleration are at right angles, so the net acceleration is found with the Pythagorean theorem:

$$a_{net} = \sqrt{a_t^2 + a_c^2} = \sqrt{\left(13 \frac{m}{s^2}\right)^2 + \left(6.25 \frac{m}{s^2}\right)^2} = 14.4 \frac{m}{s^2}$$

208. (B) The weight of the car is directed downward, and the normal force is directed perpendicular to the inclined track. Because the car is going at too great a speed and is beginning to slide, it would slide out of its current circle, or to the top of the track. The friction is thus kinetic and opposite to the slide, so it is directed down the track.

209. (D) Since the normal force and frictional force both have components directed toward the center of the circular track, they both contribute to the centripetal force acting on the car.

210. (D) The rod is uniform and has a uniform mass density that can be applied to the entire length or to a differential slice: $\dfrac{M}{L} = \dfrac{dm}{dr}$. Using this expression to substitute for dm in the integral for rotational inertia, the inertia can be found with bounds on the integral than span the length of the rod, with the zero position as the axis of rotation:

$$I = \int r^2 \, dm = \frac{M}{L} \int_{-3L/4}^{L/4} r^2 \, dr = \frac{M}{L}\left(\frac{r^3}{3}\right)\Big|_{-\frac{3L}{4}}^{\frac{L}{4}} = \frac{M}{3L}\left[\left(\frac{L}{4}\right)^3 - \left(-\frac{3L}{4}\right)^3\right] = \frac{7ML^2}{48}$$

211. (B) The rotational inertia of the rod is found by integrating along the length of the rod, with the zero position as the axis (left end) of rotation:

$$I = \int r^2 \, dm = \frac{M}{L}\int r^2 \, dr = \frac{1 \text{ kg}}{0.5 \text{ m}} \int_{0}^{0.5 \text{ m}} r^2 \, dr = 2\,\frac{\text{kg}}{\text{m}}\left(\frac{r^3}{3}\right)\Big|_{0}^{0.5 \text{ m}} = \frac{2}{3}[(0.5)^3 - 0^3)]\frac{\text{kg}}{\text{m}^2} =$$

$\dfrac{1}{12}$ kg/m^2. The torque is found from the weight of the rod acting at the center of mass,

or $\tau = rmg \sin\theta = (0.25 \text{ m})(0.5 \text{ kg})\left(10\,\dfrac{\text{m}}{\text{s}^2}\right)\sin 90 = \dfrac{5}{4}$ N m. Angular acceleration

is found from Newton's second law of rotation: $\alpha = \dfrac{\tau_{net}}{I} = \dfrac{\left(\dfrac{5}{4}\text{N m}\right)}{\dfrac{1}{12}\text{ kg /m}^2} = 15 \text{ rad/s}^2$.

212. (E) The magnitude of the centripetal force is $F_c = \dfrac{mv^2}{r} = \dfrac{(3 \text{ kg})\left(2\,\dfrac{\text{m}}{\text{s}}\right)^2}{3 \text{ m}} = 4 \text{ N}$.

Because the circle is a horizontal, level surface, the normal force is the weight of the object, and the coefficient of friction is

$$\mu = \frac{F_c}{mg} = \frac{(4 \text{ N})}{(3 \text{ kg})\left(10\,\dfrac{\text{m}}{\text{s}^2}\right)} = 0.13$$

213. (B) The angular momentum $L = mvr = (3 \text{ kg})\left(2\,\dfrac{\text{m}}{\text{s}}\right)(3 \text{ m}) = 12\,\dfrac{\text{kg m}^2}{\text{s}}$.

214. (B) The component of the force that acts perpendicular to the rod is $F\cos\theta$, so the torque acting on the rod is $FR\cos\theta$.

215. (E) The angular acceleration $\alpha = \dfrac{\tau}{I} = \dfrac{FR\cos\theta}{I}$.

216. (A) Momentum is conserved when the dancer's arms are pulled in. Because $L = I\omega$, the decrease in inertia by a factor of 4 causes the angular velocity to increase by a factor of 4. If the original rotational kinetic energy is $K = \dfrac{1}{2}I\omega^2$, the

ratio of initial to final kinetic energy is $\dfrac{K_i}{K_f} = \dfrac{\dfrac{1}{2}I\omega^2}{\dfrac{1}{2}\left(\dfrac{1}{4}I\right)(4\omega)^2} = \dfrac{1}{4}$.

217. (E) The angular acceleration of the ball is equal to the second derivative of the angle θ with respect to time.

$$\omega = \frac{d\theta}{dt} = \frac{d}{dt}(4t^2 + 3t) = 8t + 3$$

$$\alpha = \frac{d\omega}{dt} = \frac{d}{dt}(8t + 3) = 8\,\frac{\text{rad}}{\text{s}^2}$$

218. (B) The linear speed of the ball is equal to the product of the angular speed and radius at $t = 3$ s.

$$\omega = 8t + 3$$

$$v = \omega r = [8(3\text{ s}) + 3](2\text{ m}) = 54\text{ m/s}$$

219. (D) The bar is in equilibrium, so the sum of the torques around any point is zero. Summing torques around the pivot P,

$$\sum \tau = 0 = (Mg)\sin 90° - T\sin 30° = Mg - \frac{T}{2}; \text{ thus, } T = 2Mg$$

220. (A) The angular momentum of the particle corresponds to the perpendicular distance from the origin, which is x_0.

$$L = mvx_0$$

221. (A) The rotational inertia of the system is $\sum I = \frac{1}{12}mL^2 + m\left(\frac{1}{2}L\right)^2 = \frac{1}{3}mL^2$.

222. (E) The net torque is $4mgL - 3mgL = mgL$ clockwise.

223. (D) The angular acceleration $\alpha = \dfrac{\tau}{I} = \dfrac{mgL}{4mL^2 + 9mL^2} = \dfrac{g}{13L}$.

224. (A) The total kinetic energy of the hoop is converted to potential energy at the height h.

$$\frac{1}{2}mv^2 + \frac{1}{2}I\omega^2 = mgh$$

$$\frac{1}{2}mv^2 + \frac{1}{2}(mR^2)\left(\frac{v}{R}\right)^2 = mgh$$

$$h = \frac{v^2}{g}$$

225. (E) The speed of the ball at point Y is found by conservation of energy:

$$U_x + K_x = K_y$$

$$mgh + \frac{1}{2}mv_x^2 = \frac{1}{2}mv_y^2$$

$$v_y = \sqrt{2gh + v_x^2} = \sqrt{2\left(10\ \frac{m}{s^2}\right)(0.25\ m) + \left(2\ \frac{m}{s}\right)^2} = 3\ \frac{m}{s}$$

Two forces act on the ball at point Y: the tension (up) and the gravitational force (down). Applying Newton's second law, we get

$$F_{net} = \frac{mv^2}{r}$$

$$T - mg = \frac{mv^2}{R}$$

$$T = mg + \frac{mv^2}{R} = (3\ kg)\left(10\ \frac{m}{s^2}\right) + \frac{(3\ kg)\left(3\ \frac{m}{s}\right)^2}{0.25\ m} = 138\ N$$

226. (C) $\tau = rF\sin\theta = (2\ m)[(2(1\ s)^3 + \sin\pi)N]\sin 60° = 3.5\ N\ m$.

227. (C) At point C, the bottom of the circle, the force the bug has to supply to hang on has to be the greatest, since the tension is pulling away from the ball and bug. At the top of the circle, the bug would have the ball to rest on and wouldn't have to apply as much force to stay on the ball.

228. (E) At point C, the bug has to hang on with a force equal to both the centripetal force and its own weight.

$$F_c = F_{bug} - mg = m\omega^2 r$$

$$F_{bug} = m\omega^2 r + mg$$

229. (E) $\tau = rF\sin\theta = (0.1\ m)(3t^2 + 2t)\sin 90 = 0.3t^2 + 0.2t$. The angular acceleration is determined from Newton's second law: $\alpha = \dfrac{\tau_{net}}{I} = \dfrac{0.3t^2 + 0.2t}{0.05\ \text{kg/m}^2} = 6t^2 + 4t$.

The velocity can be found from integrating the acceleration function directly, given that the pulley starts at rest:

$$\Delta\omega = \omega - \omega_0 = \omega - 0 = \omega = \int_0^2 (6t^2 + 4t)\,dt = (2t^3 + 2t^2)\Big|_0^2 = 24\ \frac{\text{rad}}{\text{s}}$$

230. (E) The ratio of angular momenta is $\dfrac{L_1}{L_2} = \dfrac{I_1\omega_1}{I_2\omega_2} = \dfrac{\dfrac{1}{2}mr^2\omega}{\dfrac{1}{2}(2m)(4r)^2\omega} = \dfrac{8}{1}$.

231. (B) The rotational inertia of the system is the sum of the rotational inertias of the two balls around the pivot: $I = I_{left} + I_{right} = mL^2 + m(2L)^2 = 5mL^2$. Angular acceleration is found from Newton's second law, where the torque ($rF\sin\theta$) is from the weight of the two balls:

$$\alpha = \frac{\tau_{net}}{I} = \frac{\tau_{right} - \tau_{left}}{I} = \frac{2Lmg\sin 90° - Lmg\sin 90°}{5mL^2} = \frac{g}{5L}$$

Linear acceleration of the ball on the right is $a = r\alpha = 2L\left(\dfrac{g}{5L}\right) = \dfrac{2g}{5}$.

232. (D) The net torque is $Fr + Fr - 2F(3r) = -4Fr$. Since the question asks only for the magnitude of the torque, the net torque can be written as $4Fr$.

233. (A) The skater moves with constant velocity from A to B and C to D, indicated by zero acceleration on the first and third sections of the graph. On the curves from B to C and D to A, there is a centripetal force acting on the skater, causing a constant centripetal acceleration in these intervals, indicated by the horizontal lines in the second and fourth intervals of the graph.

234. (C) The net torque is $\tau = I\alpha = \dfrac{I(\omega_f - \omega_o)}{\Delta t}$.

235. (D) The power is related to the torque by $P = \tau\omega = \dfrac{I\omega_o}{\Delta t}\omega_o = \dfrac{I\omega_o{}^2}{\Delta t}$.

236. (D) Angular momentum is conserved as the radius is shortened, so $mv_1\, r_1 = m\, v_2\, (1/4\, r_1)$ gives $v_2 = 4\, v_1$.

237. (A) Since the ball rolls without slipping, the relationship between velocity and angular velocity is $v = r\omega$.

238. (C) Since the ball is rolling and slipping, the speed v of the ball must be less than $r\omega$, since the ball will rotate with an angular speed less than ω. In this case, the speed of the ball cannot be calculated without knowing more about the kinetic friction acting on the ball.

239. (B) Given constant acceleration and zero initial velocity, the angular velocity from kinematics is $\omega = 6t$. For a person to not slide down the wall, the static friction (in the upward direction) must equal the weight of the person. The normal force from the wall of the cylinder is found from Newton's second law: $F_n = ma_c = mr\omega^2$, given that the minimum static friction by definition is $f_s = \mu_s F_n = \mu_s mr\omega^2$. Because the static friction must at a minimum equal the weight of a rider, $\mu_s mr\omega^2 = mg$, giving

$$\omega^2 = (5t)^2 = \frac{g}{\mu_s r} = \frac{10\,\frac{m}{s^2}}{(0.05)(2\ m)} = 100\ \frac{rad^2}{s^2}\ \text{or}\ t = 2\ s$$

240. (E) Since the apparatus is floating freely in space, there are no external forces to change the momentum or angular momentum. Kinetic energy is not conserved because the clay is deformed in the inelastic collision.

241. (D) Angular momentum is conserved during the collision.

$$mvL = I\omega$$

$$\omega = \frac{mvL}{I}$$

242. (A) The weight is directed downward, the normal force is directed perpendicular to the plane, and the friction force causes a clockwise torque on the sphere by pulling the contact point up the plane.

243. (B) Using conservation of energy,

$$mgh = \frac{1}{2}mv^2 + \frac{1}{2}I\omega^2 = \frac{1}{2}mv^2 + \frac{1}{2}\left(\frac{2}{3}mR^2\right)\left(\frac{v}{R}\right)^2$$

Solving for the speed v gives $v = \sqrt{\frac{6gh}{5}}$.

244. (C) The angular speeds of the disks are not equal, but the linear velocity of each disk is the same. So $v = r_1\omega_1 = 2r_2\omega_2$, giving $\omega_2 = \frac{1}{2}\omega$.

245. (B) The change in potential energy of the stick is equal to the kinetic energy of the stick at the bottom of the swing. The change in height of the center of mass of the stick is $L/2$. So the change in potential energy as the stick swings is $\Delta U = mg\left(\frac{L}{2}\right)$, which is equal to the kinetic energy at the bottom of the swing.

$$mg\left(\frac{L}{2}\right) = \frac{1}{2}I\omega^2$$

$$\omega = \sqrt{\frac{mgL}{I}}$$

246. Applying Newton's second law to the block, we get $F_{net} = mg - T = ma = mR\alpha$, where T is the tension in the string. The downward direction is specified as positive. Applying Newton's second law to the rotation of the disk, we get $\tau_{net} = rT = I\alpha = \frac{1}{2}MR^2\alpha$ or $T = \frac{1}{2}MR\alpha$. Combining these two equations gives $mg - \frac{1}{2}MR\alpha = mR\alpha$ or $\alpha = \dfrac{mg}{R\left(m + \dfrac{1}{2}M\right)}$.

247. Using conservation of energy for the mass-pulley system, we get

$$U_g = K_r + K_t$$

$$mgh = \frac{1}{2}I\omega^2 + \frac{1}{2}mv^2 = \frac{1}{2}\left(\frac{1}{2}MR^2\right)\left(\frac{v}{R}\right)^2 + \frac{1}{2}mv^2 = \frac{1}{4}Mv^2 + \frac{1}{2}mv^2$$

$$v = \sqrt{\frac{mgh}{\frac{1}{4}M + \frac{1}{2}m}} = 2\sqrt{\frac{mgh}{M + 2m}}$$

248. This can be solved with the work-energy theorem: $W = -f_k d = \Delta K$. Thus,

$$d = -\frac{\Delta K}{f_k} = \frac{0.5 K_i}{\mu_k(mg)} = 5.3m$$

249. The total kinetic energy is

$$K_r + K_t = \frac{1}{2}I\omega^2 + \frac{1}{2}mv^2 = \frac{1}{2}\left(\frac{2}{3}MR^2\right)\left(\frac{v}{R}\right)^2 + \frac{1}{2}Mv^2 = \frac{5}{6}Mv^2.$$

250. Apply conservation of energy, and use the expression from Question 249 for total kinetic energy:

$$U_g = K$$

$$Mgh = MgL\,(\sin 10°) = \frac{5}{6}Mv^2$$

$$L = \frac{5v^2}{6g\sin 10°} = \frac{5\left(5\frac{m}{s}\right)^2}{6\left(10\frac{m}{s^2}\right)(\sin 10°)} = 12\ m$$

Chapter 6: Oscillations and Gravitation

251. (E) Apply Newton's second law of rotation to the pendulum, deflected a small angle θ from the vertical. $\tau_{net} = I\alpha$ or, with $I = \frac{1}{3}ML^2$ (see solution to Question 211), $-\frac{MgL}{2}\sin\theta = -\frac{MgL\theta}{2} = \frac{1}{3}ML^2\frac{d^2\theta}{dt^2}$, with the force of gravity for the torque applied at the center of mass of the uniform rod (at L/2) and the small angle expression $\sin\theta = \theta$. Thus, $\frac{d^2\theta}{dt^2} = -\frac{3g\theta}{2L}$. The angular position function can be described by $\theta = \theta_{max}\cos(\omega t)$, assuming no phase shift ($\varnothing = 0$). Taking the second derivative, and combining with the previous result, $\frac{d^2\theta}{dt^2} = -\omega^2\theta_{max}\cos(\omega t) = -\omega^2\theta = -\frac{3g\theta}{2L}$, By definition,

$$\omega = 2\pi f = \frac{2\pi}{T} \quad \text{or} \quad T = \frac{2\pi}{\omega} = \frac{2\pi}{\sqrt{3g/2L}} = 2\pi\sqrt{\frac{2L}{3g}}$$

252. (D) Hooke's law states that the force applied by the spring is proportional to the stretch distance, $F = -kx$. The potential energy of the spring is maximum at the amplitude, and the kinetic energy of the mass on the spring is maximum at the equilibrium. Conservation of energy dictates that PE at the amplitude is equal to the KE at the equilibrium position.

253. (E) Conservation of energy can be applied to the spring. At the point of release, the spring has gravitational potential energy only. Referencing the lowest point as 0 gravitational potential energy, at the lowest point the spring has elastic potential energy only.

$$U_g = U_s$$

$$mgh = \frac{1}{2}kh^2$$

$$h = \frac{2mg}{k} = \frac{(2)(1\text{ kg})\left(10\ \dfrac{\text{m}}{\text{s}^2}\right)}{20\ \dfrac{\text{N}}{\text{m}}} = 1\text{ m}$$

(Note that the amplitude of oscillation will be 0.5 m.)

254. (B) The period of oscillation is given by

$$T = 2\pi\sqrt{\frac{m}{k}} = 2\pi\sqrt{\frac{1}{20}} \text{ s}$$

255. (B) A freely falling object falls the first 5 m in 1 s by the equation $y = \frac{1}{2}\, gt^2$. The ball will repeatedly bounce back up to 5 m in perfectly elastic collisions with the floor.

256. (A) From the figure, the time from 1 to 3 seconds shows half of one complete cycle, or a time (2 s) of half a period; thus, the period of oscillation is 4 s. Using the period of a simple pendulum, we get

$$T = 2\pi\sqrt{L/g},\ L = g\left(\frac{T}{2\pi}\right)^2 = \left(10\ \frac{m}{s^2}\right)\left(\frac{4\ s}{2\pi}\right)^2 = 4.1 \text{ m}$$

257. (C) The mass begins at the amplitude (stretch distance x is maximum) at a time when the kinetic energy is zero and the potential energy is maximum. The kinetic energy is maximum and the potential energy is zero when the stretch distance x is zero (equilibrium position). The object's stretch distance is maximum at $t = 0$, 2, and 4, so the potential energy is maximum at those points. The cycle continues, showing a curved graph for potential energy, due to the object's acceleration throughout the cycle.

258. (D) The period T is related to the angular frequency by the equation $\omega = \frac{2\pi}{T} = 4$, so the period is $T = \frac{2\pi}{\omega} = \frac{2\pi}{4} = \frac{\pi}{2}$ s.

259. (B) The equation for the frequency f of a pendulum is $f = \frac{1}{2\pi}\sqrt{\frac{g}{L}}$, so decreasing the length to $\frac{1}{4}L$ increases the frequency by $2f$.

260. (B) Two springs connected in parallel doubles the spring constant to $2k$, which doubles the frequency and halves the period.

261. (C) A higher spring constant k indicates a stiffer spring; that is, for a higher k, it takes more force to stretch it than a spring of lower k. So the frequency of a spring of higher k will be higher than one of a lower k. Also, we could consider the equation for the frequency of an object in simple harmonic motion, $= \frac{1}{2\pi}\sqrt{\frac{k}{m}}$, showing that a higher k gives a higher frequency.

262. (A) The acceleration of the mass is caused by the spring force:

$$F_s = ma$$

$$-kx = m\frac{d^2x}{dt^2}$$

$$\frac{d^2x}{dt^2} = \frac{-k}{m}x$$

263. (C) The position of the mass as a function of time is given by the equation $x = A\cos(\omega t)$, where $\omega = \sqrt{\frac{k}{m}}$, giving $x = x_o \cos\sqrt{\frac{k}{m}}t$.

264. (B) The angular frequency ω is related to the spring constant and mass by $\omega = \sqrt{\frac{k}{m}}$, where k/m = 4. So $\omega = \sqrt{\frac{4}{1}} = 2\frac{rad}{s}$.

265. (A) Based on the equation for the angular frequency in the previous question, the mass must be 1 kg.

266. (D) The equation for the period of oscillation is given by

$$T = 2\pi\sqrt{\frac{m}{k}} = 2\pi\sqrt{\frac{1}{4}} = \pi \text{ s}$$

267. (B) According to the equation for the period of a pendulum, $T = 2\pi\sqrt{\frac{L}{g}}$, to decrease the period by ½, we must increase the acceleration due to gravity to 4 g.

268. (C) The potential energy at the amplitude x_o is equal to the maximum kinetic energy $K = \frac{1}{2}mv_{max}^2$. Setting the maximum potential energy equal to the maximum kinetic energy, we get

$$\frac{1}{2}kx_o^2 = \frac{1}{2}mv_{max}^2 \text{ gives } v_{max} = \sqrt{\frac{k}{m}}x_o$$

269. (E) Conservation of momentum gives the speed of the two masses after they collide and stick together:

$$m_1v_1 = (m_1 + m_2)v'$$

$$m_Bv_B = (m_B + m_S)v'$$

$$(1 \text{ kg})\left(4\frac{\text{m}}{\text{s}}\right) = (1 \text{ kg} + 1 \text{ kg})v'$$

$$v' = 2.0 \frac{\text{m}}{\text{s}}$$

Conservation of energy gives us the spring constant by setting the kinetic energy of the blocks equal to the potential energy in the spring.

$$\frac{1}{2}kx_o^2 = \frac{1}{2}mv^2$$

$$\frac{1}{2}k(0.5 \text{ m})^2 = \frac{1}{2}(2 \text{ kg})\left(2\frac{\text{m}}{\text{s}}\right)^2$$

$$k = 32\frac{\text{N}}{\text{m}}$$

270. (B) To find the speed of the block when it leaves the table, we set the potential energy of the compressed spring equal to the kinetic energy of the block:

$$\frac{1}{2}kx_o^2 = \frac{1}{2}mv^2$$

$$v = \sqrt{\frac{kx^2}{m}} = \sqrt{\frac{\left(5\frac{\text{N}}{\text{m}}\right)(1 \text{ m})^2}{0.5 \text{ kg}}} = 3.2\frac{\text{m}}{\text{s}}.$$ This velocity is the horizontal velocity

of the block as it leaves the table. The time for the block to fall to the floor is =

$$\sqrt{\frac{2y}{g}} = \sqrt{\frac{2(1.5 \text{ m})}{10 \text{ m/s}^2}} = 0.55 \text{ s}.$$ The block lands a distance x from the base of the table:

$$x = v_x t = \left(3.2\frac{\text{m}}{\text{s}}\right)(0.55 \text{ s}) = 1.7 \text{ m}$$

271. (C) The kinetic energy is constant before the collision as well as after the collision but is converted to potential energy in the spring during the collision, momentarily reducing the kinetic energy of the system.

272. (E) The total energy is $U_g + \frac{1}{2}mv^2 = -G\frac{mM}{2R} + \frac{1}{2}mv^2$, where v is the speed of the satellite. Newton's second law can be used to find a substitution for the speed:

$$F_c = \frac{mv^2}{r} = \frac{mv^2}{2R}$$

$$G\frac{mM}{(2R)^2} = \frac{mv^2}{2R}$$

$$G\frac{mM}{4R} = \frac{1}{2}mv^2$$

Substituting this expression into the energy equation, we get

$$-G\frac{mM}{2R} + G\frac{mM}{4R} = -G\frac{(2mM)}{4R} + G\frac{mM}{4R} = -G\frac{mM}{4R}$$

273. (D) The work done by gravity is equal to the opposite of the change in potential energy, or $W = -\Delta U$. The work done against gravity is thus equal to the potential energy change, or $\Delta U = -G\frac{mM}{2R+R} - \left(-G\frac{mM}{R}\right) = -G\frac{mM}{3R} + G\frac{3mM}{3R} = 2G\frac{mM}{3R}$.

274. (D) The angular momentum is constant throughout the entire orbit, but the kinetic energy decreases as the satellite moves farther away from the Earth. This is due to the fact that potential energy increases from A to B, and the total energy remains constant.

275. (B) Gravitational acceleration of the smaller planet can be determined from $g = G\frac{M}{R^2}$. To determine the mass of the second planet compared with the first, an equality of densities is used, approximating the volume of each planet as a sphere:

$$\rho_{2R} = \rho_R$$

$$\frac{M_{2R}}{\frac{4}{3}\pi(2R)^3} = \frac{M_R}{\frac{4}{3}\pi R^3}$$

$$\frac{M_{2R}}{8} = M_R$$

$$M_{2R} = 8M_R$$

The ratio of gravitational accelerations is then

$$\frac{g_R}{g_{2R}} = \frac{\dfrac{GM}{R^2}}{\dfrac{G(8M)}{(2R)^2}} = \frac{1}{2}$$

276. (E) The planets undergo centripetal acceleration about the star, which can be found by $a = G\dfrac{m}{r^2}$, where m and r are the mass of the star and the radius of orbit, respectively (note that the mass of the planets is not relevant). Thus,

$$\frac{a_x}{a_y} = \frac{G\dfrac{m}{R^2}}{G\dfrac{m}{(3R)^2}} = 9.$$

277. (A) The equation for the speed of a satellite orbiting at a radius R is $v = \sqrt{\dfrac{GM}{R}}$. For the speed to double to $2v$, the radius would have to decrease to $2v = \sqrt{\dfrac{GM}{\left(\dfrac{1}{4}R\right)}}$, or ¼ R.

278. (E) Angular momentum is conserved in orbit, where angular momentum is $L = rmv$; thus,

$$rmv_1 = 3rmv_2$$

$$\frac{v_1}{v_2} = 3$$

279. (C) Applying the universal law of gravity to a differential slice of the rod gives $F = -G\dfrac{mdM}{r^2}$ (the minus sign indicates that the force is attractive). Because the rod is uniform, the linear mass density is $\lambda = \dfrac{M}{L} = \dfrac{dm}{dr}$ and can be used to change the variable of integration to r. Integrating along the length of the rod, from the nearest to the furthest position from the small mass, we get

$$F = \int_d^{d+L} -\frac{Gm(\lambda dr)}{r^2} = -Gm\lambda \left(-\frac{1}{r}\right)\Big|_d^{d+L} = G\frac{mM}{L}\left(\frac{1}{d+L} - \frac{1}{d}\right)$$

$$= G\frac{mM}{L}\left[-\frac{L}{d(d+L)}\right] = -G\frac{mM}{d(d+L)}$$

280. (C) The speed of a planet in a circular orbit is $v = \sqrt{\dfrac{GM}{R}} = \dfrac{2\pi R}{T}$, where T is the period of orbit. Rearranging for the period gives $T = \sqrt{\dfrac{4\pi^2 R^3}{GM}}$.

281. (B) Angular momentum is conserved as the satellite orbits.

$$mv_a a = mv_b b$$

$$v_a = \frac{bv}{a}$$

282. (C) Gravitational potential energy is high and negative when the two masses are far apart, and it's low and negative when they are close together. The potential energy depends on $1/r$, so the graph curves upward.

283. (C) The two masses accelerate toward each other due to the increasing gravitational force between them as they approach, making answer (C) the correct U vs. t graph.

284. (B) Since the gravitational force acting on the satellite increases as it travels closer to the Earth, the acceleration also increases.

285. (B) Since the speed of the satellite is slightly too large to stay in a circular orbit, the satellite is at its closest approach to the planet at its original point. The other side of the planet becomes the farthest point, where it is moving at its slowest speed.

286. (C) Since the speed of the satellite is slightly too small to stay in a circular orbit, the satellite is at its farthest approach to the planet at its original point. The other side of the planet becomes the closest point, where it is moving at its fastest speed.

287. (E) The equation for the gravitational force between the stars is equal to the equation for centripetal force:

$$F_G = \frac{GMM}{R^2} = \frac{Mv^2}{\frac{1}{2}R}$$

$$v = \sqrt{\frac{GM}{2R}}$$

288. (A) Since the satellite is still at the same radius r for the moment, its potential energy has not changed when it changes its speed. Therefore the work done to change the satellite's orbit comes from the change in kinetic energy.

289. (D) A satellite is held in orbit by both the (negative) potential energy and (positive) kinetic energy of the satellite, and the sum of the two is the total energy of the satellite, which is zero. The potential energy at a particular orbit cannot change, so increasing the kinetic energy to exceed the potential energy will give the satellite enough energy to escape.

290. (A) Since momentum is conserved, the total momentum after the collision is equal to the total momentum before the collision.

$$2mv - mv = mv$$

So momentum is clockwise in the direction of the larger mass.

291. (E) Conservation of momentum gives

$$2mv - mv = 3mv'$$

$$v' = \frac{v}{3}$$

292. (C) The potential energy of the ball at the top of the tunnel is equal to the kinetic energy of the ball at the center of the planet.

$$\frac{GmM}{R} = \frac{1}{2}mv^2$$

$$v = \sqrt{\frac{2GM}{R}}$$

293. (E) The ball will accelerate toward the center, pass the center with maximum speed, then slow down as it approaches the other side of the planet, rising to its original height. Then it will fall back down the tunnel and repeat the process. The ball oscillates about the center of the planet, like a mass on a spring.

294. The potential energy is equal to the kinetic energy when the potential energy reaches half its original value.

$$\frac{1}{2}kx^2 = \frac{1}{2}\left(\frac{1}{2}kA^2\right)$$

$$x = \frac{A}{\sqrt{2}}$$

295. The position function of an oscillator is $x = x_{max} \cos(\omega t)$ (with 0 phase shift due to starting at the maximum amplitude). For an ideal spring, $f = \dfrac{1}{T} = \dfrac{1}{2\pi}\sqrt{\dfrac{k}{m}}$; thus, $\omega = 2\pi f = \sqrt{\dfrac{k}{m}}$. Velocity is the derivative of the position function; thus,

$$v = \frac{dv}{dt} = -\omega x_{max} \sin(\omega t) = -A\sqrt{\frac{k}{m}}\sin\left(\sqrt{\frac{k}{m}}\,t\right).$$

296. The period of oscillation is 2 s (the graph shows 1.5 cycles). Using $T = 2\pi\sqrt{\dfrac{L}{g}}$, we get $L = g\left(\dfrac{T}{2\pi}\right)^2 = \left(10\,\dfrac{\text{m}}{\text{s}^2}\right)\left(\dfrac{2\text{ s}}{2\pi}\right)^2 = 1.01$ m.

297. The amplitude of oscillation is 2 m. The equation for the position of the mass as a function of time is $x = A\cos(\omega t)$.

$$x = 2\cos(2\pi\, ft) = 2\cos(\pi t)$$

The speed is $v = \dfrac{dx}{dt} = \dfrac{d}{dt}[2\cos(\pi t)] = 2\pi\sin(\pi t)$

298. The period of the stars is the same.

$$T_1 = T_2$$

$$\sqrt{\frac{4\pi^2 r^3}{GM_2}} = \sqrt{\frac{4\pi^2(2r)^3}{GM_1}}$$

Solving for the ratio of the two masses gives

$$\frac{M_1}{M_2} = 8$$

299. The acceleration due to gravity for each star is

$$a_1 = \frac{GM}{r^2} \text{ and } a_2 = \frac{GM}{(2r)^2}, \text{ giving } \frac{a_1}{a_2} = 4.$$

300. Both stars make one revolution in the same amount of time, so $T_1 = T_2$.

Chapter 7: Electric Force, Field, Potential, Gauss's Law

301. (B) Any charge placed on a spherical conducting surface will spread out evenly around the sphere. A conductor allows the charges to move freely on the surface, and the charges repel each other until they reach equilibrium on the surface.

302. (A) All of the negative charges are on the outside of the sphere, and thus the electric field is zero inside the sphere.

303. (C) The charges will distribute themselves so that the entire surface is at the same potential; otherwise, the charges would move farther based on the difference in potential. Since potential depends on both charge and distance, this would cause charges to bunch up on the narrow portions of the conductor and spread out more on the larger portions of the conductor.

304. (C) The charges will distribute themselves so that the entire surface is at the same potential; otherwise, the charges would move farther based on the difference in potential. Since potential depends on both charge and distance, this would cause charges to bunch up on the narrow portions of the conductor and spread out more on the larger portions of the conductor to create an equipotential surface on the entire conductor.

305. (E) The total charge on the spheres is $-2\,\mu C$. When a wire connects the spheres, the charge redistributes itself so each sphere has $-1\,\mu C$ of charge. The original force between the spheres was $F = \dfrac{K(+1\mu C)(-3\mu C)}{r^2}$ and is now $F = \dfrac{K(-1\mu C)(-1\mu C)}{r^2}$, so the new force between the spheres is $\dfrac{1}{3}F$ and is repulsive, since both charges are negative.

306. (A) By symmetry, both the electric field and electric potential are zero at the center of the sphere, since the distance from each charge is the same to the center of the square, and there are two positive charges and two negative charges at the corners.

307. (B) For the electric field to point upward (positive to negative), there would need to be positive charges on the bottom of the square and negative charges on the top.

308. (C) The charges $+2Q$ and $+Q$ will apply a force down and to the right and to the right, respectively, giving a net field directed down and to the right.

309. (D) Since there is no charge inside the sphere, the electric field is zero everywhere inside the sphere. Then the electric field decreases with $1/r^2$ outside the sphere.

310. (A) Since there is no charge inside the sphere, the electric potential is equal to the potential at the surface of the sphere and remains constant everywhere inside the sphere. Then the electric potential decreases with $1/r$ outside the sphere.

311. (B) The electric field is linearly related to distance from the center of the sphere, $E = Cr$, then decreases with $1/r^2$ outside the sphere.

312. (C) Since the electric potential is proportional to the integral of the electric field with respect to distance r, the potential increases with r^2 inside the sphere, and decreases with $1/r$ outside the sphere.

313. (E) The charge enclosed in a Gaussian sphere of radius r inside the sphere is

$$Q = \int_0^r \rho \, dV = \int_0^r \beta r (4\pi r^2) dr = \beta(4\pi) \int_0^r r^3 dr = \beta \pi r^4$$

Using Gauss's law, we get

$$\int E \, dA = \frac{Q_{enc}}{\varepsilon_o}$$

$$E(4\pi r^2) = \frac{\beta \pi r^4}{\varepsilon_o}$$

$$E = \frac{\beta r^2}{4\varepsilon_o}$$

314. (A) The electric potential at the surface of the sphere of radius R can be found by integrating the electric field inside the sphere.

$$V = \int E \, dr = \int \frac{\beta r^2}{4\varepsilon_o} dr = \frac{\beta R^3}{4\varepsilon_o}$$

315. (E) Whether the positive charge is moved from A to B or from B to A, the work done is zero, since whatever energy gained on the first half of the path is lost on the second half of the path. The energy of the positive charge is the same at either of the corners.

316. (B) The electric field will apply a torque and a downward net force on the rod, since the larger charge will experience a greater counterclockwise torque and the larger charge will also produce a downward force, causing the rod and charges to accelerate downward.

317. (A) The positive charge in the center will draw the negative charges in the outside conductor to the inside surface of the sphere.

318. (A) When the grounding wire is connected to the outer sphere, more electrons will come up from the ground, since they are attracted to the positive charge in the center, making the outer sphere negatively charged.

319. (D) The electric field inside the sphere of radius a is zero, since there is no enclosed charge in the sphere. The electric field between a and b encloses a charge of $+2Q$ and decreases with $1/r^2$ outside the smaller sphere. Then the electric field outside the sphere encloses a net charge of $+Q$ and decreases with $1/r^2$ outside the sphere.

320. (A) The electric potential is constant inside the smaller sphere and is equal to the potential at the surface of the smaller sphere. Then the electric potential decreases with $1/r$ outside the smaller sphere, and again decreases with $1/r$ outside the sphere.

321. (A) The charges will distribute themselves so that the entire surface is at the same potential; otherwise, the charges would move farther based on the difference in potential. Since potential depends on both charge and distance, this would cause charges to bunch up on the narrow portions of the conductor and spread out more on the larger portions of the conductor to create an equipotential surface on the entire conductor.

322. (C) The electric field can be found by taking the negative derivative of the potential function with respect to r.

$$E = -\frac{dV}{dr} = -\frac{d}{dr}(ar^{-1}) = ar^{-2}$$

323. (D) The work done in moving a charge in an electric field is

$$W = qV = q(Ed) = (4 \ \mu C)\left(4,000\frac{N}{C}\right)(0.2 \ m) = 3,200 \ \mu J$$

324. (E) The downward force acting on the droplet is its weight

$$mg = (3.2 \times 10^{-7}\,\text{kg})\left(10\,\frac{\text{m}}{\text{s}^2}\right) = 3.2 \times 10^{-6}\,\text{N}.$$

The upward force on the droplet applied by the electric field is

$$qE = (8 \times 10^{-9}\,\text{C})\left(200\,\frac{\text{N}}{\text{C}}\right) = 1.6 \times 10^{-6}\,\text{N}.$$

The downward force is greater than the upward force, so the droplet will accelerate downward.

325. (A) The two spheres carry the same charge but are not at the same potential, since they are different sizes. The smaller sphere will have the greater surface potential since the charges are closer to each other. Current will flow from the smaller sphere at higher potential to the larger sphere at lower potential.

326. (E) All of the charge on the ring is the same distance from the point on the axis. The distance from any charge on the ring to the point on the axis is the hypotenuse r of the right triangle, and is given by the Pythagorean theorem,

$$r = \sqrt{R^2 + 9d^2}$$

The potential at the point on the axis is then $V = \dfrac{kQ}{r} = \dfrac{kQ}{\sqrt{R^2 + 9d^2}}$.

327. (A) Along the axis, the electric field to the left of the ring is practically zero far away, then increases negatively until it reaches a maximum, and then decreases to zero at the center of the ring. Then the electric field becomes positive just to the right of the ring, and the pattern repeats in reverse.

328. (E) Gauss's law states that the electric flux $\int E \cdot dA$ is proportional to the charge enclosed in a closed surface. If the net charge in a closed surface is zero, the flux through the surface is zero, even though the electric field passing through that surface may not be zero.

329. (A) If an electric field is caused by a charge located outside a closed surface, electric field lines would pass through the surface, but the flux into the surface would equal the flux out of the surface, so the net flux would be zero.

330. (B) Electric potential depends on the type of charge (positive or negative) and how far away they are. Electric potential is the work per unit charge done to move a charge through an electric field. Potential is a scalar quantity and does not depend on direction.

331. (E) The electric field outside of the smaller sphere is $E = \dfrac{kQ}{R^2}$. For the same charge Q on both spheres, the electric field outside of the sphere of radius $4R$ is $E = \dfrac{kQ}{(4R)^2} = E = \dfrac{kQ}{16R^2}$, or 1/16 of the electric field due to the smaller sphere.

332. (E) The electric potential outside of the smaller sphere is $V = \dfrac{kQ}{R}$. For the same charge Q on both spheres, the electric potential outside of the sphere of radius $4R$ is $= \dfrac{kQ}{4R}$, or 1/4 of the electric potential due to the smaller sphere.

333. (C) Electric field lines are always perpendicular to equipotential lines and are directed from higher potential to lower potential.

334. (A) Electric field lines are defined as pointing in the direction a positive charge would move in that field, from higher potential (more positive) to lower potential (more negative).

335. (B) Since the electric field is constant between the plates, the potential decreases at a constant rate as a charge moves from top to bottom. The equipotential lines would be horizontal and evenly spaced, much like a hiker descending down a mountain with a constant slope.

336. (B) Electric field is determined by applying Gauss's law—in this case, by integrating the flux integral from zero to a to find the electric field inside the sphere, and then again outside the sphere to find the electric field at $r > a$. The electric field outside the sphere is the sum of these two integrals.

337. (D) Once you've determined the electric field both inside and outside the sphere, the electric potential inside the sphere is determined by beginning far away from the sphere and integrating the electric field function outside the sphere from infinity to a, then integrating the electric field function inside the sphere from a to x_1. The electric potential at x_1 is the sum of these two integrals.

338. (D) When the student touches the negative knob, electrons will leave the electroscope through her finger to ground, leaving a net positive charge on the electroscope. When the rod and finger are removed, the charge will distribute throughout the electroscope, making the knob and leaves negatively charged.

339. (A) Since the electric field is greater when it exits the cube compared to when it entered the cube, there must be a charge enclosed in the cube adding to the electric field as it passes through.

340. (D) According to Gauss's law, the electric flux exiting the cube is due to the charge enclosed in the cube.

$$EA = \frac{q_{enc}}{\varepsilon_o}$$

$$q_{enc} = \varepsilon_o EA = \varepsilon_o(ba^2)(a^2) = \varepsilon_o ba^4$$

341. (E) Since the charge on the larger cylinder is on the inside surface of the cylinder, there is no electric field outside the larger cylinder. Equivalently, the net charge in a Gaussian cylinder around the outside of the cylinders is zero, so the electric field on the outside is zero.

342. (A) Applying Gauss's law between the cylinders gives

$$EA = \frac{q_{enc}}{\varepsilon_o}$$

$$E(2\pi r_2 L) = \frac{Q}{\varepsilon_o}$$

$$E = \frac{Q}{2\pi\varepsilon_o r_2 L}$$

343. (B) Gauss's law is most convenient to use when the charges are arranged symmetrically, such as on a sphere or cylinder.

344. (C) Gauss's law can be derived from the inverse square law ($1/r^2$), such as the electric force between electric charges, the gravitational force between masses, and the magnetic force.

345. The total electric potential is the sum of the individual electrical potentials. Potential is a scalar quantity.

$$V = k\frac{q_1}{3r} + k\frac{q_2}{r} = 4k\frac{Q}{3r}$$

346. The work done is equal to the opposite of the potential energy changes in bringing the charge from infinitely far away to this location.

$$W = U - 0 = \left[k\frac{q_1 q_3}{3r} + \left(k\frac{q_2 q_3}{r}\right)\right] = \frac{kq_3}{3r}(q_1 + 3q_2)$$

347. Momentum will be conserved, and before release the total momentum of the two charge system is zero; thus, $mv_1 = 2mv_2$ or $v_1 = 2v_2$. Energy is also conserved before release and after release.

$$U = K$$

$$k\frac{q_1 q_2}{4r} = \frac{1}{2}mv_1^2 + \frac{1}{2}mv_2^2$$

$$\frac{kq^2}{2r} = mv_1^2 + (2m)\left(\frac{v_1}{2}\right)^2 = \frac{3mv_1^2}{2}$$

$$v_1 = \sqrt{\frac{kq^2}{3m}}$$

348. The electric flux is given as $\Phi = 1\times10^6 \dfrac{Nm^2}{C}$ in the region from 0 to a. Using Gauss's law, we get $q = \varepsilon_0 \Phi = 8.85\times10^{-12}\dfrac{F}{m}*1\times10^6\dfrac{Nm^2}{C} = 8.85\times10^{-6}\ C$

349. As in Question 348, the total charge enclosed inside a Gaussian surface $r > b$ is

$q = \varepsilon_0 \Phi = 8.85\times10^{-12}\dfrac{F}{m}*\left(-2\times10^6\dfrac{Nm^2}{C}\right) = -17.7\times10^{-6}\ C$. Since the electric field inside a conductor is zero (as indicated by the zero flux on the plot), the charge enclosed in the region $a < r < b$ must be zero. Since there is $8.85\times10^{-6}\ C$ at the center (the point charge; see Question 348), there must be $-8.85\times10^{-6}\ C$ along the surface of the shell at $r = a$.

The total charge enclosed ($-17.7\times10^{-6}\ C$) in a shell $r > b$ is thus made up of the point charge, the charge on the inner surface of the spherical shell, and the charge on the outer surface of the spherical shell. Thus, $-17.7\times10^{-6}\ C = 8.85\times10^{-6}\ C - 8.85\times10^{-6}\ C + Q_b$ and the charge on the outer surface of the shell is $-17.7\times10^{-6}\ C$. The net charge is the sum of the charge on the inner and outer surfaces, or $26.55\times10^{-6}\ C$.

350. The charge density in the insulating sphere is the total charge divided by the volume, or $\rho = -\dfrac{2Q}{\dfrac{4}{3}\pi R^3}$. Thus, for a distance r from the center of the sphere, the charge enclosed is the charge density multiplied by volume of the enclosed sphere, or $q_{in} = \rho * \dfrac{4}{3} \pi r^3 = -\dfrac{2Q}{\frac{4}{3}\pi R^3} * \dfrac{4}{3}\pi r^3 = -2Q\dfrac{r^3}{R^3}$. Using Gauss's law, with a spherical

Gaussian surface, $EA = \dfrac{q_{in}}{\varepsilon_0}$, or $E = \dfrac{q_{in}}{A\varepsilon_0} = \dfrac{-2Q\dfrac{r^3}{R^3}}{4\pi r^2 \varepsilon_0} = \dfrac{1}{4\pi\varepsilon_0}\left(-\dfrac{2Qr}{R^3}\right)$.

Chapter 8: Electric Circuits, Capacitors, Dielectrics

351. (E) The resistance between a and b for circuits 1 and 5 is 2 Ω.

352. (C) Since the two resistors on that branch are equal, they will each have the same voltage across them. The total resistance of the parallel arrangement is $\dfrac{1}{2\Omega} + \dfrac{1}{4\Omega} = \dfrac{3}{4\Omega}$, giving $R_P = \dfrac{4}{3\Omega}$. The total resistance in the circuit is $R_t = 2\Omega + \dfrac{4}{3\Omega} = \dfrac{10}{3\Omega}\Omega$. The parallel voltage is 4/10 of the total voltage, or $\dfrac{4}{10}(12\text{ V}) = 4.8$ V. The voltage across the 2-ohm resistor in the right branch is half of this voltage, giving 2.4 V.

353. (B) The voltage across the resistor in the left branch is 4.8 V. The ammeter will read the current as $I = \dfrac{4.8\text{ V}}{2\Omega} = 2.4$ A.

354. (B) Adding another resistor in parallel decreases the resistance in the circuit, so the current and the reading on the ammeter would increase when another resistor is added in parallel.

355. (A) The emf ε is the slope of the graph of power vs. current, or

$$\varepsilon = \dfrac{\Delta P}{\Delta I} = \dfrac{20\text{ W}}{4\text{ A}} = 5\text{ V}$$

356. (C) When the power is 10 W, the current is 2 A. The resistance is $R = \dfrac{P}{I^2} = \dfrac{10\text{ W}}{(2\text{ A})^2} = 2.5$ Ω

357. (D) The equation for the resistance of a conductor is $R = \dfrac{\rho L}{A}$, where ρ is resistivity, L is the length of the conductor, and A is the area through which the current passes. Since all of the conductors are the same length and resistivity, the conductor with the smallest area has the highest resistance.

358. (B) The resistance of the two 2-ohm resistors in parallel is $1\,\Omega$. Since 1 A of current is passing through the 2-ohm resistor on the far right, the current through the other 2-ohm resistor must also be 1 A, giving a total current in the circuit of 2 A. According to Ohm's law,

$$R = \frac{V}{I}$$

$$3\,\Omega + 1\,\Omega + r = \frac{12\text{ V}}{2.0\text{ A}}$$

$$r = 2\,\Omega$$

359. (D) Charge is related to current by $q = \displaystyle\int_0^2 I\,dt = \int_0^2 4t^3\,dt = t^4\big|_0^2 = 16$ C.

360. (B) A voltmeter across the battery and its internal resistance would read $6\text{ V} - Ir = 6\text{ V} - (1\text{ A})(2\,\Omega) = 4$ V.

361. (D) The arrangement that dissipates the most power is related to the equation $P = \dfrac{V^2}{R}$. For answer (D), this equation gives the most power, 12 W.

362. (C) Since 2 A of current is entering point a and 1 A is leaving point a, there must be 1 A of current passing through the middle branch and through the 3-ohm resistor. So a voltmeter connected across a and b would read $6\text{ V} + (1\text{ A})(3\,\Omega) = 9$ V.

363. (B) Power is high when resistance is low and drops off with 1/R with constant emf.

364. (A) The arrangement that dissipates the most power is related to the equation $P = \dfrac{V^2}{R}$. For answer (A), this equation gives a power of 9 W.

365. (A) Bulb 1 will burn the brightest, since it is in a position for the total current to pass through it. The other bulbs only get part of the total current.

366. (C) Bulbs 2 and 3 will not change their brightness, since bulb 4 was connected in parallel to them. Bulbs 2 and 3 still have the same voltage applied across them.

367. (C) Circuit I will not discharge its charge when the battery is removed because it is an open circuit and will retain its charge. Circuit II is still a complete circuit when the battery is removed and will discharge through the resistor.

368. (E) The equation for the capacitance of parallel plates is $C = \dfrac{\varepsilon_o A}{d}$. Changing the quantities as described gives $C = \dfrac{\varepsilon_o (4A)}{\left(\dfrac{1}{2}d\right)} = 8\,C$.

369. (C) Charge, capacitance, and voltage are related by $V = \dfrac{q}{C}$. Setting the voltage across each capacitor equal to each other gives $\dfrac{q_o}{C_o} = \dfrac{q_2}{2C_o}$ gives $\dfrac{q_2}{q_o} = 2$.

370. (D) The 8-μF capacitors are in parallel. Capacitors in parallel add for an equivalent capacitance—in this case, $8\ \mu\text{F} + 8\ \mu\text{F} = 16\ \mu\text{F}$. This equivalent capacitance is in series with the 2-μF and 4-μF capacitors. Capacitors in series add as reciprocals, giving $\dfrac{1}{C_{eq}} = \dfrac{1}{2} + \dfrac{1}{16} + \dfrac{1}{4} = \dfrac{13}{16\ \mu\text{F}}$; thus, $C_{eq} = \dfrac{16}{13}\ \mu\text{F}$.

371. (C) For capacitors in series, the charge is equal on each capacitor. Thus, the equivalent capacitance can be used to find the charge distributed into the circuit, which would be the charge on each capacitor in series: $Q = CV = \left(\dfrac{16}{13}\ \mu\text{F}\right)(120\text{ V}) = 148\ \mu\text{C}$.

372. (A) Current is the flow of charge, and any charge entering a junction must exit that junction. This is a statement of conservation of charge.

373. (D) Since $E = \dfrac{V}{d}$, we now have $E = \dfrac{V}{2d}$, giving half the electric field.

374. (D) The energy stored in the capacitor is $U = \dfrac{1}{2}CV^2 = \dfrac{1}{2}(10\ \mu\text{F})(12\text{ V})^2 = 720\ \mu\text{J}$.

375. (D) When the switch is closed, current flows freely through the uncharged capacitor, so the current begins high. As the capacitor charges, it resists the flow of current, and the current decreases exponentially.

376. (D) The graph for the voltage across the resistor will match the graph for the current through the resistor, as in the explanation for the previous question.

377. (B) The voltage across the capacitor begins at zero since it is uncharged. As current decreases in the circuit due to the charging of the capacitor, the voltage across the charged capacitor rises exponentially in the opposite direction of the battery.

378. (E) Capacitors in parallel can be added: $C_t = 10 \ \mu F + 10 \ \mu F + 10 \ \mu F = 30 \ \mu F$.

379. (E) The total capacitance in series is given by $\dfrac{1}{C_t} = \dfrac{1}{9 \ \mu F} + \dfrac{1}{9 \ \mu F} + \dfrac{1}{9 \ \mu F} = \dfrac{3}{9 \ \mu F}$, or $C_t = 3 \ \mu F$. Since the capacitors are in series, they each receive the same charge, which is equal to the total charge in the circuit: $q = CV = (3 \ \mu F)(9 \ V) = 27 \ \mu C$.

380. (E) Since the capacitors are connected in series, each capacitor will have 2 V across it. The energy stored in one of the capacitors is
$$U = \frac{1}{2}CV^2 = \frac{1}{2}(6 \ \mu F)(2 \ V)^2 = 12 \ \mu J.$$

381. (D) Filling a capacitor with a dielectric increases the capacitance of the capacitor, allowing it to store more charge.

382. (B) Placing another resistor in parallel will decrease the total resistance and increase the current through the circuit, increasing the rate at which the capacitor charges.

383. (B) The maximum current through the resistor is given by Ohm's law. Using the maximum voltage from the battery gives $I = \dfrac{\varepsilon}{R}$.

384. (D) The current starts at zero and increases rapidly as the capacitor begins to charge. The current decreases to zero as the capacitor charges, and when the switch is connected to b, the capacitor discharges, with the current dropping off exponentially.

385. (C) Gauss's law states that $EA = \dfrac{q_{enc}}{\varepsilon_o}$. The charge enclosed can be written as CV, where $V = Ed$. Rearranging gives the equation for capacitance, $C = \dfrac{\varepsilon_o A}{d}$.

386. (C) A parallel-plate capacitor with a dielectric is given by
$$C = \frac{\kappa \varepsilon_o A}{d} = \frac{4\varepsilon_o A}{\frac{1}{2}d} = 8 \ C.$$

387. (A) Gauss's law states that

$$\int E\,dA = \frac{Q_{enc}}{\varepsilon_o}.$$ Solving for E:

$$E(4\pi r^2) = \frac{Q}{\varepsilon_o} \text{ gives } E = \frac{Q}{4\pi\varepsilon_o r^2}$$

388. (B) They are connected in parallel because the positive top half is connected to the positive bottom half, and the negative top half is connected to the negative bottom half.

389. (C) Since the capacitors are connected in parallel, their capacitances can be added:

$$C_t = \frac{1}{2}C_o + \frac{1}{2}(3C_o) = 2C_o$$

390. (C) Applying Gauss's law between the cylinders gives

$$EA = \frac{q_{enc}}{\varepsilon_o}$$

$$E(2\pi rL) = \frac{Q}{\varepsilon_o}$$

$$E = \frac{Q}{2\pi\varepsilon_o rL}$$

391. (B) They are connected in parallel because the positive larger right-side third is connected to the positive left-side two-thirds, and the negative right-side third is connected to the negative left-side two-thirds.

392. (D) Since the capacitors are connected in parallel, their capacitances can be added:

$$C_t = \frac{2}{3}C_o + \frac{1}{3}(3C_o) = \frac{5}{3}C_o$$

393. (C) When a dielectric is inserted between the plates, a charge is induced inside the dielectric at the tip and the bottom. The induced charge is opposite to the charge on the plates, so they create an electric field opposite to the original electric field between the plates, thus decreasing the net electric field between the plates.

394. The total voltage in the circuit is 6 V − 3 V = 3 V, since they face opposite directions. Using Ohm's law, 3 V = (2 A)(0.2 Ω + 0.1 Ω + 1.0 Ω + R), giving R = 0.2 Ω.

395. Taking the top half of the loop, the voltmeter will read −3V − (2 A)(0.2 Ω) − (2 A)(0.1 Ω) = −5.4 V, or 5.4 V, depending on how the voltmeter is connected across a and b.

396. The power dissipated through the 0.1-ohm resistor is $P = I^2 R =$ $(2\ A)^2 (0.1 Ω) = 0.4$ W. The energy is given by the product of power and time, $E = Pt = (0.4\ \text{W})(30\ \text{s}) = 12$ J.

397. The maximum charge occurs when $t = 0$, leaving $q_{max} = 6$ C.

398. The charge and current are related by $I = \dfrac{dq}{dt} = \dfrac{d}{dt}\left(6e^{\frac{-t}{4}}\right) = -\dfrac{3}{2}e^{\frac{-t}{4}}$.

399. The number 4 is in the place of the product RC in the general equation for the current produced by a discharging capacitor. The product RC has units of time.

400. The product RC has units of Ω, F = V/A, C/V = C/C/s = seconds.

Chapter 9: Magnetic Fields and Forces

401. (D) The magnetic field around the wire at a radius r is given by Ampere's law, $B = \dfrac{\mu_o I}{2\pi r}$, directed out of the page by the right-hand rule.

402. (C) The magnetic field produced by a current flowing through a wire is proportional to $\dfrac{I}{r}$. The magnetic field produced by each wire is $\dfrac{2I}{r}$ and $\dfrac{4I}{2r}$, giving equal magnetic fields.

403. (A) By the right-hand rule applied to each wire, one of the wires produces a magnetic field directed out of the page, and the other produces a magnetic field into the page, giving a net magnetic field of zero.

404. (C) By Newton's third law, the wires exert equal and opposite forces on each other.

405. (B) The magnetic fields produced by opposite currents exert an attractive force on each other.

406. (A) By the right-hand rule, the force on the top of the loop is downward and the force on the bottom of the loop is upward, creating a clockwise torque on the loop and a clockwise rotation.

407. (D) The current through the spring coil creates a magnetic field that interacts with the magnetic field due to the magnet in which the coil rests. The coil experiences a force and a torque, turning proportionally to the current and rotating to make the needle move the proper distance on the meter.

408. (A) Since the currents are in opposite directions, the magnetic fields produced are in the same direction, causing the loops to repel.

409. (E) Since the magnetic force between current-carrying wires depends on the product of the currents, twice the current in each loop will produce four times the force between them.

410. (C) By the right-hand rule, the magnetic field produced by the current in the loop curls to the left on the outside of the loop and to the right through the center of the loop.

411. (C) By the right-hand rule, thumb in the direction of the velocity, fingers in the direction of the magnetic field (into the page), and the force comes out of the palm, up to the top of the page.

412. (D) The current in the loop at the top will experience an upward force by the right-hand rule. The current at the bottom of the loop will experience a downward force. Similarly, the current in the 3:00 and 9:00 positions will contribute to the expansion of the loop.

413. (A) Each wire creates an equal and opposite magnetic field at point P, giving a net magnetic field of zero.

414. (E) Both currents create magnetic fields with components to the right, giving a net magnetic field at point N to the right.

415. (C) Using the left-hand rule, since the charge is negative, the force is up to the top of the page.

416. (B) The magnetic force on the electron becomes a centripetal force, causing it to travel in a circular path.

417. (E) The magnetic force is always perpendicular to the velocity of the electron and therefore cannot change its kinetic energy.

418. (C) By the right-hand rule, the thumb is pointed out of the page and the palm faces up and to the left, giving a magnetic field in the direction of your fingers down and to the right.

419. (C) Since the particle enters the magnetic field at an angle, it moves in a circular path while also moving forward, creating a spiral-shaped path.

420. (D) The magnetic field due to wire 1 is $B_1 = \dfrac{\mu_o I}{2\pi d}$, and the magnetic field due to wire 2 is $B_1 = \dfrac{\mu_o I}{2\pi(2d)}$. Both magnetic fields are in the same direction by the right-hand rule, so the sum of the magnetic fields is $\dfrac{3}{2}B_1$.

421. (C) The magnetic force is given by $F = qvB = (2 \times 10^{-6}\text{ C})\left(2 \times 10^6\,\dfrac{\text{m}}{\text{s}}\right)$ $(0.2\text{ T}) = 0.8\text{ N}$ to the right by the right-hand rule.

422. (D) Since the positive charge experiences a magnetic force to the right, the electric field must be established to apply an electric force on the charge to the left. Thus, the electric field must be directed to the left.

423. (A) Using the left-hand rule for the negative charge, the magnetic force acting on the charge is directed down toward the bottom of the page. Thus, the electric field, which points in the direction a positive charge would experience a force, must be also directed downward.

424. (B) For the charge to follow a straight-line path in the electric and magnetic fields, the net force acting on the charge must be zero. Setting the electric force equal to the magnetic force, we get

$$F_E = F_B$$

$$qE = qvB$$

$$E = vB = \left(8 \times 10^6\,\dfrac{\text{m}}{\text{s}}\right)(0.5\text{ T}) = 4 \times 10^6\,\dfrac{\text{N}}{\text{C}}$$

425. (A) If you follow a positive charge from the top of the sheet to the bottom, it will experience a force to the right by the right-hand rule. Thus, point X becomes positive and has a higher potential than point Y. This is called the Hall effect.

426. (C) Ampere's law states that $\int B \cdot dl = \mu_o I_{enc}$, giving $B(2\pi r) = \mu_o I$.

427. (D) Using Ampere's law, the equation for the magnetic field as a function of distance r from the wire is $\dfrac{\mu_o I}{2\pi r}$, so the magnetic field varies inversely with distance from the wire, giving answer (D).

428. (A) In a perfect solenoid, all of the magnetic field produced by the current is inside the solenoid, so the magnetic field outside the solenoid is zero.

429. (D) Using the right-hand rule, the direction of the magnetic field inside the solenoid is found by curling your fingers around in the direction of the current, and the magnetic field points in the direction of your thumb.

430. (B) Since the only segment in the area where there is a magnetic field is a to b, the integral from a to b is the best choice.

431. (E) The magnetic force becomes the centripetal force acting on the charge:

$$F_B = F_C$$

$$qvB = \frac{mv^2}{r}$$

$$\frac{q}{m} = \frac{v}{rB}$$

432. (A) Since the magnetic force is perpendicular to the velocity of the charge, the magnetic force cannot do any work on the charge or change its kinetic energy.

433. (C) According to Ampere's law, the radius r and magnetic field B are inversely related, giving graph (C).

434. (D) The current is the charge per unit time, $I = \dfrac{Q}{T}$.

435. (E) Since the rotation of the charges (current) is clockwise, the magnetic field inside the loop is to the right by the right-hand rule.

436. (D) The magnetic field anywhere on the axis of the ring is to the left by the right-hand rule.

437. (D) Current density is defined as the current per unit area, $J = \dfrac{I}{A} = \dfrac{I}{ab}$.

438. (B) The best symmetry for this situation calls for a rectangular loop for Ampere's law.

439. (B) Using the right-hand rule, put the thumb in the direction of the current (outward) and the fingers curl around to point to the left at point X and to the right at point Y.

440. (D) Using the right-hand rule, put the thumb in the direction of the current (outward) and the fingers curl around to point up and to the left at point M.

441. (E) Using the right-hand rule, put the thumb in the direction of the current (outward) and the fingers curl around to point to the right at point N.

442. (A) Since the two currents are equal and in opposite directions, the net enclosed current is zero and the net magnetic field produced at point P is zero.

443. (E) The magnetic field inside the cylinder of radius a is linear with respect to distance r from the center of the cylinder, then falls off with $1/r$ between a and b, and then eventually drops to zero outside the larger cylinder, since the currents are in opposite directions.

444. (E) For any device to register a magnetic field, there has to be relative velocity between the device and the moving charge, in this case a compass. If the compass is moving with the charge, there is no relative velocity, and the compass will not deflect.

445. For the region outside the cylinder, the magnetic field produced is the same as if the cylinder were simply a current-carrying wire. Ampere's law then gives $B = \dfrac{\mu_o I}{2\pi r}$.

446. Applying Ampere's law at a distance r from the center of the cylinder gives $\int \boldsymbol{B} \cdot \boldsymbol{dl} = \mu_o I_{enc}$, where I_{enc} is related to the ratio of current passing through the area enclosed by r and the area enclosed by a:

$$B(2\pi r) = \mu_o I \left(\frac{\pi r^2}{\pi a^2} \right), \text{ giving } B = \frac{\mu_o I r}{2\pi a^2}$$

447. The magnetic field inside the conductor is proportional to the distance r from the center, so the first segment of the graph is linear. Then the magnetic field drops off with $1/r$ outside the conductor.

448. The electric potential difference ΔV is related to the work done on the charge, which is equal to the change in kinetic energy of the charge.

$$W = \Delta KE$$

$$q\Delta V = \frac{1}{2}mv^2$$

$$\Delta V = \frac{mv^2}{2q}$$

449. Since the electron enters the magnetic field perpendicularly, we can use the left-hand rule to determine that the force on the charge is up to the top of the page, and causes the electron to travel in a circular path labeled A.

450. The magnetic force becomes the centripetal force acting on the charge:

$$F_B = F_C$$

$$qvB = \frac{mv^2}{r}$$

$$r = \frac{mv}{qB}$$

Chapter 10: Electromagnetic Induction, Inductance, and Maxwell's Equations

451. (D) According to Faraday's law of induction, the magnetic flux must be changing for a current to be induced in a loop. Either the magnetic field can be changing or the area through which it passes can be changing.

452. (D) According to Ohm's law, $I = \frac{\varepsilon}{R}$. The induced emf in the loop is

$$\varepsilon = \frac{-\Delta\Phi}{\Delta t} = \frac{-B\Delta A}{\Delta t} = \frac{-BL\Delta w}{\Delta t} = BLv. \text{ The current is then } I = \frac{\varepsilon}{R} = \frac{BLv}{R}.$$

453. (D) Since the flux is decreasing through the loop as the loop exits the magnetic field, the induced current in the loop will reinforce the magnetic flux through the loop by creating a current that produces an outward magnetic flux through the loop. Thus, the current must be counterclockwise in the loop according to the right-hand rule.

454. (C) The magnetic flux must change through the loop, and in this situation, the magnetic field is moving downward, which does not change the flux through the loop.

455. (B) The change in magnetic flux through the loop is $\Delta\Phi = \Delta BA = B\Delta A = (0.3 \text{ T})(0.4 \text{ m}^2) = 0.12 \text{ T m}^2$.

456. (A) The induced emf is $\varepsilon = \dfrac{-\Delta\Phi}{\Delta t} = \dfrac{0.12 \text{ T m}^2}{0.2 \text{ s}} = 0.006 \text{ V}$.

457. (E) For the flux through the smaller loop to change, the area of the loop has to be decreased. This cannot be accomplished by rotating it around the x-axis.

458. (C) The magnetic flux through the loop is increasing into the loop. By Lenz's law, current will be induced in the wire to oppose the change that produced it. A counterclockwise current will oppose the change in magnetic flux through the loop by the right-hand rule.

459. (D) As the bar falls, its speed increases. The induced emf is related to the speed of the bar by the equation $\varepsilon = BLv$. The speed increases (relatively) linearly as it falls. So, the induced emf in the rod is proportional to the falling velocity, and increases linearly with the speed.

460. (C) The emf produced in the loop is $\varepsilon = \dfrac{-d\Phi}{dt} = A\dfrac{-dB}{dt} = ab\dfrac{-dB}{dt}$. Dropping the negative sign, the rate of change in magnetic field is $\dfrac{dB}{dt} = \dfrac{\varepsilon}{ab} = \dfrac{IR}{ab}$.

461. (B) The flux through the closed loop is increasing inward, since the area through which the flux passes is increasing, so the induced current in the bar is to the right to oppose the change in flux by Lenz's law.

462. (C) The magnetic force acting on the bar is $F = ILB = \dfrac{BLv}{R}LB = \dfrac{B^2L^2v}{R}$.

463. (A) As the front of the loop enters the magnetic field, the flux begins to increase through the loop. Since the speed is constant, the change in flux area increases at a constant rate from zero to w. The flux is constant while the entire loop is in the magnetic field; then the flux decreases constantly as the loop exits the magnetic field. The flux is zero after the loop completely exits the field.

464. (A) By Lenz's law, the magnetic force produced by the induced current will oppose the motion of the loop, somewhat like friction.

465. (C) The magnitude of the induced emf in the loop is $\varepsilon = \dfrac{\Delta\Phi}{\Delta t} = \dfrac{A\Delta B}{\Delta t} = \dfrac{(0.2 \text{ m})^2 (0.1 \text{ T})}{4\text{s}} = 0.001$ V. The induced current is then $I = \dfrac{\varepsilon}{R} = \dfrac{0.001 \text{ V}}{0.5\Omega} = 0.002$ A.

466. (A) As the north pole of the magnet is pushed into the loop, the magnetic flux is increasing into the loop, producing an induced current into the page that will oppose the change in flux. Then as the magnet is pulled out of the loop, the induced current will produce a magnetic flux that opposes the decrease in flux, and reverse its direction, coming out of the page.

467. (C) The component of the weight directed down the incline is $mg\sin\theta$ and is the force causing the acceleration of the bar.

$$F_{net} = mg\sin\theta = ma$$

$$a = g\sin\theta = \left(10\frac{\text{m}}{\text{s}^2}\right)(\sin 30°) = 5\frac{\text{m}}{\text{s}^2}$$

468. (C) A component of gravity points down the incline, and an opposing magnetic force is produced by the induced current in the bar as it moves down the rails.

469. (E) When the bar reaches its final speed, it is no longer accelerating, and the magnetic force is equal to $mg\sin\theta$.

$$mg\sin\theta = ILB$$

$$I = \frac{mg\sin\theta}{LB} = \frac{(0.2 \text{ kg})\left(10\frac{\text{m}}{\text{s}^2}\right)(\sin 30°)}{(0.3 \text{ m})(0.3 \text{ T})} = 10 \text{ A}$$

470. (A) The magnetic flux through the loop is $\Phi = BA\cos\theta = (0.3 \text{ T})(0.3 \text{ m})(0.6 \text{ m})\cos 30° = 0.0078 \text{ T m}^2$.

471. (D) The rate of change of magnetic flux is $\dfrac{-d\Phi}{dt} = A\dfrac{dB}{dt} = s^2\dfrac{dB}{dt} = s^2\dfrac{d}{dt}(k+Ct) = s^2 C$.

472. (D) Ohm's law states that $I = \dfrac{\varepsilon}{R}$ and the magnitude of the induced emf is $\varepsilon = \dfrac{d\Phi}{dt} = s^2 C$. The current is $I = \dfrac{s^2 C}{R}$.

473. (E) By the right-hand rule, the current (thumb) on the near side is to the right, the magnetic field (fingers) is down to the bottom of the page, and the force (palm) on the wire is into the page away from you.

474. (D) The induced emf in the loop is related to the change in flux by the equation $\varepsilon = \dfrac{d\Phi}{dt} = A\dfrac{dB}{dt} = \pi r^2 \dfrac{dB}{dt} = k\pi r^2 t^{\frac{3}{2}}$. Solving for the rate of change of magnetic field gives $\dfrac{dB}{dt} = kt^{\frac{3}{2}}$.

Separating variables and integrating the magnetic field gives

$$B = \int dB = \int kt^{\frac{3}{2}} dt = \frac{2}{3} kt^{\frac{5}{2}}.$$

475. (A) For the loop to remain suspended in equilibrium, the upward magnetic force must equal the weight downward.

$$F_B = F_C$$

$$IaB = mg$$

$$I = \frac{mg}{aB}$$

476. (B) The current is induced in the wire because the magnetic flux is changing.

$$\varepsilon = \frac{d\Phi}{dt} = A\frac{dB}{dt} = \pi r^2 \frac{dB}{dt} = \pi r^2 \frac{d}{dt}(B_o - kt) = -k\pi r^2$$

Using Ohm's law, we get

$$I = \frac{\varepsilon}{R} = \frac{k\pi r^2}{R}$$

477. (B) There is an induced current due to the decreasing magnetic field: $B = B_0 - kt$. This magnetic field is zero when $B = 0$, which occurs at $t = \dfrac{B_0}{k}$. For times greater than this, the magnetic field is then increasing coming out of the page, causing a reversal of the current direction.

478. (C) The magnetic flux as a function of time is

$$\Phi = BA = A(4e^{-2t}) = 4Ae^{-2t}$$

479. (C) The induced emf can be found by

$$\varepsilon = \frac{-d\Phi}{dt} = -A\frac{dB}{dt} = -A\frac{d}{dt}(4e^{-2t}) = 8Ae^{-2t}$$

By Ohm's law,

$$I = \frac{\varepsilon}{R} = \frac{8Ae^{-2t}}{R}$$

480. (E) Energy is the product of power and time, or in this case $\int_0^\infty P\,dt = \int_0^\infty I^2R\,dt$.

481. (A) When $bt > 1$, the current in the wire is positive and decreasing, producing a flux through the loop that is decreasing. The magnetic field due to the current-carrying wire is out of the page by the right-hand rule.

482. (D) The flux integral $\int B \cdot dA$ begins at y and goes to $y + s$, since this is the region of space occupied by the loop.

483. (A) When the switch is closed, the inductor first greatly opposes the voltage from the battery by Lenz's law, so the voltage is low across the resistor. As current begins to flow, the inductor opposes the battery voltage with less back emf until the current in the circuit is constant, and the voltage across the resistor is equal to the emf provided by the battery. When the current is steady, the inductor does not oppose the emf from the battery and current flows freely through it.

484. (C) According to Lenz's law, the inductor will oppose a *change* in current. Since the *change* in current is high when the switch is first closed, the back emf from the inductor is high to oppose the change. The back emf in the inductor then decreases as the current in the circuit becomes more steady (less change). Eventually, the voltage across the inductor is zero when the current is steady.

485. (C) Inductance L is measured in Henrys, and resistance is measured in ohms.

So, $\dfrac{H}{\Omega} = \dfrac{\frac{V}{A/s}}{\Omega} = \dfrac{A\Omega}{\Omega A/s} = \text{seconds}$.

486. (C) The back emf due to the changing current is found by

$$\varepsilon_L = -L\frac{dI}{dt} = -L\frac{d}{dt}(3t^2) = -L(6t) = -(0.5\ \mathrm{H})[6(2\ \mathrm{s})] = -6\ \mathrm{V}$$

487. (A) According to the loop rule, the sum of the voltages around the circuit is zero. The voltage ε rises through the battery, then drops across the resistor $(-IR)$, and then drops through the inductor $\left(-L\dfrac{dI}{dt}\right)$.

488. (D) After a long time, the inductor stores magnetic energy, so when the switch is connected to b, the emf across the inductor causes current to continue to flow through the two resistors $(2R)$. Using the loop rule, the sum of the voltage drops around the circuit and gives $-2IR - L\dfrac{dI}{dt} = 0$.

489. (C) This is called an LC circuit, and the energy oscillates between the capacitor and the inductor. Sometimes this circuit is called an oscillating circuit.

490. (B) The flux of magnetic field through a closed surface is zero, since any field lines exiting the closed surface from the north pole of the magnet will reenter the closed surface into the south pole. The magnetic flux would not be zero if there was only one pole enclosed in the surface.

491. (A) Gauss's law for electrostatics states that the flux of electric field through a closed surface is caused by the charge enclosed in the surface.

492. (C) Ampere's law states that the magnetic field integrated around a closed path is related to the current enclosed in that path.

493. (D) Faraday's law of induction relates the induced emf ε to changing magnetic flux $d\Phi/dt$. Integrating the electric field along a path gives the emf ε and the rate of change of magnetic flux.

494. (E) Gauss's law can be applied to gravity, since the gravitation force and acceleration are inverse square laws. We can say that the flux of the gravitational field g is related to the mass enclosed in a closed surface.

495. Since the flux is increasing outward, the current induced in the loop will create a change in flux that opposes the increasing magnetic flux, producing a current that is clockwise by the right-hand rule.

496. Ohm's law states that $I = \dfrac{\varepsilon}{R} = \dfrac{A\dfrac{dB}{dt}}{R} = \dfrac{\pi a^2}{R}\dfrac{dB}{dt}$.

497. The induced current of the loop at radius $2a$ is $I = \dfrac{\varepsilon}{R} = \dfrac{A\dfrac{dB}{dt}}{R} = \dfrac{\pi(2a)^2}{R}\dfrac{dB}{dt}$.

498. When the switch is connected at a, the back emf is highest and is equal and opposite to the battery emf, 6V.

499. After a long time, the current is steady and the inductor provides no back emf. The current is given by Ohm's law:

$$I = \frac{\varepsilon}{R} = \frac{6 \text{ V}}{2\Omega} = 3\text{A}$$

500. When the current is a steady 3 A, the energy stored in the inductor is

$$U = \frac{1}{2}LI^2 = \frac{1}{2}(0.1 \text{ H})(3\text{A})^2 = 0.45 \text{ J}$$

NOTES

NOTES

NOTES

NOTES